BRian W. ALDISS

MODERN MASTERS OF SCIENCE FICTION

Edited by Gary K. Wolfe

Science fiction often anticipates the consequences of scientific discoveries. The immense strides made by science since World War II have been matched step by step by writers who gave equal attention to scientific principles, human imagination, and the craft of fiction. The respect for science fiction won by Jules Verne and H. G. Wells was further increased by Isaac Asimov, Arthur C. Clarke, Robert Heinlein, Ursula K. Le Guin, Joanna Russ, and Ray Bradbury. Modern Masters of Science Fiction is devoted to books that survey the work of individual authors who continue to inspire and advance science fiction.

A list of books in the series appears at the end of this book.

BRIAN W. ALDISS

Paul Kincaid

UNIVERSITY OF
ILLINOIS PRESS
Urbana, Chicago, and Springfield

Cataloging data available from the Library of Congress
LCCN 2021058921
ISBN 978-0-252-04448-9 (cloth : alk.)
ISBN 978-0-252-08655-7 (paper : alk.)
ISBN 978-0-252-05347-4 (ebook)

contents

ACKNOWLEDGMENTS

There is almost too much to be said about Brian Aldiss. Anyone taking on the task of writing an overview of his sixty-year career faces a daunting task. So I want to thank, first of all, friends including John and Judith Clute, Nina Allan and Christopher Priest, and Paul March-Russell, not to mention my long-suffering wife Maureen Kincaid Speller for conversations, probably now long forgotten, which helped convince me that I had something to say on the subject and further helped me focus on what that something was.

When I was full of doubt, my editor at the University of Illinois Press read my very rough first draft of Chapter 1 and assured me I was on the right track.

Andrew Mazibrada and Maureen Kincaid Speller both took on the unenviable task of reading my chapters and providing invaluable comments that helped make this better than it may otherwise have been.

My Aldiss bibliography clearly owes an incalculable debt to the work of Margaret Aldiss and also to the International Science Fiction Data Base.

Abbreviations

AoE	*The Airs of Earth*
BBA	*The Book of Brian Aldiss*
BF	*Bodily Functions*
BfH	*Barefoot in the Head*
BHS	*Bury My Heart at W. H. Smith's*
BoH	*Brothers of the Head*
BSF1	*Best Science Fiction Stories of Brian W. Aldiss*
BSF2	*Best Science Fiction Stories of Brian W. Aldiss (rev. ed.)*
BSF3	*Best SF Stories of Brian W. Aldiss (3rd ed.)*
BYS	*Billion Year Spree*
CaC	*Cracken at Critical*
CB	*Cultural Breaks*
CSS50	*The Complete Short Stories: The 1950s*
CSS60.1	*The Complete Short Stories: The 1960s, Part 1*
CSS60.2	*The Complete Short Stories: The 1960s, Part 2*
CSS60.3	*The Complete Short Stories: The 1960s, Part 3*
CSS60.4	*The Complete Short Stories: The 1960s, Part 4*
CT	*The Canopy of Time*
CZ	*Cryptozoic*
DLY	*The Dark Light Years*
DU	*Dracula Unbound*
EMH	*The Eighty Minute Hour*
EoS	*Enemies of the System*
EQ	*Equator and Segregation*
EW	*Earthworks*
FB	*Foreign Bodies: Stories*
FM	*Finches of Mars*
FU	*Frankenstein Unbound*
GB	*Greybeard*
GGS	*Galaxies Like Grains of Sand*
HA	*HARM*
HC	*Hell's Cartographers*
HH	*Hothouse*
HSp	*Helliconia Spring*

HSu	Helliconia Summer
HW	Helliconia Winter
IH	The Invention of Happiness.
II	Intangibles, Inc. and Other Stories
LO	Last Orders and Other Stories
MoE	The Moment of Eclipse
MOI	Moreau's Other Island
MoP	The Magic of the Past
MT	The Malacia Tapestry
NAOE	New Arrivals, Old Encounters
N-S	Non-Stop
PU	The Primal Urge
RoE	A Romance of the Equator: Best Fantasy Stories
RPA	Report on Probability A
SFT	The Shape of Further Things
SiF	Seasons in Flight
SLAS	Supertoys Last All Summer Long and Other Stories of Future Time
SoB	The Secret of This Book
SS	Starswarm
ST	The Saliva Tree and Other Strange Growths
STAN	Space, Time and Nathaniel
Su-S	Super-State
ToE	The Twinkling of an Eye, or My Life as an Englishman
TTF	A Tupolev Too Far and Other Stories
WM	White Mars, or The Mind Set Free, a 21st-Century Utopia

BRIAN W. ALDISS

CHAPTER 1

WARRIOR

In July 1944, still more than a month shy of his nineteenth birthday, Brian Aldiss went to war.

He had joined the army directly after leaving school the summer before and now, after a year of basic training, was Signalman Aldiss of the Royal Signals Regiment. The troopship he boarded in Glasgow, a former luxury liner called the *Otranto*, would take him not to France, where the "second front" had been opened only a month earlier, but to India. From there he joined the self-styled "Forgotten Army" on its final advance against the Japanese across the razor-edged ridges, precipitous slopes, dried-up river beds, and mosquito-infested jungles of Burma. The war in Burma, toxic, secret, and brutal, was a fight many soldiers were eager to avoid, but Aldiss seems to have almost welcomed the prospect. "I had left behind, not only England, but an inadequate earlier self" (*ToE*, 10), he wrote in his autobiography, *The Twinkling of an Eye* (1998), throughout which he made repeated comments about becoming a man, for instance: "I was growing throughout the campaign, a plant flourishing in poor soil" (*ToE*, 174). And his loving descriptions of the awfulness of some of the army camps in India and Burma are always offset by suggestions that his schooldays were worse: "After ten years at boarding schools, Burma was no real hardship" (*ToE*, 174).

Aldiss was a gangling teenager, awkward in most situations, who hid his public school background from his fellow soldiers for fear it would disrupt the first genuine comradeship he seems to have known in his life. At the same time, he was taking enthusiastic advantage of the prostitutes to be found near each of the army camps where he served. These women "afforded me no particular training in virtue" (*ToE*, 389), as he put it with unusual coyness, though they did help establish the model of priapic masculinity that would be a constant and at times unfortunate feature of both his work and his life. War was bad, but the army had its advantages.

Even after the Japanese surrender, it would be two years before Aldiss returned home. First he was posted to Sumatra, where the remnants of Japan's Twenty-Fifth Army maintained a fragile peace in a country in which rebel forces were fighting to prevent the reintroduction of Dutch rule. From there Aldiss went on to Hong Kong before finally being repatriated to Britain in the summer of 1947.

By then, Britain no longer felt like home; he had returned "to what was then, and in a curious way has remained ever since, a foreign land" (*ToE*, 199). He had exchanged the color, heat, and sexual freedom he had found in the East for a world that was gray, cold, austere, and prudish. "The English . . . became a lesser race after the war" (*ToE*, 25), Aldiss has said, and in comparison to what he had known in the army, "English life was thin gruel" (*ToE*, 200).

It would be wrong to say that these experiences made Aldiss a writer. He had been scribbling stories since the age of three and had refined his talents at public school, where he used storytelling as a way of winning friends and fending off homosexual interest in the dormitory. Harold Boyer, his form master at West Buckland School, recalled him being "a much sought-after entertainer and story-teller."[1] And a former comrade-in-arms, Dave Seager, has reported that Aldiss's stories and rhymes, which he turned out with seeming ease, made him a popular entertainer among the troops crowded aboard the *Otranto*.[2] Nevertheless, the type of writer he would become, the themes and images he would employ throughout his career, would be informed by the contrasting worlds of wartime Burma and postwar Britain.

Sometimes, these influences are explicit. Novels such as *A Soldier Erect* (1971) and *Forgotten Life* (1988) draw directly on the war in Burma as he knew it. And the culture shock of his return to Britain is spelled out even in such relatively late stories as "Just Back from Java" (1980), whose hero, Alan Morbey, finds Britain cold, frosty, and damp. His grandmother imagines that her home is being flooded, his wife has left him, and he dreams of "jungles and warm nights" (*RoE*, 163).

More commonly, these experiences contributed to the inescapable metaphorical underpinnings of Aldiss's work. For instance, stories as varied as *Non-Stop* (1958), "Equator" (1958), and "The Gods in Flight" (1984) draw quite closely on his time in Burma and Sumatra. Others deal with war more generally; in fact, it is part of the background of almost everything he wrote, from *Bow Down to Nul* (1960) and *Greybeard* (1964) to *The Malacia Tapestry* (1976) and *HARM* (2007). He shared the view, common among front-line soldiers, that war was the ultimate failure of humanity, the irrefutable proof of collective madness. As he said later, when he feared being recalled to the army at the time of the Korean War, "The idea haunted me then, and has troubled me ever since, that humanity may be a few apples short of the tree of knowledge" (*ToE*, 213). In late and relatively minor works such as *Super-State* (2002), he would continue to make the same point: "If war is declared," one character announces, "it is proof once more that mankind is mad" (*Su-S*, 32). Yet precisely because war was too terrible to contemplate, too brutal an image of collective insanity, he believed that war was an inevitable part of human affairs.

This notion of the madness of civilization is connected also with the sense of despair and alienation that Aldiss felt on his return to Britain. He found the West to be both unwelcoming and undeserving, condemned by its austerity, its attitude toward sex, and its coldness, both physical and metaphorical. Of course, as with other British writers associated with the New Wave, alienation was a part of his literary armory. But there is a savagery in his depiction of modern British life in works as varied as *The Primal Urge* (1961), *Cryptozoic* (1967), *Report on Probability A* (1968), and *Barefoot in the Head* (1969), a sense of the perceived worthlessness of the culture, that is peculiarly his own.

This antagonism toward the West is accompanied by an exoticizing of the East. Although many of his stories are explicitly anticolonial—for example, "Segregation" (1958), "The Under-Privileged" (1963), and *The Dark Light Years* (1964)—there is still an orientalist attitude, the sense that the East is a place of warmth, comfort, and sexual liberality for the Westerner, or at least for Brian Aldiss. He was overwhelmed by the light, color, heat, sounds, and smells of India, where "a thousand worlds seemed to be contained, with fascinations inexhaustible" (*ToE*, 8). In particular, two images of nature at its most profuse captivated him. The first was an immense banyan tree he saw in India that would directly inform the overgrown planet he described in *Hothouse* (1962). The second was the dense jungle through which he fought in Burma, the trees "festooned in all manner of climbers and epiphytes" (*ToE*, 170), where making any progress without hacking your way through with a *kukri* was impossible. This would in turn appear as the clogged passageways of *Non-Stop*. Apart from the innumerable short stories that are set in places like Sumatra, Singapore, India, and Hong Kong where he saw service, all of this gave rise to recurring images of Nature overwhelming mankind in stories from "The Saliva Tree" (1965) to the Helliconia Trilogy (1982–1985).

This uneasy sense of the East as something to be observed from the outside is apparent in a story that Aldiss tells in *Bury My Heart at W. H. Smith's* (1990). He describes taking a train journey across India and watching peasants in the field: "They appeared motionless, like figures on a frieze. . . . Monotony was their lot" (*BHS*, 11). What caught his attention was not so much the poverty of their lives as its unchanging and repetitive nature. This image, coupled with a sense that the hidebound English society to which he returned after the war was in its own way constrained within tightly prescribed and repetitive limits, leads to a recurring sense of stasis in his work, seen, for example, in *Report on Probability A*, *The Malacia Tapestry*, *Cryptozoic*, and *Enemies of the System* (1978).

There are contrasts and contradictions in all I have summarized in these last few paragraphs. For Aldiss, the East was a place of desire, of longing, of freedom, yet he never sought to return there except for brief trips that often seemed to involve trying to locate the prostitutes he had known. For all his caustic views about the culture and civilization of the West, particularly of a diminished and disheartened Britain, he chose to remain there and become a part of the cultural establishment. War was madness, yet it had also given him perhaps the happiest time of his life. And it is, I argue, precisely in these contradictions, and others, that the distinctive qualities that made Aldiss the writer he would become were born.

Brian Aldiss was a writer whose work was easier to admire than to love. He stood four-square in the history of science fiction. He was a colossus, unmistakable and unavoidable, who shaped not only science fiction but how science fiction perceived itself. He saw himself, I argue, as the new H. G. Wells, not only in his work, which frequently echoed that of his predecessor, but also, perhaps, in his lifestyle, or at least in his sexual conquests. And yet (with Aldiss there always seems to be an "and yet") he was always in some way distanced from science fiction, just as he was a self-proclaimed Englishman who was distanced from England. The closer he came to working within the familiar generic frameworks, the more he seemed to be slumming. The more adventurous and daring his work, the more it stretched ideas of what science fiction might be, sometimes to breaking point. He was one of the guiding spirits of the New Wave in Britain but was never entirely comfortable in that milieu. He produced the essential narrative history of the genre at a time when, as he told the story, he had largely lost interest in writing science fiction. He sought and enjoyed literary respectability, and for most of what might loosely be called the literary establishment he was the acceptable face of science fiction, all while science fiction itself was at its most anti-establishment.

It is impossible to write about Brian Aldiss without coming face to face with these contradictions. He is, for that very reason, not an easy person to write about. He produced at least as many abject failures as he did towering achievements, yet which works will belong in which category will depend entirely on the reader. He remains controversial, difficult, infuriating. And yet it is as hard to imagine postwar British science fiction without him as it is to imagine British science fiction in general without Wells.

★   ★   ★

In a career of sixty years Brian Aldiss produced over eighty books and more than four hundred short stories, not counting his numerous poems, plays, and other occasional writings. It would take a work several times the length of this book to give equal weight to them all, so I have pursued a largely thematic approach in this study. The themes allow me to pursue the continuities in his work as much as the contradictions, and so the chapters, arranged in roughly chronological order, each pick up on a key theme, which often is pursued beyond the strictly chronological bounds of the chapter.

This first chapter, "Warrior," covers the early years of his career while taking as its theme the interconnected influences of his time in the army and the disillusionment engendered by his return to Britain. These influences are particularly at play in novels like *Non-Stop* and *The Primal Urge*, but they would have a long-lasting effect on all of his writing, and every subsequent chapter will hark back to this theme. The other effect of Aldiss's time in the East was a fascination with lush and overabundant vegetation, an interest that became more focused following the publication of Rachel Carson's *Silent Spring* (1962). Chapter 2, "Naturalist," takes this as its theme while primarily covering the early 1960s, ranging from *Hothouse* to *Cryptozoic*. Overlapping with this period was a time of fundamental change in the character of British science fiction beginning when Michael Moorcock assumed the editorship of *New Worlds*. Chapter 3, "Experimentalist," looks at the way Aldiss became one of the key voices of the New Wave through works such as *Report on Probability A* and *Barefoot in the Head*. Thematically, however, the chapter goes against most established critical perspectives by arguing that Aldiss was less interested in the New Wave than he was in the opportunities it gave him to experiment, and so the chapter follows him beyond the New Wave to other experimental writings, from *The Eighty Minute Hour* (1974) to the various Enigmas.

One persistent story perpetuated not only by Aldiss but also by other critics of his work is that he was so disappointed by the poor reception of *Barefoot in the Head* that he effectively abandoned science fiction. In Chapter 4, "Historian," I show that this is an unconvincing account and that his next major work, *Billion Year Spree* (1973), was an attempt to reconcile his interest in generic science fiction with New Wave experimentalism. His engagement with the history of the genre also prompted much of his own fiction through the 1970s and on into the 1990s, covering works such as *Frankenstein Unbound* (1973), *Moreau's Other Island* (1980), *Dracula Unbound* (1991), and *The Malacia Tapestry*. Chapter 5, "Scientist," takes the story from the late 1970s—*Enemies of the System* and *Brothers of the Head* (1977)—to the mid-1980s, focusing on the Helliconia Trilogy. Thematically, the chapter considers how these works used science as both a prop and an inspiration, though it also draws heavily on themes already explored, particularly in Chapters 1 and 2. Finally, Chapter 6, "Utopian," traces what is, in effect, the dying fall of the last years of his career. Here we find works like *Super-State* that echo earlier novels but lack their vivacity; books that attempt a new direction, such as *White Mars* (1999), though the utopian tone does not convince after the misanthropy of practically all his earlier works; and occasional late flowerings, such as *HARM*, though they do not quite recapture the passion that made his earliest work so memorable. Throughout this book I engage with other critics, especially the authors of the three earlier books on Aldiss—Richard Mathews, Michael Collings, and Brian Griffin and David Wingrove—although none of them appeared later than the halfway mark in Aldiss's career. It may already be apparent, however, that I am inclined to take a far more contrarian view of Aldiss than any of these commentators allow themselves.

* * *

Brian Wilson Aldiss was born in East Dereham, Norfolk, on August 18, 1925. His grandfather, H. H. Aldiss, owned a large department store in the town; Brian's father, Stanley, familiarly known as Bill, ran one of the departments, and the family lived in a flat on the premises.

Aldiss's account of his childhood is filled with images of rejection and exclusion. From an early age, his mother Elizabeth (known as Dot) told him that there had been an older sister who had died when she was six months old and that she had always wanted another girl, not a boy. Many years passed before Aldiss discovered that this older sister had actually died at birth rather than at six months and had never been christened. Five years later, when his younger sister Betty was born, Brian was suffering from whooping cough, which, at the time, could prove fatal to young babies. The moment Betty was born, therefore, he was hustled away to stay with Grandma Wilson, his mother's mother, in Peterborough. Though he long remembered this exile as lasting six months, in fact it was only six weeks until he was no longer infectious. Nevertheless, he was too young to understand anything other than that this was an unwanted exclusion from the family that coincided with the arrival of the daughter his mother had always wanted. He also records how his mother would emotionally manipulate him by threatening to run away from home and take Betty with her, something she actually appeared to do on at least one occasion. He includes an account of this incident in his autobiographical novel *The Hand-Reared Boy* (1970), and a variation of the story would also appear in *Cryptozoic* when the child, Edward Bush, is locked out in the garden by his mother, who tells him she no longer loves him. (Aldiss's autobiography, *The Twinkling of an Eye*, contains too many easily refutable errors of fact to be totally reliable; nevertheless, we should probably accept that in retelling these stories many years later, Aldiss was recalling actual events rather than his later fictionalization of them.)

An even worse experience of exile was to follow. In 1933 H. H. Aldiss died, and though he left the business jointly to Bill and his older brother, the two did not get along, and Bill almost immediately sold his share in the store and moved the family to the coastal town of Gorleston. It was a very obvious reduction in circumstances, but Aldiss didn't have much time to get used to it because in that same year he was sent away to St. Peter's Court Preparatory School, and from there, in 1936, he moved on to Framlingham College in Suffolk, which he hated. This ejection from the much-loved family home and then from the family itself can only have exacerbated Aldiss's feelings of isolation and alienation. When war broke out in 1939, Bill decided that Gorleston would be on an invasion route and abruptly moved the family to Devon. There they lived for a while in a caravan before Bill and Dot took over a small post office and general store in the village of Bickington. Although Dot seems to have been happier there than she ever was in East Dereham, this was clearly a step down socially and, presumably, economically. Nevertheless, they found the money to move Brian to another minor public school, West Buckland, on the fringes of Exmoor. It was from there that Brian Aldiss left to join the army in September 1943.

★ ★ ★

By the end of the war Aldiss's parents had moved to Barnstaple, where his father worked in a gentlemen's outfitters, and it was there that Aldiss attempted to write his first novel. *Hunter Leaves the Herd* was based on a true story he had heard in Sumatra about a British soldier fighting rebels there who had deserted to join the rebel side. The novel was never finished, Aldiss reports: "I flinched from its unreality and threw it away" (*ToE*, 200). But I do wonder whether his later short novel *Equator* (1961), which is set in Sumatra and involves a complex series of betrayals, might contain a faint echo of that early abortive novel.

After abandoning *Hunter Leaves the Herd*, Aldiss "said goodbye to the family, caught a train, came to Oxford, and found employment in a book shop" (*ToE*, 201). This is a brief and breezy account of something that must have been rather more complex. Why Oxford, a place he had visited only once, briefly, years earlier, and why a book shop? He does not say. And because on his "first weekend in Oxford" (*ToE*, 201) his new employer was showing him around the city, he seems to have stepped into the job virtually the moment he stepped off the train. This job was at Sanders & Co. on the High Street, where he stayed until the early 1950s, when he moved to a better-paying job at another Oxford bookseller, Parker's.

In 1948 he married Olive Fortescue, who would encourage his writing and type up his manuscripts. His attempts to write at this time included another mainstream novel, *Shouting Down a Cliff*, which he completed but never submitted. Meanwhile, as an avid reader of science fiction, he was also trying his hand at genre stories, and having discovered the British sf magazine *Nebula*, he wrote a short story, "T" ("It remains my shortest title," he noted [*BHS*, 46]). The story was completed in January 1953, sold in 1955, and published in *Nebula* 18, November 1956, by which time his first book had come out, a collection of short stories was all set to go, and he had quit the bookshop to become a full-time writer.

"T," which would be included in that first collection, *Space, Time and Nathaniel* (1957), is a good example of the way Aldiss's early work would appear to conform to the genre conventions of the time while subtly undermining those conventions in a way that made the work appear fresh and innovative. It is a story of aliens, space war, and time travel with a twist ending that almost seems like the punchline of a joke; all were familiar elements in any sf story of the mid-1950s. But in this story the reader's sympathy is directed toward the legless, one-armed alien T, who is locked within a machine that "regulate[s him] so that he neither [grows] nor waste[s]" (*STAN*, 21). He is, in a way that would become familiar in Aldiss's work, diminished physically and therefore mentally. He is a passive figure, carried by the machine though not really part of it, yet "loneliness [is] one of the innumerable concepts which his creators arranged he should never sense" (*STAN*, 21–22). He is a weapon, one of twelve sent back in time by his race to destroy the home world of their enemy before that enemy can evolve. The enemy is humankind, the target is Earth, and they are aiming for the seventh planet from the edge of the solar system. T reaches his target and destroys it but the aliens have miscalculated. The planet T has destroyed becomes the asteroid belt, while in the swamps of Earth, which has only now become the seventh planet from the edge, life begins to stir. It's not a great story. It's too one-dimensional, too reliant on its twist ending, but it is a crude example of the way Aldiss would upset the conventions of the genre.

★ ★ ★

But what turned Aldiss into a professional writer was not science fiction. Early in 1954, on the strength of a short piece he had written for *The Bookseller*, the magazine of the book trade, he was able to persuade the magazine to let him write a weekly column. This column was a lightly fictionalized account of life as an assistant in a small bookshop, based on his experiences at Sanders & Co. The first of the Brightfount Diaries, written under the pen name Peter Pica, was published in *The Bookseller* of June 12, 1954, with twenty-one more following before the last appeared in March 1955. The columns, firmly in the mode of popular fictions at the time, were mildly humorous, gently satirical, and flattering to the reader, who was expected to be familiar with the literary and artistic world portrayed. Before the end of the year, publishers were clamoring to bring the columns out in book form. The first to contact Aldiss was Charles Montieth of Faber and Faber, a prestigious house then best known as the home of T. S. Eliot. So it was Faber that published *The Brightfount Diaries* in the autumn of 1955.

Just a month after the first of the Brightfount Diaries appeared, Aldiss's first published science fiction story, "Criminal Record," appeared in *Science Fantasy*, then at the end of the year "Not for an Age" won third prize in the Christmas competition run by the *Observer* for stories set in AD 2500. It was published in the *Observer* in January 1955, at the same time "Outside" appeared in *New Worlds*. *New Worlds* and its sister publication, *Science Fantasy*, were two of the most popular magazines in what was, at the time, quite a crowded British sf market. So Aldiss, seven years after his first attempt to write a novel, was suddenly a very visible writer. Though Kingsley Amis would later say that "Outside" was "about the finest science fiction short since Wells,"[3] these were not exactly world-shattering stories. They were distinctive, however, and they did proclaim a new writer worth paying attention to. They were also beginning to attract the attention of science fiction editors and readers.

The prevailing aesthetic in science fiction still reflected John W. Campbell's insistence that humans must always prove superior to any problem, any alien. It was a literature of competent men, and yet Aldiss's experience in the war, his sense of the failure of the West, of a world diminished equally by war and by austerity, meant that the literature of competent men was something that he simply could not write. In "Not for an Age," for instance, a university lecturer in 1950s Britain, just living his normal life, becomes an object of comedy to people from the future who discover a means to watch events in the past, while in "Criminal Record" the two central characters, for all their technological ability, prove to be no match for the nonhuman future. Though "Outside" might seem to conform to the model of human superiority, it is not quite so simple as that. The story concerns a group of characters living out a dull, repetitious existence in an old house. When one of the group ventures outside we discover that they are, in fact, aliens disguised as humans. To those who observe them, their alienness is betrayed by their failure to reproduce human individuality. Yet we must wonder whether this lack of individuality isn't itself part of their perfect mimicry of humans, because the same trait is sourly true of a number of human characters in Aldiss stories from around this time. For instance, in "Panel Game" we are introduced to Rick, of whom we are told, "As far as he might be said to have a character, his character was cheerful" (STAN, 172). This lack of character, of individuality, is a direct consequence of the excessive consumer society that holds sway: everything is subsumed into television advertising, which "did away with unemployment, over-employment, strikes, neuroses, wars, housing problems, crime and football pools" (STAN, 179). Thus was encapsulated the diminishment of postwar British society.

By the time *The Brightfount Diaries* was published late in 1955, five more stories had been published, in *Science Fantasy*, *Nebula*, *Authentic Science Fiction*, and *New Worlds*. During 1956 this rate of production increased enough for Aldiss to give up his job at Parker's to become a full-time writer. The following year he joined the *Oxford Mail* newspaper as literary editor, a position he held until 1969, but this was essentially a part-time role, and throughout this time his principal occupation was as novelist and short story writer. By the end of 1956 he had published sixteen short science fiction stories, enough for him to approach Faber with the idea of a collection. (His introduction to the first edition of the book is dated April 1956, perhaps suggesting how early he was putting the collection together in his mind, at least.) *Space, Time and Nathaniel*, which appeared in 1957, gathered together fourteen of these early stories.

Most science fiction collections at this time had titles that made sweeping declarations about space and time, but appending the name Nathaniel adds a touch of bathos that stands in earnest of Aldiss's desire to be different from his contemporaries. It marked, he has said, "the fact that I did not intend to follow a trail worn by other British SF writers. None of them wrote well enough, to my mind, except J. G. Ballard" (*BHS*, 46–47). (Ballard's first two stories appeared simultaneously in December 1956, so it is unlikely that his work had made any real impact on Aldiss's thinking at this time.) In his introduction to the 1979 edition of the book, Aldiss notes, "Much of my art was and has remained mildly deflationary . . . letting the air out of the tyres of galactic epics" (*STAN*, 10). One might query the use of the word "mildly." More important, I think, the use of the name Nathaniel brings into focus the humanity, the interest in the individual, that was rather more central to his work. In the introduction to the first edition, he argues that the purpose of the science in science fiction is that it "reveals us continually to ourselves, and the more clearly the picture is seen, the more mysterious it is seen to be" (*STAN*, 16).

The humanity that is revealed to us in these stories, of course, is not elevated or special but is marked more by failure and incomprehension, and the mystery is often that humanity survives at all. The human instinct for war is an instinct for our own destruction, as in "Our Kind of Knowledge," which records an encounter between militaristic humans, inclined to shoot first and ask questions later, and a hybrid of humans and their greatest enemies. These crossbreeds are ethereal, peaceful, and powerful: the way to the future is to become one with the enemy rather than to fight them. The typical Aldiss character, as in "The Failed Men," must "hide the fused, dead feeling inside. . . . But he had also to try and hide the deadness from himself" (*STAN*, 109).

The story concerns time travelers arriving in a far distant future when mankind's descendants have lapsed into a profound failure. There's a suggestion (no more) that the failure is itself a way of responding to the visitors from the past, something perhaps triggered by the colonialist character of the time travelers. The essence of the story, as of so many others, is the inability of one culture to understand another and the sense that all roads lead to failure. In "There Is a Tide," the consequence of human technological tinkering is that "Africa [is] ruptured at her very heart, beyond man's mending" (*STAN*, 151). As the narrator puts it: "Although I had always 'known' man was puny, it was the sight of that vast collapsing slab of mountain which had driven the fact into my marrow" (*STAN*, 147). Failure, puniness, diminishment, the message over and over again from these early, often very simple stories is that humankind has not fitted itself for its own future. And as we trace echoes of "Our Kind of Knowledge" in *The Dark Light Years*, of "The Failed Men" in *Cryptozoic*, and of "There Is a Tide" perhaps in Helliconia, we recognize that it is a message that would recur throughout the ever more sophisticated work that would follow.

*   *   *

One of Aldiss's stories, published in *Science Fantasy* in February 1956, would not be included in *Space, Time and Nathaniel* because it was already being expanded into his first novel, *Non-Stop*.

I discuss later in this study the extent of Aldiss's debt to the science fiction that had gone before and his acute awareness of this debt. His fiction, particularly that written during the 1950s and 1960s, is littered with references to fans and fellow authors, and works by other authors frequently inform his own stories. *Non-Stop* is a case in point. In 1941, Robert A. Heinlein's "Universe" and its sequel, "Common Sense" (also 1941), were published in *Astounding* and would later be conjoined as the novel *Orphans of the Sky* (1963). It is credited with being the first appearance of a generation starship in science fiction. In Heinlein's story, the people on board have forgotten that they are on a ship, and their society has degenerated into one of ritual and superstition. Aldiss's novel is clearly in dialogue with Heinlein's story. *Non-Stop* deliberately echoes its predecessor, introducing us to people aboard a generation starship who have forgotten that they are on a ship, and whose society has degenerated similarly. But whereas Heinlein's hero is an archetypal competent man who discovers the true nature of the ship and leads a few of his fellows to escape and land on a new world, Aldiss presents a very different scenario.

In the note that opens the novel, Aldiss declares that "a community which cannot or will not realize how insignificant a part of the universe it occupies is not truly civilized" (*N-S*, 9). The use of the word "universe" is obviously intentional, but the critical word for our purposes is "insignificant." As is often the case in Aldiss's work, there has been a war—there are still, in fact, ongoing battles, as we shall see—whose after-effects, felt long after any conflict, are a diminishment of what makes us human—literally, in this case, for the people aboard the ship are significantly smaller than normal Earth-bound humans.

When the book appeared in the United States the title was changed to *Starship*. It has been argued that this title gave away the surprise ending of the novel—indeed, Aldiss himself complained about it in *Bury My Heart at W. H. Smith's*—but that is a misreading of the book. There are repeated references to quarters, decks, companionways, compartments, and corridors. The corridors are overgrown with a bamboo-like growth called "ponics," a word we quickly recognize as being derived from "hydroponics." In fact, the notion that they are aboard a ship is part of the theology of the priest Marapper, and the protagonist, Roy Complain, is told much the same thing by the old explorer, Bergass. That all of this takes place aboard a starship is no secret to either the reader or the characters; what is important is that the characters don't understand the significance of this knowledge. The novel is a form of *bildungsroman* in which the spiritual education of Complain lies in coming to understand what it means to be on this particular ship.

The Greene tribe, to which Complain belongs at the start of the novel, is a nomadic society that is regularly clearing a way through the dense ponics, which provide food, medicine and other helpful things for the community, so they can move into a new section of corridor. They constantly face "disease and death and attacks by other tribes" (*N-S*, 25). In such circumstances cooperation would work for the good of all, but that is not in Aldiss's worldview. Instead, as Complain realizes, "They [are] isolated, and every man's hand [is] against his neighbour" (*N-S*, 35). The community is rigid in its structures, discouraging "any sort of thought not on severely practical lines" (*N-S*, 19). This prohibits any theorizing about their situation or their world, and we see strict rules about separation of children from their parents, while "sentiment [is] one of the weaknesses the Greene tribe [strives] to eradicate" (*N-S*, 23). Consequently, "the virtues by which men survived . . . [are] . . . cunning, greed, self-seeking" (*N-S*, 37). This is the view of someone disillusioned, someone who, when looking at the world, thinks that mankind cannot summon the virtues necessary to recover from war, let alone avoid war in future.

The people on this ship have lost their way, both literally and socially; being without purpose means they are also without community. Thus, when Complain recognizes that he and Roffrey joined Marapper's expedition for similar reasons, it provokes not fellow feeling, but quite the opposite: "Complain decided he must more than ever beware of the man, for if they had similar objectives, they were the more likely to clash" (*N-S*, 95). And when Complain later joins the Forwards, one of the first lessons he learns is: "You need not think because someone shows friendliness they mean you harm" (*N-S*, 165). This failure of community, this sense that everyone is necessarily isolated from everyone else, seems typical of the worldview that Aldiss expresses in his stories. It is surely significant that within the Greene tribe Complain is at odds with his wife and his mother and seems to have no easy relationship with anyone else he comes into contact with. And the five members of Marapper's expedition are constantly battling each other, just as they battle everything they come across in the world around them. Roffrey disappears after the encounter with the Giants; Wantage goes mad and attacks both Fermour and Complain before being killed by the Forwards; Marapper resorts to prayer rather than action, finding "some sort of mental refuge from this crisis by turning to the routines of priesthood" (*N-S*, 119), a personification of the futility they all feel. As David Pringle puts it, "*All* the characters are mean and petty, hemmed in by their peculiar circumstances."[4]

Aldiss wanted to recapture what he regarded as the wonder and the alienness of the East that he had fallen in love with during the war, and yet this is a place where the lushness of vegetation is threatening and where man's hand can only be turned against his neighbor. It is surely not reading too much into the novel to see Burma translated into the corridors of the ship, where the dense vegetation hides endless dangers. In their study of Aldiss's writing, *Apertures* (1984), Brian Griffin and David Wingrove state unequivocally that "none of [his wartime experiences] came wholly to the surface in Aldiss's writing until 1978, when *A Rude Awakening* was published,"[5] yet much of his earlier writing is suffused with those experiences. Here, for instance, there is a scene where the expedition has to cut its way through what had once been a mess hall, but the furniture had been raised up by the ponics to make a surreal obstacle: "As if in a nightmare, they cut their way past chairs and tables, half-blinded by midges which rose like dust from the foliage and settled on their faces. The thicket grew worse. Whole clumps of ponic had collapsed under this self-imposed strain and were rotting in slimy clumps, on top of which more plants grew. A blight had settled in, a blue blight sticky to the touch, which soon made the party's knives difficult to handle" (*N-S*,114). The dense foliage, the insects, and the heat make this read like a straightforward transposition of an encounter in the Burmese jungle, where "standing in that heat was like standing in a jelly" (*N-S*, 115).

And like the young Brian Aldiss growing up in the course of the Burma campaign, so Roy Complain is "rapidly sloughing the dry husk that limited Greene tribe thinking" (*N-S*, 127) with each new discovery, each new encounter. But just as Aldiss found England diminishing as he grew, so others are "changing into lower beings" (*N-S*, 251). *Non-Stop* is an echo of Aldiss's wartime experience, making visible his conclusion that as violence spreads through the ship it leaves only madness and self-destruction. And unlike Robert Heinlein's generation starship story, there is no way out at the end.

As the story nears its climax, Complain and his companion from the Forwards, Vyann, reach the command center of the ship and also acquire the diary of Gregory Complain, the first captain of the ship as it departed Procyon. From the command center they learn that the ship is orbiting Earth, which, Fredric Jameson tells us, transforms the story "from a pseudo-cosmological adventure story of explorations within the strange world of the ship, to a *political fable* of man's manipulation of his fellow man."[6] From the diary they learn that the homeward journey to Earth was intended to take seven generations; they are now the twenty-third generation. They also learn that the catastrophe that has changed the population, filled the ship with hydroponic plants, and raised the rats to intelligence is the result of a previously unknown amino acid brought on board in the water they took on from Procyon. These changes include an increased metabolic rate: people on the ship are smaller than normal humans, live four days in one day, and tend to die by around age twenty. As Complain observes, they are no longer human: "All that we've suffered, hoped, done, loved . . . it's not been real. We're just funny little mechanical things, twitching in a frenzy, dolls activated by chemicals" (N-S, 261). The reason they have spent generations in Earth orbit is that their acquired inhumanity renders them unable to live on the planet. The giants that have been seen throughout Complain's journey are normal humans from Earth, keeping watch on the ship and its inhabitants. But neither Complain nor any of his fellows can go home, for there is no home to go to. In part this is because, physiologically, they simply could not survive on Earth, but one senses also that Jameson's calling the book a political fable is a way of saying that everyone on board the ship is at war and in reality there is no way home from war. Aldiss returned to find an England that he felt was not his home any more; here that sense is dramatized in the final destruction of the ship.

Non-Stop was generally, if not universally, well received. Damon Knight, writing at the start of the 1960s, said that all "we have seen so far . . . [of Aldiss's novels] . . . are pot boilers,"[7] within which group he presumably includes Non-Stop, but he seems to have been something of an outlier. Nevertheless, it does appear to be a book that has grown in stature as the years have gone by. Perhaps when Pringle praises the book for refusing to "resolve itself into a happy, wish-fulfilling ending,"[8] we get a glimpse of a mood and approach that are more in tune with a later generation of science fiction readers than those of the 1950s, a later generation, of course, that was in part shaped by the fictions of Brian Aldiss. To put it another way, for Jameson the novel "has the effect of discrediting all our . . . generic expectations,"[9] and until the New Wave came along, in which Aldiss would play a leading role, readers tended to be more comfortable with the certainties of Heinlein than with the uncertainties of Aldiss.

★   ★   ★

Of course, Knight was correct. If we exclude Non-Stop, which I think was both more ambitious and more successful in achieving its ambitions than the term "pot boiler" would imply, then Aldiss's next few novels were indeed pot boilers. But the ambition was still there, and in the late 1950s and early 1960s it was revealed mostly in the profusion of short stories he was still writing.

The title of *Space, Time and Nathaniel* wasn't the only thing that marked that first collection out from other collections of the time. Aldiss very carefully set out the stories in a group of four (Space), a group of four (Time), and a group of six (Nathaniel), rather like a sonnet of two quatrains and a sestet. This arrangement suggests that Aldiss was well aware of how he wanted his stories to be presented. And much the same awareness informs his next two collections, although in each case this intent was initially foiled by his publisher.

His second collection was conceived as a sort of chronicle of the future consisting of eleven stories linked by "expository narrative" (*GGS*, 5) that together would present an episodic account of the coming millennia. Unfortunately, the linking material was removed for the first British publication in 1959, thus transforming it into a disconnected set of stories under the title *The Canopy of Time*. The American edition, which came out the following year under the title *Galaxies Like Grains of Sand*, replaced the first story, "Three's a Cloud" (1959), with "Out of Reach" (1957) and omitted three stories altogether—"Blighted Profile" (1958), "Judas Danced" (1958), and "They Shall Inherit" (1958)—although it did reinstate the linking material. The closest we have to Aldiss's original intention for the book is the 1979 British edition from Gollancz, which followed the form of the American edition but reinstated "Blighted Profile." This convoluted history is typical of Aldiss's early years as a writer, when most of his books underwent at least a title change between editions.

To the extent that *Galaxies Like Grains of Sand* is a fix-up, a collection of linked short stories that have been engineered in such a way as to compose a novel, the book acts as a future history. A future history is any sequence of linked stories or novels that together project a (seemingly) consistent history covering an extended period of the future. At the time Aldiss was writing these stories, the most famous future history was that which Robert A. Heinlein had been compiling since the 1940s and which would continue to provide a framework for much of his work well into the 1960s. Aldiss's collection, therefore, might be seen, like its near-contemporary, *Non-Stop*, as an impish response to Heinlein. But there was another model for a future history, provided before World War II by the sprawling philosophical epic that was *Last and First Men* by Olaf Stapledon (1930). This was a survey of the future covering millions of years during which the human race rose and declined, was remade and declined, time and again. Because of its scale and its perspective, it was almost completely devoid of character and the sort of human dramas that constitute most fiction. *Galaxies Like Grains of Sand* falls somewhere between these two models. The expository narrative echoes Stapledon in its broad and character-less survey of successive millennia: the War Millennia, the Robot Millennia, the Dark Millennia, the Ultimate Millennia, and so forth. The stories that are linked by such passages, however, are human dramas that record events concerning one set of characters within a moment of that millennium. There are no continuing characters; settings and circumstances change from one story to the next, so as much as anything it is down to the perceptions of the readers whether they are reading a set of linked or unrelated stories, but the linking material seems to me to make the whole greater than the sum of its parts.

As is the case often with Aldiss, though these are not themselves war stories, war is both the background and the impulse for the majority of them. War "fitted like a light harness over everyman's affairs, binding together the civilized universe as an ivy will cover a giant sequoia" (*GGS*, 99)—this is neither the first nor the last time Aldiss specifically links war and civilization. As he puts it at one point: "Man—it is at once his making and his undoing—is a competitive animal" (*GGS*, 98). Or as one character refers to human history: "Blood; war; lost causes; forgotten hopes; ages in chaos and days when even desperation died. It is no history to be proud of" (*GGS*, 107), an outline of history that is almost identical to the one we will see laid out in *Helliconia Winter* (1985). It is, therefore, no coincidence that the first age of mankind covered in the book is the War Millennia. In "Out of Reach" the world is being torn apart by war, and while some escape to the other planets and beyond—"the spores blown by the winds of war that established man in every cell of the honeycomb galaxy" (*GGS*, 50)—others escape by turning inwards, living in Dreameries. One such is Milton, whose vivid dream involves his visiting the world of the alien Solites, who have recently visited Earth. The dream, so vivid that it is obviously a memory, involves his marrying one of the Solites and being taken with her to their world, but there he encounters another Earthman, Chun Hwa, who happens to be from the other side in the war. (Chun Hwa and the Solites reappear in a later story, "Blighted Profile," which suggests that Aldiss was intentionally linking the stories even as he composed them, but in that story they are not the sophisticated time travelers seen in "Out of Reach.") Milton's rage is such that he accidentally kills his wife and is exiled back to his own world, only to discover that in truth the Solites are from Earth's future, from the time after it has been nearly destroyed by the war. In some ways, this story recalls "The Failed Men," in which humans travelling into their own future are unable to fully comprehend or adequately communicate with the people they find there; all that they bring with them is a form of death wish.

After war come the Sterile Millennia, followed, as humanity starts to lose its grip on its own world, by the Robot Millennia and what is perhaps the most often anthologized story that Aldiss wrote, "Who Can Replace a Man?" Most of the other stories in this collection are overemphatic, too obvious in the point they are making, and often surprisingly straightforward for Aldiss, but "Who Can Replace a Man?" is subtle and tender, and it manages to evoke sympathy and fellow-feeling for what is, in essence, a piece of farm machinery. The land is exhausted, yet still the robots tend the ground until the day when no orders arrive from the city. Logically they conclude that all men have broken down, because "if a machine had broken down, it would have been quickly replaced. But who can replace a man?" (*GGS*, 53). There is a strict hierarchy of machine intelligence, and those with higher intelligence assume leadership. As we often see in Aldiss, here are characters struggling to make the best of their situation but hampered by restrictions that are generally not of their making. A group of robots set off into the Badlands, where they might be safe from threats. But there they encounter a lone surviving man and instantly revert to their servile roles. Mankind is not the answer, but since no one can replace a man, there is no answer.

As the collection marches ever onward into the future, the same message is repeated in one form or another. Over the course of the millennia humans spread across space, where "stars and planets [hang] like dew amid spiders' webs" (*GGS*, 111), an image that we will see curiously literalized in *Hothouse*. The further they go, the more they lose touch with Earth, with each other, with what has made them human, but always what they carry with them is war (as in "Incentive") and an inability to understand anyone who is not like themselves (as in "O Ishrail!"). Eventually this lack of understanding and propensity for war come together in the Ultimate Millennia: in "Visiting Amoeba" a man from a strange world beyond the galactic rim foments an attack on Earth. The attack is defeated by the overwhelming power of the old order, but the man is unfazed because he is not human; he is the next stage in evolution. The galaxy is coming to an end, and his message to all the human worlds is that his kind will be the basis for a new order of existence that arises from the ruins. War is what has kept human civilization going, and it is how it will end. "Visiting Amoeba" is not a particularly good story—like many others in this collection it is overly formulaic—but it encapsulates the view of humanity that guides much of Aldiss's work.

★   ★   ★

The complex structure of *Galaxies Like Grains of Sand* was something Aldiss tried to replicate in his next collection, only to encounter exactly the same issues. The first version of the collection was published by Faber in 1963 under the title *The Airs of Earth*. It contained eight stories but no linking material. The U.S. edition, published a year later, also contained eight stories, but three were different from those in the U.K. edition and another story, "How to Be a Soldier," appeared under a different title, "Hearts and Engines." *Starswarm*, as the U.S. edition was retitled, also contained the sort of linking material that had appeared in *Galaxies Like Grains of Sand*. This has become the standard edition of the collection, though a 1984 publication by Baen Books in the United States added a ninth story, "Intangibles, Inc." (1959).

It is hard to imagine that *The Airs of Earth* was Aldiss's own title for the book, since the linking material makes it plain that each story represents a different sector of a galactic cluster, so that the collection as a whole comprises a survey of "a handful of the myriad civilizations, all contemporary in one sense, all isolated in another, that go to make up our galactic cluster" (*SS*, 7). The link between the two collections, not only in structure but in intent, is made explicit in the way the last section of expository material in *Galaxies Like Grains of Sand* began, "Again we must use the symbol: Time passed" (*GGS*, 157) while the first section of exposition in *Starswarm* begins: "The most simple statement you can make is also the most profound: Time passes" (*SS*, 7). This doesn't simply establish that the two books have similar concerns; it is also a statement of Aldiss's repeated interest in time, or more precisely, in the long view. The opening of *Starswarm* continues: "A million centuries—give or take a dozen—have elapsed" (*SS*, 7), a distance that Aldiss's imagination has overleapt, only to discover at the end of that immensity of time that man remains the same, that war is the shaping mechanism, and that the story he has to tell, save for a few mechanical details, could be anywhen. This is something we will discover again in *Hothouse, Cryptozoic, Enemies of the System*, Helliconia, and elsewhere. Time, Aldiss suggests, changes nothing, but changes everything; yet in its essential and mostly undesirable characteristics, time stays the same.

The stories, with one exception, are no more impressive than those in *Galaxies Like Grains of Sand*, but as in that collection they provide a broad, basic view of the idea Aldiss sought to present. In "Hearts and Engines," for instance, there is a joke that Aldiss is so fond of that he uses it twice: "Every day someone somewhere is inventing gunpowder" (*SS*, 33). It is, on the surface, a joke about the spread of humanity across the galaxy, so that "diversity is everywhere; originality nowhere" (*SS*, 33), but more tellingly it reflects his view that humanity is most inventive when creating weapons of war. And this is yet another story about the human cost of war. In this instance, drawing on an idea from H. G. Wells's story "The New Accelerator" (1901), it concerns a drug that speeds soldiers up so that the enemy has no chance to react to them but does so at a dreadful cost to the soldiers affected.

Presumably because of his time in the East, Aldiss often expressed anti-colonialist views long before they became a familiar stance in science fiction. Here they emerge in such stories as "The Under-Privileged," in which a devolved group of humans have, of necessity, become reptilian, cold-blooded, in order to survive on their planet. They are reached by a superior group, the Warms, and despite their consciousness of being underprivileged they work hard to earn the right to move to the capital of the warm-blooded humans. When they get there, having been taken under the wing of a friendly local called Slen Kater (a play on the name of prominent fan and bookseller, Ken Slater, one of the innumerable examples of the way Aldiss incorporated the names of people he knew into his fiction), they are drugged to make them happy and don't realize that they have become exhibits in a sort of zoo. And in "The Game of God," an early version of the novelette "Segregation," a survey party arrives on a planet prior to colonization. They find a human who has been there for twenty years, worshipped as a god by the vicious cayman-headed natives. But it turns out that he has been a virtual prisoner all that time, afraid to go out and learn the truth, and everything he says has been derived from the colorful adventure films made about his life. The fact that the survey party discovers the truth about the planet does nothing to stop the oncoming colonists and "their depredations on 'new' planets" (*SS*, 104).

One of the more emotionally powerful of the stories collected here, a harbinger, perhaps, of the emotionally searching stories that were to come later in the decade, is "O Moon of My Delight," which is set on a moon where ships that travel faster than the speed of light can land. The entire moon is girdled by the Flange, a device for absorbing the velocity of the ship, but the knock-on effect is that the moon's orbit is shifted with each landing, so time on the moon is constantly being readjusted. It's the story of Murrag, who labors on a farm while he writes his book about the moon and who is in love with the Flange and the sight of an FTL ship landing. He conveys this excitement to Fay, the six-year-old daughter of the farmer for whom he works. The farmer is about to take his family and leave the moon, and Fay wants to have her first and last chance to see a ship landing. So she runs away to the Flange, unaware of the elaborate protection measures that enclose it, and is killed. The emotional kicker is that no one is really bothered by her death: the farmer and his family are too excited about leaving the moon, and Murrag is too excited by the idea of his book.

The one truly outstanding story in the collection is "Old Hundredth," which was specially commissioned by John "Ted" Carnell for the one hundredth issue of *New Worlds* in 1960. The title refers to the hymn "All creatures that on Earth do dwell," which is set to a tune that had previously been used for Psalm 100; it is appropriate, because the creatures *have* inherited the Earth. The story is set on a far-future dying Earth, though this future also reflects the distant past; surviving structures were "the essence of man. They were man—all that remained of him on Earth" (*SS*, 184). Here again we can see that man is a creature of war: "When the first flint, the first shell, was shaped into a weapon, that action shaped man" (*SS*, 184). Among the upgraded creatures that now populate the humanless planet (including the viewpoint character, Dandi, who is a giant sloth), the only ones that are feared are the bears, "the only creatures to show signs of wishing to emulate man's old aggressiveness" (*SS*, 187).

★   ★   ★

These three collections barely scraped the surface of what Aldiss was writing at this time. Between 1954, when "Criminal Record" first appeared, and the end of 1959, he published fifty-six short stories (excluding the various Brightfount Diaries he wrote for *The Bookseller*). Most of these appeared in *New Worlds*, though he was also a regular in *Science Fantasy* and *Nebula*, and in January 1958 his story "The New Father Christmas" was the occasion of his first appearance in the *Magazine of Fantasy and Science Fiction*.

These stories were attracting attention. In 1959, at the Seventeenth World Science Fiction Convention, Detention, staged in Detroit, Michigan, Aldiss was shortlisted for a Hugo Award for Best New Author, alongside another British writer, Pauline Ashwell, and three American writers, Rosel George Brown, Louis Charbonneau, and Kit Reed. As it turned out, no award was presented, though the nominees appear to have received a plaque that would later mislead Margaret Aldiss into thinking he had won.[10]

Many of these stories would be as thematically interesting as the stories we have looked at so far, but not all. Aldiss had been reading science fiction since the days of space operas, and though he would campaign for the acceptance of science fiction as literature, he also had a taste for its cruder expressions. There is here a contradiction that would become more evident as his career progressed in the way he would expect much of his own fiction to be taken seriously as literature while celebrating the "hokum,"[11] as he called it, of sf at its most generic and quoting, with evident approval, a remark attributed to Dena Brown about putting science fiction "back in the gutter where it belongs."[12] Some of Aldiss's stories, therefore, would represent a joyful embrace of the most hackneyed forms of the genre, often under pseudonyms such as Jael Cracken.

This form of sf extended to his next two short novels. As is typical of Aldiss's work around this time, their publishing history was rather complex. The first appeared as a two-part serial in *New Worlds* in September and October 1958 under the title "Equator"; it was then published in the United States as part of an Ace Double (with *The Changeling Worlds* by Ken Bulmer) under the title *Vanguard from Alpha*, and after that it was coupled with the novelette "Segregation" in a U.K. paperback titled *Equator: A Human Time Bomb from the Moon*. Much later, a heavily revised version of *Equator* was incorporated into a novel variously titled *The Year Before Yesterday* and *Cracken at Critical* (1987). The second began as a serial in *New Worlds* between March and May 1960 under the title "X for Exploitation" before appearing as *Bow Down to Nul* as part of an Ace Double (with *The Dark Destroyers* by Manly Wade Wellman) and finally becoming *The Interpreter* for its British paperback publication.

Neither of these could be counted as particularly good novels (Margaret Aldiss considers *Bow Down to Nul* as "probably Aldiss's least successful novel" though there are, admittedly, other contenders for that title).[13] *Equator* has the advantage of being set largely in Sumatra, a place Aldiss knew from his military service, and there is quite a vivid sense of place. The story concerns an astronaut, Tyne Leslie, who finds himself caught in a three-way struggle between two differing factions of the alien settlers, the Rosk, and a variety of Earth agents, without ever being entirely sure which he can trust. The version of the story that was later incorporated into *Cracken at Critical* was extensively tidied up, yet those changes did nothing to enhance the quality or increase the complexity of a novel that is basically a breathless mélange of violence, hair's-breadth escapes, coincidences, and sudden revelations that change everything. As Damon Knight concedes, however, "even in his comic-book writing, Aldiss is more perceptive than most."[14]

If *Equator* takes Aldiss back to his military experience on Sumatra (and perhaps some faint echo of *Hunter Leaves the Herd*), *The Interpreter* reminds us that he served in the Signals Regiment. The story is "an analogue of what Western imperialism had done to India and Indonesia"[15] in which one man, the Interpreter of the title, stands between humanity and the alien Nul, controlling the nature of their relationship by the way he interprets or misinterprets their communications.

★   ★   ★

It is tempting to wonder whether Aldiss found the crudity of these two novels unsatisfactory, because he turned away from the broad, baroque realms of science fiction toward the mainstream with his next two novels. More accurately, we might say, with his next three novels, because it was at this time that he wrote the first version of what became *Report on Probability A*, but that is discussed elsewhere in this book.

The first of the pair, *The Male Response* (1961), involves an indecisive technician sent to install a powerful computer in the newly independent African state of Goya, who then finds himself embroiled in what Griffin and Wingrove aptly sum up as "James Bond-type skulduggery."[16] The sexual promiscuity that was apparently enough to get the novel banned in South Africa (though this may have had more to do with interracial relationships than sexual ones) is perhaps the first appearance of what I have called the priapic masculinity that is to become a key aspect of many of Aldiss's male characters.

This aspect is even more to the fore in the second of this pair of novels, *The Primal Urge*. This is a more overtly science-fictional novel because it involves a shiny metal disc known as an Emotional Register (ER) that is inserted into the forehead and glows pink when the wearer feels sexual attraction for someone. These devices are intended to "enable the id for the first time to communicate direct [*sic*], without the intervention of the ego" (*PU*, 23), a reversion to the primal, though not the primitive, that will "set us free from all the accumulation of five thousand years of petty convention" (*PU*, 24). It is, in effect, an assault on the traditional conservatism and prudery of the English, part of the hated narrowness that Aldiss had encountered on his return from his sexually liberal years in the army, an assault in which, "under the first concerted frontal attack it had ever faced, that prudery collapsed; it had been a poor, frail thing, a middle class myth of hardly more than a century's standing" (*PU*, 55). The novel's focus on sexual desire prompts Richard Mathews to call it a satire on "the new permissiveness,"[17] but when it was published in 1961 it had been barely a year since the verdict had been delivered in the trial of Penguin Books over the publication of the unexpurgated *Lady Chatterley's Lover* (1928) by D. H. Lawrence. This trial ushered in a more liberal era in publishing, but it wasn't exactly the launch of the permissive society, which wouldn't really get going in Britain until after the Profumo Scandal in 1963, so in that sense there was nothing for Aldiss to satirize.

The Primal Urge is very pointedly set in the present. Aldiss asserts that this is a "contemporary picture" (*PU*, 7), and he makes more use of real people, products, and institutions such as Air Chief Marshall Dowding, Bertrand Russell, Arthur Koestler, J. B. Priestley, Aldous Huxley, Kosset Carpets, Oxford

Marmalade, Dickens and Jones, and the National Book League than in any of his other works. This narrow-minded, self-satisfied country, Aldiss is saying, is in desperate need of a jolt of the sexual liberation he enjoyed in the East. This connection is made explicit when he talks of "waves of sex flow[ing] out overpoweringly above the audience, drowning them like a breeze from an Indian village" (*PU*, 175).

That the novel is addressed to the young generation struggling to liberate themselves from the strictures of contemporary British society is further suggested by the name of the protagonist, Jimmy Solent, which calls to mind the central character in John Osborne's play *Look Back in Anger* (1956), Jimmy Porter (the Solent being the strait upon which stands Portsmouth, which in turn perhaps suggests Porter). This identification is reinforced by the character of Alyson, echoing that play's Alison. Osborne's characters, however, never would have displayed the attitudes that Aldiss's characters do. For instance, Alyson begins the novel by bemoaning the fact that she's a member of "the generation that missed the war" (*PU*, 16). In other words, those too young to have been in the war are presented as feeling that they missed out on something, or perhaps it might be more accurate to say that those who fought in the war (such as Aldiss) regard themselves as having been made special by the experience, and so everyone else must regret missing it. This was not exactly a universal feeling among the youth of the late 1950s and 1960s, but it pinpoints Aldiss's own attitudes precisely. As we will see elsewhere, Aldiss, already approaching forty as he wrote this novel, was never exactly in tune with the younger generation.

I have a feeling that this novel, weak as it is in many ways, is like *The Hand-Reared Boy* and its sequels in more closely matching Aldiss's own feelings and ideas than does much of his other work. For instance, religion and belief play a more positive role in most of the books than they do in Aldiss's own thought, but in *Primal Urge* it boils down to this contrast between Jimmy and his stuffed-shirt brother Aubrey: "I know you've got a good old Christian theory that any natural instinct is wrong, but I've got a good old pagan idea that what a man wants is ultimately the best thing he can have" (*PU*, 140). I think that, for Aldiss, religion was an unnecessary restraint on humanity's natural instincts and behaviors, which were overwhelmingly sexual. As elsewhere in his work, this is a very masculine world. There is a rare suggestion of homosexuality when Jimmy's friend Donald, is bitchy about a colleague: "It was, of course, the result of Donald's being what he was, and of the law's attitude to what he was" (*PU*, 48). And although there is a suggestion that the Emotional Register will cause the decriminalization of homosexuality, when Jimmy meets, and fancies, a lesbian, he thinks, "You never knew when a spot of physiotherapy might not convert these borderline cases" (*PU*, 109), an attitude that seems typical not only of the times but also of Aldiss. His valorization of sex is primarily heterosexual and male-centered. There is, unusually, a strong, independent, and clever woman in the shape of Rose English, Jimmy's first lust object, who turns out to have been the inventor of the ER. But she, for her cleverness, for her indifference to the desires of men, is looked at askance by the prominent male characters. With regard to sex she behaves as casually as the men would wish to, and in keeping with the mores of the period she is damned for it.

The flirtations with the crudeness of genre fiction and with the sexualization of mainstream literature suggested by these works would evolve and bear fruit in the coming years. For now, however, Aldiss's career was about to take a new turn, but it was one that still had roots in his wartime experiences.

CHAPTER 2

NATURALIST

The tree was in the Calcutta Botanical Gardens, where a notice "proclaimed it to be the biggest tree in the world" (*HH*, 270). Brian Aldiss had left the nearby army camp and crossed the River Hoogley in order to spend an afternoon just gazing at this banyan tree. When, later, he returned to Britain he discovered that in the 1920s the evolutionary biologist Julian Huxley had written about the tree in an article called "The Meaning of Death." Huxley's juxtaposition of this startling example of profuse vegetation with death is something that would have resonated with Aldiss, whose other experience of profuse vegetation, in the jungles of Burma, had also been intimately associated with death. Those jungles had made an oblique appearance in *Non-Stop*, but "that Dali-like banyan . . . remained ineradically [*sic*] in mind" (*HH*, 271).

In his article Huxley had said that the tree covered two acres. Aldiss wondered how many more acres it covered by the time he saw it and began to speculate that, as the sun began to go nova and the world grew warmer, the tree might cover the whole globe. The result was a story titled "Hothouse" that appeared in the *Magazine of Fantasy and Science Fiction* in February 1961. The story was an immediate hit with readers, and four more stories, "Nomansland," "Undergrowth," "Timberline," and "Evergreen" would appear in the magazine during 1961. The editor at the time, Avram Davidson, reputedly revived the term "science-fantasy" specifically to cover the "Hothouse" series because neither "fantasy" nor "science fiction" seemed an appropriate category.[1] It was this series, rather than the revision of the stories that became the novel *Hothouse*, that won the Hugo Award for Best Short Story at the 1962 Worldcon, the only time a series rather than an individual story has won that particular award. It was Aldiss's first major award for his fiction.

Parenthetically, in his 2008 afterword to *Hothouse*, Aldiss repeats a story he tells in *Bury My Heart at W. H. Smith's*, *The Twinkling of an Eye*, and his last essay collection, *An Exile from Planet Earth* (2012). One morning in 1962 his girlfriend, Margaret Mason, who would become his second wife, found a strange object on the doorstep wrapped in an Irish newspaper. This proved to be the Hugo Award for "Hothouse." Presumably, it had been carried back from the Worldcon, held that year in Chicago, by one of the Irish fans present, who had then posted it for the last part of its journey. Aldiss insists, "I hadn't even heard of Hugos at that time" (*ToE*, 235), but, like much else in his autobiography, this claim needs to be taken with a pinch of salt. By 1962 he had, after all, already received a plaque when he was shortlisted for a Best New Writer Hugo only three years earlier. Moreover, his active engagement in the science fiction fandom of the time, including helping found the British Science Fiction Association in 1958 (he held Membership Number 1 throughout his life and served as president from 1960), makes such ignorance of the Hugo Awards highly unlikely.

The five "Hothouse" stories were quickly revised and combined into the novel *Hothouse*, published in 1962. (Despite the popularity of the "Hothouse" stories among American fans, the American publisher, Signet, chose to abridge the book and retitle it *The Long Afternoon of Earth*, apparently for fear that booksellers might otherwise shelve it among gardening titles.) It is one of the key works of Aldiss's career. After what we might take to be the disappointment of the four preceding novels it is interesting how, in this book, Aldiss directs our attention back to *Non-Stop*. It is not merely that the corridor-clogging ponics of *Non-Stop* find an echo in the world-spanning tree of *Hothouse*, or the fact that in both novels the humans are physically diminished, but the name of the protagonist, Gren, clearly recalls the Greene tribe of the earlier novel.

In keeping with Huxley's juxtaposition of the banyan and death, the novel opens with five-year-old Clat falling and being taken by a trappersnapper before she can be rescued. The death is not mourned: "It was the way," they say, and besides, "Clat's was not the first death they had witnessed" (*HH*, 5). This is not so much an indifference toward death as an acceptance of it. This is a world where death awaits at every turn and there is little point in making a fuss about it: "In the forest when one fell to the green there was scarcely ever a bone surviving to be buried" (*HH*, 8), so at birth the male parent carved a wooden "soul" to be interred in place of the body.

In a letter to Michael Collings, Aldiss says that his "successful novels" offer "symbolist landscapes" to which "the writer/reader must create his own key or map or else perish."[2] There is no great problem in devising the key to this particular novel. *Non-Stop* may have referenced Aldiss's wartime experiences, but of all his science fiction it is probably *Hothouse* that most directly recapitulated those experiences: the jungle, the dangers hidden all around, the constant presence of death, and the sense of the necessary insignificance of mankind. When a comrade dies there is nothing to be done but move on, because whatever killed him is waiting to do the same to you. It is tempting, also, to trace a link with *The Inheritors* by William Golding (1955), which had appeared to ecstatic reviews—Arthur Koestler had called it "an earthquake in the petrified forests of the English novel,"[3] a comment that certainly would have aroused Aldiss's interest. Though one is set at the very beginning of humankind's time on Earth and the other at the very end, both begin with a death and deal with a diminished people struggling to make sense of a world that is bigger and more complex than they can realize.

This world is overwhelmed by vegetation: "No bare places existed" (*HH*, 6), and humans, "the last animal species in the all-conquering vegetable world" (*HH*, 7), are barely avoiding extinction. Virtually all of the creatures that are encountered in the novel are plants that have evolved an independent, mobile existence and mimic birds, butterflies, insects, and other beings. Within this unrelenting landscape, Aldiss's humans are "the merest footnotes to humanity's greater story, one flickering downturn in humanity's fortunes before its story begins again."[4] The novel consists of various encounters with the different grotesqueries of this world, so that it comes across as a series of metaphors for jungle warfare. One form of mobile plant is the traverser, "that gross vegetable equivalent of a spider" (HH, 15), which has spun webs that tie Earth to the now motionless moon. This means that Earth is literally festooned with cobwebs, a familiar representation of decay and abandonment. As we saw in Non-Stop and will see again in Earthworks, The Malacia Tapestry, and Enemies of the System, this is a world in which time has effectively come to a stop.

We have seen repeatedly that for Aldiss the British whom he encountered on his return in 1947 were a "lesser race," and that diminishment has already appeared in Non-Stop and The Primal Urge; here again this stasis has resulted in the devolution of humankind. As the morel, the parasitic fungus that has acquired intelligence, says to Gren of the long-ago times when mankind ruled Earth: "You were large beings then, five times as tall as you are now" (HH, 88), and with this comes a reduction in human understanding, which "trickled shallow these days. It was the way" (HH, 17). Later, in works such as Report on Probability A and the Helliconia Trilogy, Aldiss consistently shows that such stasis brings with it hollowness, monotony, and passivity, recalling the people he had seen from the train in India, whose unchanging life "requires endurance, born of centuries of fatalistic courage, passive acceptance, qualities scarce in the unsleeping West" (BHS, 12). These farmers are specifically recalled toward the end of this novel when Sodal Ye says of the Arablers that they had "lost the notion of passing time. . . . For them there was simply the individual life span. It was—it is, the only time span they are capable of recognizing: the period-of-being" (HH, 245).

As is appropriate in a tale of an unchanging future, the story is episodic; there is no great dramatic arc, no great revelation, no world-changing event. The society that we find among the trees is matriarchal, and Gren is exiled because he is disruptive and disobedient. But, alone in this unforgiving environment, he falls victim to a parasitic fungus. This morel is able to access race memories in Gren and his mate Poyly that the two humans aren't even aware of: "It was the first creature in a billion years to be able to look back down the long avenues of time" (*HH*, 95). Groping "among the very shards of human memory" (*HH*, 115), the morel discovers (or at least claims to have discovered) that early man achieved intelligence by means of a symbiotic relationship with fungi and over time evolved a larger skull capacity so that "vulnerable morels were able to move inside, to become truly a part of the people, to improve their own abilities under a curving shelter of bone" (*HH*, 117). But as the sun became hotter, giving off stronger radiation, the morel symbiots could not survive, and so human intelligence was drastically reduced at a stroke.

There are other suggestions that human intelligence is a result of symbiosis. For instance, the Fishers are colonized by the "Tummy-trees," which connect themselves to the Fishers by a long tail. The Tummy-trees keep the Fishers safe, guide them in their fishing, and provide them with a limited intelligence. When Gren and Poyly cut off the tail of one of the Fishers he becomes incomprehensible in his speech and anxious to return to the tree in the hope of acquiring a new tail. But recalling Aldiss's short story "Our Kind of Knowledge," which implies that the way to survive the future is to breed with the enemy, we should perhaps conclude that such symbiotic relationships are merely the most efficient way to survive in this future. The morel that parasitizes Gren is not particularly reliable, but Gren is not equipped to question the things he is told. The death of Poyly is the turning point for the morel: to this moment its aim has been to acquire power through Gren; afterwards its aim is to acquire power despite Gren. When Gren, his new partner Yattmur, and their baby Laren are living in the mountain cave, it becomes feral, evil, and affects Gren so that he behaves "in a curiously slack way as if his nervous system was having to respond to two rival centres of control. . . . In his eyes hung a blind look like a curtain" (*HH*, 211). The conflict within the novel here centers on the battle to free Gren from the influence of the morel, but when Gren is able to trick the morel into leaving him, he in turn comes under the influence of Sodal Ye, an intelligent dolphin-like being. From Sodal Ye we learn how quickly Earth is approaching its end. Acting on this knowledge, members of Gren's former tribe, who have traveled the webs between the worlds, set out into space aboard a traverser with the morel installed as its governor. But Gren will not join them; his journey ends back in the world tree, where life continues as though nothing had happened. As

C. N. Manlove points out, this is hardly a story of development "from an unthinking to a more thinking state[;] . . . that thinking will be largely useless as thought, for it will only enable him the more surely to stay alive, not to create anything new."[5] In fact, Gren chooses the path to the old, to certain death; novelty is the choice of the older members of his tribe who are on their way into space.

The Hugo Award is testimony to how well *Hothouse* was received at the time, while in other circles Kingsley Amis proclaimed in the *Observer* that it was "a work of genuine creative imagination."[6] The book's reputation has not faded over the years. In 1977 Andrew Darlington called it "wide-screen baroque at its most outlandishly extravagant and breath-taking."[7] For David Pringle, in 1985, it was "a novel of prodigious inventiveness and linguistic dexterity, marred by occasional whimsicalities."[8] And in 2016 Adam Roberts declared that "summary cannot do justice to the brilliant, mind-gripping, sparkling *oddness* of this book."[9] It is obvious from these comments that what first attracts the attention of commentators is the book's pyrotechnic language. In truth, there was still something of the 1950s in Aldiss's prose, a formality, a rather studied humor (and an occasional old-fashioned attitude, shall we say, as when he reports that Poyly had "a womanly gift for irrelevance that eons of time had not quenched" [*HH*, 96]), but he was starting to develop the more inventive use of language that would form a greater part of his work as the decade progressed. It was perhaps easier, however, to draw attention to the language than to what Roberts so succinctly calls the "oddness" of the book. Anyone who tried to examine the novel in terms of the verities of science fiction at that time might conclude, as James Blish (writing as William Atheling Jr.) did, that *Hothouse* was "a sadly damaged piece of goods. Aldiss had a marvellous idea; he clothed it in highly personal, highly cadenced prose; he filled it with lovely ingenuities; and he lost control of it."[10] Aldiss had a ready response to such criticism. In a privately circulated journal called *Proceedings of the Institute for Twenty-First Century Studies* he wrote: "I am a surrealist at heart; that is, I'm none too sure whether the reality of the world agrees with its appearance. Only in sf, or near sf, can you express this feeling in words."[11] Although *Hothouse* is, perhaps, too coherent to fully take on the way surrealism traditionally expresses the unconscious, nevertheless the prose, particularly in its use of playful neologisms and extravagant invention, at least venture toward the surreal. In this Aldiss was, along with his friend J. G. Ballard, starting to invent the New Wave, but that was still a few years away.

★   ★   ★

Hothouse, still widely considered to be one of Aldiss's best novels, also occupies a pivotal position both in terms of his career and within the history of science fiction. Yet as Aldiss stated, it was "a novel from which I always feel distanced, perhaps recalling the miserable circumstances under which it was written" (*HC*, 206). At the end of the 1950s, not long after his second child, Wendy, was born, his marriage to Olive fell apart. They had been drifting away from each other for some time; by his own admission, Aldiss seems to have been neither the most faithful of husbands nor the easiest person to live with. But he was devastated when the marriage failed. Olive and the children moved to the Isle of Wight, and for a long time Aldiss felt that he would never see Wendy or his son Clive again. At the same time, he was now living in somewhat reduced circumstances while starting to build a relationship with Margaret Mason. In 1962, the year *Hothouse* appeared, Mason published *Item Forty-Three*, the first step toward what would become her comprehensive bibliography of Aldiss's work.

The novels and stories Aldiss wrote at this time would for him, therefore, be tainted by the anxieties and circumstances in which they were written. Despite this, or perhaps because of a more focused concentration on his writing, these were also years in which he produced some of his best work. But only one novel directly expressed the fear of never seeing his children again: *Greybeard*. That the novel is dedicated to his children is a tacit acknowledgement of this fact.

For once, the publishing history of this novel is uncomplicated: it is not a fix-up from earlier stories, there was no serialization, and it didn't appear under variant titles or with wildly differing texts. It eschews the exuberance of earlier works, the wild invention, the moments of comedy that Aldiss seemed powerless to resist even when he was trying to be at his most serious. It was, in all, a somber, powerful, moving account of a world without children.

As we have seen, images of overgrown vegetation, stasis, and diminishment consistently appear in Aldiss's portrayals of a world that has failed. It is, therefore, no surprise that such images all play their part in *Greybeard* as well. Thus, in the opening scene, a family of stoats crosses a field that had once produced a good crop of wheat, but "during a period of neglect, weeds had sprung up and choked the cereal. Later, fire spread across the fields, burning the thistles, parsleys, and giant grasses which had overtaken the wheat" (*GB*, 7). With not a single person in the scene, nature is once again repossessing what had been the work of man. "Even in the wilderness, the pattern of a way of life when man had been master was still evident," (*GB*, 8), telling us is that man is no longer master: "Man had gone, and the great interlocking world of living species had already knitted over the space he once occupied" (*GB*, 181). We are five paragraphs into the novel before there is a suggestion that humans still occupy this world, and when it comes, we see that their existence is indicated by "the raw stumps of trees, the piles of sawdust, and an axe biting deep into a log" (*GB*, 8). Humans are identified by their destruction of what nature is reclaiming; they are unnatural. Two years earlier, in the same year *Hothouse* appeared, Rachel Carson's *Silent Spring* had been published. In *Greybeard*, as in *Hothouse* and particularly in *Earthworks* (1965), Aldiss showed an awareness of the environmental concerns that Carson had raised, an awareness that would be explored in even greater depth in later works such as the Helliconia Trilogy.

We can extend this notion that humans and nature stand on opposite sides to say that mankind brings unnatural color into the world, and what we see in Aldiss's work is that the failure of humanity is marked by a sense of colorlessness. Here, for instance, "the vertical red and orange stripes of the old man's garment furnished the only splash of colour on the entire bedraggled landscape" (*GB*, 8). And when the villagers of Sparcot assemble, "the general effect [is] colourless" (*GB*, 24). There has been a war, of course, and the war has wrought the destruction not only of human life but of color. We see much the same in *Barefoot in the Head*, for instance, in which the benighted postwar Britain is similarly colorless, and "hedges and trees [have] no hint of green" (*BfH*, 87).

This colorlessness reflects the stasis of this world. Algy Timberlane, commonly known as Greybeard, the protagonist of the novel, looks out on the natural world and declares that "everything that can still multiply is doing so" (*GB*, 20). Only the humans are not multiplying: The nuclear weapons used so cavalierly in the war have rendered humanity sterile, and so their world is running down to an ultimate stillness. Sparcot, which here serves as the world in miniature, has become "a citadel for the ailments: arthritis, lumbago, rheumatism, cataract, pneumonia, influenza, sciatica, dizziness" (GB, 24). These are not merely the afflictions of age in a world without youth; they are ailments that make the sufferer stiffen and become still. As Richard Mathews says, this is a place "where time is standing still as the elderly remnants of the race wait out their days, constantly on guard against the outside world."[12] And within this stasis we see, yet again, the diminishment of humankind. When, toward the end of the novel, Jingadangelow offers a cynical view of the present—"Is not this rag-taggle present preferable to that other mechanized, organized, deodorized present we might have found ourselves in, simply because in this present we can live on a human scale?" (GB, 125)—it is apparent that the human scale is much smaller than pre-war humanity aspired to and achieved. As always in Aldiss, the only effect of war is to make lesser beings of us all.

Greybeard follows two branching paths. Starting from Sparcot, an imaginary village on the Thames outside Oxford, one path takes us forward in time as Greybeard and a small group of unlikely companions journey down the river toward London. The other path follows much the same geographical journey (Sparcot, Oxford, London) but in reverse chronological order. This reverse journey does not attempt to uncover the origins of the catastrophe (that is obvious: it is war) but rather to trace the developing understanding of what the catastrophe means. In London, at the start of the journey but the end of the book, Algy is one of the last children born after "that deliberate act men called the Accident" (GB, 134). Here, with his life and therefore hope still ahead of him, Algy begins his lifelong relationship with the woman who will, in time, become his wife, Martha. It is symbolic, I think, that in the aftermath of his failed marriage Aldiss presented practically the only happy, enduring, and companionable marriage in his entire body of work. Not unconnected to this, I am sure, is the fact that this is one of the few novels to feature a woman who is strong, calm, competent, ready to act decisively when needed. She reflects that men were "the seat of the whole sickness. They invented these situations. They needed them—torturer or tortured, they needed them . . . they were united in an algolagnia beyond woman's cure or understanding" (GB, 64). ("Algolagnia" is another word for sadomasochism.) And it is Martha who spells out the underlying theme of the novel when she declares: "Our society, our biosphere, has been sick for forty years now. How can the individual remain healthy in it?" (GB, 74).

The key section in this backwards journey through time takes place in Oxford. Here Algy is part of an international effort to monitor and record these final days of mankind. But Oxford is under military rule, for even as humanity staggers toward its end the urge to fight and to control is unabated. The deep and inescapable despising of war that is in all of Aldiss's work is expressed with particular force in this novel. When forces continue to use battlefield nuclear weapons after the Accident that rendered all higher mammals infertile, he asks bitterly: "What were several fewer species of animals compared with a hundred-mile advance and another medal on another general[?]" (GB, 144). In such a militarized atmosphere, Algy can only conclude that his mission is worthless: not only will there be no one coming after to learn from his recordings, but humankind has shown itself to be utterly unworthy of such memorializing.

So Algy abandons his quest, which is what brings him and Martha to Sparcot, where the novel opens. But Sparcot is a dead end; there is nothing there but waiting impatiently for surcease. When Algy explores a deserted house and discovers an old photograph of a boy he starts to cry: "Childhood itself lay in the rotting drawers of the world, a memory that could not stand permanently against time" (GB, 47). Bearing in mind Martha's strictures regarding remaining healthy when the entire world around you is sick, Algy concludes that he must leave Sparcot. He, Martha, and a few others set out with no particular goal in mind other than perhaps to reach the mouth of the Thames. It is, though they would never think of it in these terms, an attempt to restart the clocks. Their journey does not begin auspiciously. The first thing the group encounters is the body of someone who has taken his own life. Algy's response is to ask: "Why did he kill himself? It can't have been for want of food" (GB, 45). It is odd that he doesn't consider want of company or want of hope as a reason for suicide.

A more significant encounter follows at Swifford Fair, another fictional addition to the geography of Oxfordshire, where they come upon Doctor Jingadangelow, a comic name for a far-from-comic character. Jingadangelow offers a treatment promising rejuvenation and immortality. At his stall, there is a youth—"The effect on Greybeard was like a shock of cold water" (*GB*, 118)—but Algy quickly realizes that the "boy" is an old man who has been made up to appear young. Youth is a commodity in this world, and something that evokes almost religious awe. Indeed, the next time Algy and Martha encounter Jingadangelow, as they reach London and the end of their journey, he has transformed himself from a purveyor of quack medicines into the leader of a religious cult.

But it is through Jingadangelow that Algy discovers a genuine child. They are there, we learn, living away from adult society, hidden in the wild places where they are unlikely to be found. They are not fully human, at least not in the way Algy and his fellows are, for they know nothing of the old society, the old ways in which the measure of mankind was reckoned in terms of destructive power. Previously, in such stories as "Old Hundredth" and "Visiting Amoeba," Aldiss had suggested that humanity must be swept away and replaced with something else; here the children will replace humanity. After all that has gone before, the novel ends on a surprising note of optimism (which is itself unusual in Aldiss's work, and which may owe something to the bleakness of Aldiss's state of mind when he wrote the book) as Martha tends an injured child and Greybeard gazes ahead "at the horizon where the hills were" (*GB*, 272). The novel ends as it began, with the landscape, but now the landscape represents the future.

The novel was well received. Harry Harrison, for instance, called it "a powerful work of art" that conveys "the emotions of the characters so well that I partook of them and made them mine."[13] This may not have been a universal opinion—Ron Goulart, for instance, called it "one more turkey"[14]—but it remains, with *Hothouse*, one of the novels that is consistently rated among Aldiss's best.

★   ★   ★

But Aldiss was always a restless writer, unwilling or unable to repeat himself. Throughout his career he would ricochet between the somber and the brightly colored, between thoughtful literariness and garish cliché, between genre at its most extroverted and genre at its most introverted. Thus *Greybeard* was bracketed by two novels that were startlingly different from its quiet humanity. Before it came the story of an encounter between the brutishly human and the grossly alien, and after it came a novel that Colin Greenland describes as "exhausted and misanthropic."[15] In truth, *misanthropic* seems like an appropriate term for both *The Dark Light Years* and *Earthworks*.

Griffin and Wingrove consider *The Dark Light Years* to be "one of Aldiss's most memorable novels, if also the one which suffers most from the surface demands of the genre and the resultant artistic compromise."[16] I don't agree, in part because he wrote many novels that were much more memorable, but mostly because I don't see Aldiss as an author who would be at all prepared to compromise artistically for the sake of genre, certainly not at a time when he had recently written *Report on Probability A* and *Hothouse* and would shortly write *Greybeard* and *Barefoot in the Head*. On the contrary, I think that what we might see as the generic crudity of the novel is a deliberate artistic choice; this is, after all, a novel about shit. (One contemporary critic wrote: "When [Aldiss] was writing this, he must have felt in need of a mental laxative. It's a pity he excreted in print.")[17]

I think one of the things that Brian Aldiss delighted in was being out-rageous. Just as *The Primal Urge* insisted on attacking the sexual narrow-mindedness of 1950s Britain, so *The Dark Light Years* attacks the coyness with which all bodily functions were regarded. Thus the spaceship that first encoun-ters the alien utods is named the *Mariestopes*, after the pioneer in sexual health who was almost universally regarded with abhorrence by decent society in the years when Aldiss was growing up and was still considered with distaste in postwar Britain. The reference to Marie Stopes is particularly ironic given that the purpose of the expedition is to find planets suitable for coloniza-tion. Expanding on the critique of colonialism he had already made in such stories as "The Under-Privileged" and "Segregation," he proclaims that the colonists would turn any new planet "into a heaven of dirt-farming and semi-detacheds. Fertility was the curse of the human race, Ainson thought. Too much procreation went on: Earth's teeming loins had to ejaculate once again, ejaculate its unwanted progeny on to the virgin planets that lay awaiting" (*DLY*, 22–23). Aldiss is being deliberately provocative in comparing colonialism with a lack of sexual restraint. Without the birth control that Marie Stopes championed, there would always be younger children to be sent out to distant colonies. To Aldiss, empire wasn't a place of riches but a dumping ground for the unwanted. As Ainson later muses, one goes in search of other planets "because life on Earth [is] such hell, because, to be quite precise, living with other human beings [is] such a messy job" (*DLY*, 110). As Mihaly realizes, however, "there [is] no 'away,' only—even in the most distant galaxy—endless locations haunted by the self" (*DLY*, 111). The novel is mainly concerned with examining the nature of that haunting.

Crucial to such an examination is alterity, an other to which humanity can be opposed. The utods of the planet Dapdrof, a race forever misunderstood, are largely incomprehensible to the humans who encounter them (though they, similarly, do not understand the humans; this is yet another Aldiss novel in which failure of communication is a key). They are beings who wallow in their excreta, whose droppings "suppl[y] valuable oils which seeped into their hides, making them soft" (*DLY*, 9). In a typical pun, Aldiss has a saying of the utods: "Do to others as you would be dung by" (*DLY*, 11). When the utods first land on the planet they call Grudgrodd, their way of claiming the planet is by defecating into the planet's soil and creating a wallow. For the utods, we learn, defecation is both holy and connected with fertility: sunlight is considered "the droppings of the suns" (*DLY*, 15), which makes it both absurd and miraculous, and therefore "they must never get exalted or puffed up; for were not even their gods formed in the divine shape of a turdling?" (*DLY*, 15). The fact that these apparently disgusting creatures have developed space travel is used as a way of questioning humanity's "much-vaunted intelligence, the one thing that most clearly distinguishes [it] from the animals" (*DLY*, 63).

The *Mariestopes* arrives on Grudgrodd not long after the utods do. The captain of the ship, Bargerone, is the epitome of the stiff, stupid conformist that Aldiss has consistently attacked, a member the officer class constantly lampooned by the common soldiers with whom he served, and of course Bargerone informs us, "There is a war on . . . and I have my orders" (*DLY*, 20). The first thing the crew of the *Mariestopes* does when encountering the utods is shoot them for sport, later trying to justify these actions by repeatedly saying that there was no choice. But the killers don't notice anything outside themselves; it is left to Ainson to discover the utod spaceship. Ainson, the explorer, is our sympathetic viewpoint character because (like Aldiss?) he has nothing but contempt for humanity. Not that he is a particularly good model of humanity, being arrogant, paranoid, distant toward his wife, and disengaged from his son. When he dismissively considers his wife Enid a "poor specimen," he imagines her married to "a shopkeeper in a busy country town. Banbury. Diss. East Dereham" (*DLY*, 61). This makes Enid an analogue for Aldiss's mother, Dot, and thus Ainson is presumably an analogue for his father, Bill, who was indeed a shopkeeper in East Dereham.

Nevertheless, it is thanks to Ainson that a few of the utods are rescued and taken back to Earth, where they are imprisoned in the Exozoo. The role that defecation plays in the social, philosophical, and interpersonal life of the utods makes them an object of disgust and incomprehension to their human observers. Despite the fact that the utod spaceship has been discovered, to the humans they cannot possibly be intelligent beings. When one of the aliens is being dissected in order to determine whether it can feel pain, Mihaly, the director of the Exozoo, feels that this is "how man will treat any intelligent opposition it meets out there"; "beneath the scientific etiquette" he hears "the savage drums of ancient man, still beating away like mad for a blood-letting session" (*DLY*, 123). Vivisection is thus the pinnacle of human civilization; as Hilary Warhoon says, "Our civilization may be built not on our best, but on our worst: on fear . . . or on greed" (*DLY*, 79) and that therefore "we aren't mature enough to deal with our [aliens]" (*DLY*, 84). Once again, lack of maturity is the defining characteristic of humanity.

A major influence on this novel was a book called *Madkind: The Origin and Development of the Mind* (1962) by Charles Berg, which, according to Aldiss, supplied the "curare for the tip of *The Dark Light Years*, my flight of sixties fancy" (*ToE*, 138). Berg argued that people are unable to fully comprehend reality because there is a delusional difference between our dreams and the limiting reality of our society. Our frustration at this conflict is expressed as madness. So great was the influence of Berg's study on Aldiss that we will see its echoes in a number of his later works; this, however, was the first. For the utods, the importance of defecation puts them in intimate contact with their land and with themselves. Although they are technologically advanced, they are not divorced from Nature. Because there is thus no conflict between dreams and reality, they are not inherently mad. Nor, strictly speaking, are they civilized in human terms, because to be civilized is to be mad.

To the humans, of course, or at least the majority of them, the utods are dirty, dumb, and fit only to be shot for sport. The humans do not see how the things that make utods dirty in their eyes are precisely the things that bring them close to Nature and hence keep them sane. In contrast, human-kind is divorced from Nature and therefore from all that might make them fully human. All we see of the environment on Earth, for instance, is urban: pedestrians in London wear a street mask "which alone guarantee[s] that they [do] not fall swooning from the waste gases pouring out of the cars snorting at their elbows" (*DLY*, 83). Berg here comes together with Rachel Carson to demonstrate what we will see time and again in Aldiss, namely, that civilization divorces us from ourselves.

As the novel ends, Ainson's son has been alone on Dapdrof for forty years, studying the utods and building a rapport with them. Then a ship from Earth arrives to take him back home, although it will not quite be home since Great Britain was destroyed in the latest renewal of all-out war. The utods, it turns out, are now "practically extinct, eradicated by the hazards of war" (*DLY*, 158), revealing the same contemptuous view of warfare on Aldiss's part that we see, for instance, in *Greybeard* when Algy muses on the "several fewer species of animals" killed to place "another medal on another general" (*GB*, 144). As the younger Ainson is hurried away by the crew of the ship, anxious to get away from the stink of the utods, his arsenal is left behind in the hut where he had lived. When he is gone, the utods examine the armory, and one thinks that "he had remained patiently captive for a small fraction of his life. Now it was time that he thought about freedom" (*DLY*, 159). The implication is that the utods will use these weapons to fight off any further human depredations. What is unsaid is how effective they might be and, more telling, what will become of utod culture if their only hope of survival is to become as warlike as the humans.

The Dark Light Years is a dyspeptic novel written, we are told, because of rage at "inhumane human experiments on dolphins."[18] There are places where it works better as polemic than novel, though the focus of the anger is familiar from numerous other novels and stories by Aldiss. In keeping with its genesis, it is a book that shows signs of being rushed. The plotting is often reliant on coincidence, characters tend to serve as sketchy mouthpieces rather than the more complex and developed figures we encounter in *Hothouse* and *Greybeard*, and the book is littered with in-jokes and references, what we might now call "fan service." For instance, the female scientist Hilary Warhoon is named for the fanzine edited by Richard Bergeron and published intermittently between

1952 and 1985, to which Aldiss was a contributor, and the American survey ship is called *Gansas*, recalling the wild geese that carry the protagonist to the Moon in Francis Godwin's *The Man in the Moone* (1638).

★   ★   ★

If *The Dark Light Years* explored the distance between, on one hand, nature, peace, and reason, and on the other, civilization, war, and madness, *Earthworks* explores a world in which there is, in effect, no nature left. That the novel is meant as an allegory, at least in part, is shown by the name of the protagonist, Knowle Noland: Know No Land, a name that suggests a Flying Dutchman, condemned always to roam. Humanity has deprived itself of its place in the world by the familiar evils of the nascent 1960s environmental movement: overpopulation, overfarming, and the poisonous use of pesticides. Once Rachel Carson's *Silent Spring* had alerted the world to the perils of pesticides and had kickstarted modern environmentalism, her ideas and those of other campaigners who followed in her wake were taken up quickly by sf writers in the mid-to-late 1960s, notably in such works as *The Clone* (1965) by Theodore L. Thomas and Kate Wilhelm, *Make Room! Make Room!* (1966) by Harry Harrison, *Stand on Zanzibar* (1968) by John Brunner, and *Garbage World* (1967) by Charles Platt. But Aldiss, building naturally on ideas already expressed in *Hothouse* and *Greybeard*, was one of the first to take up the notion that Earth was already in its death throes.

The novel starts with one of the most dramatic visual images in Aldiss's work to date:

> The dead man drifted along in the breeze. He walked upright on his hind legs. . . . A few flies of ripe dimension stayed with him, although he was far from land, travelling light above the surface of the complacent South Atlantic. . . . He was coming out from Africa, moving steadily for me. (*EW*, 5)

The dead man is strapped to a personal anti-gravity device that didn't stop working when its owner died and now carries him upright across the ocean toward the *Trieste Star*, which is captained by Noland. The title Captain is little more than a convenient fiction; the ship is fully automated, and the crew has no proper function. It is a metaphor for the world: a sterile environment in which people lead a purposeless existence. And, to carry the metaphor one stage further, it is a locus of sickness in this sick world. One crewman is confined to his bunk with unspecified allergies; another breaks out in a rash after touching the dead man; the doctor, Thunderpeck, is agoraphobic; and Noland sees visions as a result of childhood food poisoning that affected parts of his brain and retinas. The world is sick, diseased, hungry, overcrowded, its natural resources depleted: "Even religion has become subordinate to hunger, as everything else has" (EW, 12). The ship, significantly, is heading for the Skeleton Coast of Africa, where Noland will crash it onto the shore when the automatic navigation system is turned off at a crucial moment.

There is no relief in this world. Death is all around, hovering, waiting, an unavoidable presence. It is a world that has been so depleted that there is no other way ahead. Through flashbacks we learn that Noland was previously a convict, a landsman, as they are called, on a prison farm: "Those years were made of hardship. . . . Death was there, too, that other great deliverer of man from his monotony" (EW, 33). Aldiss's work is full of grand pronouncements about "man," though here, as in Non-Stop, Hothouse, and Greybeard, man is diminished, tormented by a ruined world beyond his control. The reason farming is now a job only for prisoners is that it has become so dangerous. In a clear reference to Silent Spring we are told that vegetables are raised using "phosphates, potassiums, magnesiums . . . insecticides and arsenicals" (EW, 44). Every week spent washing these chemicals off the plants means a year off a man's life, while cattle are raised with growth enhancers that are carcinogenic and create flesh that is "pulpy and obviously lack[s] key nutrients" (EW, 44). In this arid, exhausted future, even the food people eat has become a source of disease rather than health, an image that we will see recurring in another work from the same year, "The Saliva Tree."

On one occasion Noland leaves his work detail and is captured by the Travellers, an outlaw band of escaped landsmen led by a man called Jess whose face has "acquired in its starved lines an asceticism that transcended hunger . . . a man whose spirit had transmuted the suffering into something finer" (EW, 42). Jess is a Christ figure who has kept alive "all that [is] left of the nobler codes of an earlier way of life" (EW, 46). This is possibly the most direct expression of the sense that a nobler aspect of humanity has been lost, a theme that runs throughout Aldiss's work. That nobility lay in the comradeship of his army buddies, and it is reflected here in the Travellers, who move across the countryside silently, "two abreast, the couples spaced apart" (*EW*, 46), recalling the way his army patrols would have moved through enemy territory. The loss of that nobility was reflected in the narrow, pinched way of life that Aldiss found on his return to Britain. By this measure, the environmental collapse that has taken place long before this novel opens is yet one more aspect of postwar austerity.

Consequently, the disease that afflicts the world is not only the result of a denatured Earth failing to produce healthful and sustaining food but is also a moral and social collapse. As we are told: "The health of character is securely tied to the health of an age; dissolution produces dissolution, betrayal betrayal, and trust is no neighbour for fear" (*EW*, 98). The Travellers are the nearest thing to society that Noland encounters, but when they are captured by the authorities he has no problem playing Judas to Jess. As a reward, he is given command of the *Trieste Star*, only to run the ship aground on the barren coast of Africa.

In this world, Africa is the only place with any vigor left in its soils, so it is the only place in which dynamic, effective societies survive. It is here, in this relatively rich land, that he meets Justine. She had been the author of letters carried by the dead man who approached the ship at the beginning of the novel. Seeking her out is the closest thing to a purpose that Noland now has. When Justine appears, she is described in a way that makes her a female reincarnation of Jess: "The usual look of illness that marked most of the world's undernourished population was stamped upon her . . . [but in her it was] . . . as much a spiritual characteristic as a physical one" (*EW*, 68). Far from being another savior, however, Justine is embroiled in conspiracies, and since he is rootless and directionless and eager to assuage the guilt he continues to feel over his betrayal of Jess, it is easy for Noland to become entangled in the plot. They are going to assassinate one of the most powerful African leaders, with the intent of fomenting a war that they see as the only possible answer to overpopulation and worldwide starvation. The books ends with Noland striving to bring about this "new way of living": "Ignoring the rumbling of my empty stomach, I cradled the rifle under one arm and crawled towards the nearest window slit" (*EW*, 126). The novel therefore closes with the same unresolved issues as *The Dark Light Years*: Will this act of violence work, and is war any kind of solution?

Earthworks feels, in many ways, like a companion piece to *The Dark Light Years*. It is short, brutal, and bleak. It is a hymn of despair, the cry of a man who has no time for so-called civilization and all it might bring. And it feels like something written quickly with a polemical point to make but no coherent story or fully realized characters with which to convey that angry message. Madkind, to call on the work of Charles Berg that clearly informed this novel as fully as it did *The Dark Light Years*, deserves no better than its own destruction. And the novel's misanthropic tone inspired a bitter response. Charles Platt, who would shortly write his own parody of environmental concerns, *Garbage World*, considered the book awful: "If you're given a copy, don't open it. It's just not worth the trouble."[19] He wasn't alone.

★   ★   ★

Despite the often wild variations in his work, and the way reviews of his fiction even from within the field swung from elation to excoriation, by the mid-1960s Aldiss was generally being hailed as the best science fiction writer in Britain. In 1965 the World Science Fiction Convention was staged in London, and Aldiss was the guest of honor. It was only the second time a British writer had been given such a distinction at a Worldcon, following Arthur C. Clarke in 1956. To coincide with this, and to mark ten years since the appearance of his first published story, a collection called *Best Science Fiction Stories of Brian W. Aldiss* was hastily assembled. It was the first of three volumes to appear over the course of the following two decades that would all have exactly the same title, although their contents would vary markedly.

The year 1965 was also the centenary of the birth of H. G. Wells, a writer with whom, as I have suggested, Aldiss felt a great affinity, one that would become more pronounced as time went on. Both were from a family of shop-keepers. Both began their careers, in earnest, when they were thirty. Both were seen as major innovators within the world of science fiction. In time, both would achieve equal success in the mainstream as well as in science fiction, and both would write acclaimed histories. Both had a failed first marriage and a second marriage to a woman who provided a stable base without overly stifling their sexual adventures (though I suspect that Margaret was somewhat less forgiving than Wells's wife, Jane). To mark this centenary, Aldiss wrote a novella in the manner of Wells, "The Saliva Tree" (1965), which not only counts as one of his finest works of short fiction but also fits neatly with the concerns and imagery of *Earthworks*, *Hothouse*, and *Greybeard*.

"The Saliva Tree" is one of the very few works that Aldiss set specifically in the county of his birth. It was only much later in his career, after the deaths of his parents, that the county began to provide a key, if generally disturbing, setting for scenes in *Brothers of the Head* and *Super-State*, though its most notable appearance is probably in the story "North Scarning" (1986). Briefly, before the Aldiss family left East Dereham, they lived in a house called St. Withburga that they came to believe was haunted. All the family reported hearing footsteps upstairs when there was no one else in the house. It was such an unnerving experience that they were relieved to move to Gorleston. Years later, when Aldiss revisited East Dereham for a family funeral, he found that the house had been converted into council offices, but the council workers were disturbed by the same noise of footsteps upstairs. Aldiss incorporated this wholesale into "North Scarning," in which a writer, Tom Bridges, returns to the Norfolk home where he was born. The place is now derelict, and the ghost of the previous occupant, who had eventually driven Tom and his parents away, is still there. At one point, Tom muses: "Have I never escaped from my childhood? Were all those adult years just a dream?" (*RoE*, 306). The notion of being trapped by the inescapability of childhood memories gives "North Scarning" an almost confessional feel. But what is notable about it is the way the Norfolk landscape is used to evoke unease. And that is exactly the sensation that the landscape of Norfolk generates in "The Saliva Tree," as if there is a shiver of dis-ease with every glance back at where Aldiss came from.

"The Saliva Tree" wears its homage to Wells on its sleeve, crowding the story with casual references to him and his fiction. When the unnatural produce first begins to appear on the farm it is referred to as the food of the gods, and later, when the protagonist, Gregory, has a dream about the saliva tree it is described as "the shape of things to come" (*BSF3*, 137).

The story begins, like *The War of the Worlds* (1896), with a meteor crashing into a pond on a farm in Norfolk. At first, its arrival has no consequences other than a couple of incidents that seem to involve something invisible. But in the following spring all the animals produce far more offspring than they can possibly feed and raise, the fruit trees are overloaded with fruit, and everything about the farm is marked with an unnatural abundance: "'Course, they ent all going to live,' the farmer said. 'The old sows ent got enough dugs to feed that brood'" (*BSF3*, 99).

Gregory, a young man of independent means and scientific bent who is a correspondent of Wells's, is at first a welcome visitor to the farm, but as he begins to detect an air of unease about the place, he becomes progressively less welcome. Returning after a brief absence, he finds the farm nearly overgrown with wildlife and birds fluttering everywhere, "yet the impression he receive[s is] one of death rather than life" (*BSF3*, 109). When the farmer's pregnant wife gives birth to nine children, even "the wallpaper pattern [takes] on a diseased and livid look as if the house itself embodied sickness" (*BSF3*, 110). At first the farmer welcomes this profusion: times are hard, and he will have a lot more produce to sell. But the milk his cows produce is sour, the newborn piglets have an odd and unpleasant taste, and the fruits are inedible; they have become like the unnatural and unnourishing foods of *Earthworks*. Or at least, they are to everyone else; the farmer and his family seem to detect nothing unusual in the flavor of their food. Then the invisible thing that arrived on the meteor, having engineered everything to suit its own particular tastes, begins to feast. It is noticeable that whenever Aldiss writes of nature in profusion, here as in *Hothouse* and *Greybeard*, for example, it is to the detriment of humanity, as if there is no balance to be achieved between humankind and nature.

★　★　★

In 1966 "The Saliva Tree" won the first Nebula Award for Best Novella, which it shared with "He Who Shapes" by Roger Zelazny. Aldiss had dug back into the history of the genre, something he would increasingly do later in his career, while simultaneously establishing himself as a lauded exponent of familiar science fiction. Yet at this very moment the genre was changing, a new tone of voice, a new attitude, a new approach emerging in the pages of *New Worlds*. Brian Aldiss had graced that magazine since his second published sf story, but now it had a new, young, and iconoclastic editor, Michael Moorcock, and was forging an identity that would become known as the New Wave. Aldiss was to become, perhaps unexpectedly, one of the most recognizable and influential voices of the New Wave, as we will see. But it was almost as if he had two parallel careers going on at the same time. For all his distinctive New Wave work, he was still regularly producing fiction that was firmly in an older and more familiar mode. When his new short story collection, *The Saliva Tree and Other Strange Growths*, appeared in 1966, only one of the ten stories reflected the characteristics of the New Wave (though that story, "The Girl and the Robot with Flowers" [1965], would definitively mark the dividing line between the old and the new science fictions, as we shall see shortly), while the next novel, published in Britain as *An Age* and in the United States as *Cryptozoic*, hovered rather awkwardly somewhere between the two. By marrying the New Wave-ish notion of mind travel with more traditional structure and imagery, it was, as Griffin and Wingrove suggest, "as if Aldiss, aware that he was on the brink of radical literary experimentation, was proving to himself just how far he could stretch the old sf-adventure formulae to express what he had to say, in order to disprove and quieten in advance any accusation of wilful perversity."[20]

The novel, which is essentially about the perception of time, is an actualization of Kierkegaard's oft-quoted dictum that life can only be understood backwards, but it must be lived forwards. As such, the novel is full of references to beginnings and endings that are confused or the wrong way around. The opening scene, set in the distant past on a Devonian beach with its near-motionless sea, red mud, and lobe-finned fish struggling out of the mud in search of insects, deliberately recalls the final scene of Wells's *The Time Machine* (1895), which takes place on the final beach awaiting the death of Earth. As a member of the biker gang says: "I look at this sea and I can't help thinking we're at the *end* of the world, not the beginning" (CZ, 20). Such reversals appear throughout the novel. Thus, when the protagonist, Bush, learns that his dead mother had lost her faith after some mysterious incident when she was six, he concludes: "The rest of her life was anti-climax, and she'd have done better to live her days backwards, with the cancer healing and her getting young again and eventually gaining her baby faith!" (CZ, 71). Another time he remembers an incident when, during his military training, he was obliged to take part in the beating and torture of another man—"the worst act of his life" (CZ, 102)—and also a time in childhood when his mother had locked him out of the house for a day, which he now sees as appropriate punishment for the beating: "Typical that they should be reversed in order, as if he symbolically lived his life backwards" (CZ, 102).

This is all deliberate because time actually is reversed within the novel. When the story takes us deep into the Cryptozoic and Bush thinks that this is how the world began, Silverstone corrects him: the Cryptozoic "stands at the end of Earth's history, not at the beginning as you have believed" (CZ, 149). Silverstone's theory is that "the flow of time in fact moves in the opposite direction to its apparent one" (CZ, 150), so people do live backwards, and what they interpret as failure to foresee the future is actually their forgetting what happened. By this reckoning, humankind will, in the blink of a cosmic second, devolve into simpler creatures; as is so often the case in Aldiss, devolution is what lies ahead for humanity.

In *Cryptozoic*, people have learned the trick of apparently traveling in time, but the concept of timeflow "is in the human consciousness, not in the external universe" (CZ, 86). As a consequence, they are not time travelers but mind travelers, and their travel is effected by the use of a drug, "CSD," which is obviously meant to recall LSD and perhaps a hint of what would become the Acid-Head War stories, the first of which would appear that same year. If this travel through time takes place in the mind as a result of drugs, we might question the reality of the experience, but such questioning never occurs within the book. There is a phantasmagorical air to the scenes set in other times: mind travelers have no direct interaction with the period they visit. They touch nothing, hear nothing, and smell nothing, and other time travelers from different ages seem ghostly, so that the plain that Bush observes is covered with "the misty obstructions of future time" where "two faint phantasms of men [walk] through him, deep in conversation, not a decibel of which leak[s] through the time-entropy barrier to him" (CZ, 39). And yet the solidity of that plain is never in doubt. It is an observed reality; only the observers are shadowy. When Silverstone explains his new view of the world, he says: "What mankind has never taken into account until now is the extent to which the observer has managed to distort the external object" (CZ,149), but what we see more of in the novel is the way the external object distorts the observer.

Equally shadowy, equally distorting, is the motivation for mind traveling. From one perspective it would seem to be artistic. Bush is a painter, and the ability to mind travel has had a transformative effect on society: "The human consciousness had now widened so alarmingly, was so busy transforming everything on Earth into its own peculiar tones, that no art could exist that did not take proper cognisance of the fact" (*CZ*, 14). Art itself, however, seems to belong firmly in the past. Bush consistently refers to other painters as "old Claude Monet" (*CZ*, 14) or "old Joseph Mallord William Turner" (*CZ*, 15), and when his long-time friend Borrow shows Bush some pictures that Bush recognizes as genius, suddenly he becomes "old Borrow" (*CZ*, 43). Art, clearly, is not of the moment.

From another perspective, mind travel is about sex. We are told, for instance, that a survey of 2080 "showed how strong incest-motivation is in mind-travellers. It's the force behind the predisposition to look back" (*CZ*, 29). This is pure Freud, a view that informs the role of sex in many of Aldiss's novels: "Man first became homo sapiens when he put a ban on . . . endogamy, the custom forbidding marriage outside the familial group. Exogamy was man's very first painful step forward" (29). This marked humanity's growing separation from nature, and time and again, in *Hothouse*, for example, we see that humanity grows closer to nature only by a process of devolution.

Yet there is a third motivation, hinted at but never made explicit in the novel: the hatefulness of the present. When Bush returns to his present, 2093, he finds a run-down Britain, a fascistic state, and talk of a revolution that took place while he was away (of course there was). The military regime of General Bolt has been bloodily overthrown and replaced with the military regime of Admiral Gleeson, but nothing changes. Bush is now to be an assassin who must seek out Silverstone, once an assistant to the creator of mind travel, who has a new and, to the regime, dangerous theory of mind travel. Suddenly the novel takes on the coloration of a rather crude action adventure. There are chases and escapes, coincidences abound, and things that are supposedly impossible become, for the sake of the plot, easy. Early in the novel, for instance, we are told that Bush held the record for travel to the most recent past with a journey into the Bronze Age and that anything more recent cannot be done, suddenly he finds himself in 1930. Here, in a village called Breedale near Darlington, he discovers a large, poor family that are his ancestors. After witnessing a family tragedy—the mother dying after a miscarriage, the father committing suicide after bringing on that event through violence—Bush then travels further back in history to London at the time of the Great Exhibition, 1851, where he finds himself playing hide-and-seek with other mind travelers.

It is a novel that loses track of itself, as if Aldiss started out trying to write something, considering the drugs and the mind travel, that fit within the New Wave spirit of the age. But before long he seems to have lost confidence in that approach and reverted to something more familiar. Ironically, given Aldiss's own later comments on 1950s British science fiction, J. G. Ballard deemed it "well-told but suffocatingly cosy."[21] It would seem that the only way he could find into the revolutionary excitement of the New Wave was to say goodbye to the more familiar plots and tropes of science fiction.

CHAPTER 3

EXPERIMENTALIST

In September 1965, the same month the *Magazine of Fantasy and Science Fiction* first published "The Saliva Tree," *New Worlds* presented a special issue focused on Brian Aldiss. It contained appreciations by Edmund Crispin and Peter White and two stories by Aldiss. One of these, "Old Time's Sake," disappeared almost as quickly as it appeared, but the other would define Aldiss's relationship with the New Wave that *New Worlds* now represented. Originally published as "Girl and Robot with Flowers," it was almost immediately retitled "The Girl and the Robot with Flowers," and if not Aldiss's best short story, it must be, I believe, close to the top. It is not, of course, a science fiction story, though it is a story about science fiction. It is also such a crucial work in laying out the distinction, at least as Aldiss saw it, between traditional forms of sf and what the New Wave wanted to explore that it is worth examining this story at some length.[1]

The narrator of the story is a science fiction writer living in Oxford. The writer is unnamed, but during the course of the story he mentions, familiarly, Jim Ballard, Poul Anderson, Fred Pohl, Mike Moorcock, and the author of a book called *War with the Robots*, which was a 1962 short story collection by Harry Harrison. This is the circle within which Oxford resident Brian Aldiss was moving at the time, so if not actually autobiographical, it certainly edges close to that territory.

In the first paragraph, the narrator (I am tempted to call him Brian, but that is perhaps presumptuous) announces to his wife Marion: "I've started another story" (*BSF3*, 75). At the time, Aldiss had been separated from his first wife, Olive, for some years, and the divorce that finally came through in 1965 would allow him to marry his second wife, Margaret, in December of that year. Marion is, therefore, a politely fictionalized version of Margaret, and though she does not particularly care for science fiction, "she is full of love, and it may lend her enough empathy to make her feel as sincerely delighted as I do when another story is on the way" (*BSF3*, 75). No sooner have we been told that this new story is about robots than the refrigerator starts to rumble, clearly annoying the narrator. He complains: "'It just sits there gobbling electricity like a—' 'A robot?' Marion suggested" (*BSF3*, 75).

The sense of joy at the start of a new piece of fiction quickly fades. Abruptly, the mood becomes one of discontent, doubt, uncertainty. The author now wants to talk over his story, which is clearly not his usual practice. "Don't your robots surprise you?" Marion asks, and he replies: "Maybe Jim Ballard's right and they are old hat, worked to death" (*BSF3*, 76). This discontent is not with his writing—his abilities are never questioned here—but with his subject matter, with the character of science fiction. In *The Twinkling of an Eye* Aldiss reports that when he, Ballard, and Moorcock got together in the early 1960s, "much as we argued, we had a basic point of agreement: we thought most of British SF boring, and determined to change it" (*ToE*, 257). Aldiss believed this so strongly that ten years later he was repeating much the same point, describing sf as a "beautiful tender place . . . betrayed by the practitioners of pulp science fiction (who use it for thick-arm adventure and jackboot philosophy)."[2] "The Girl and the Robot with Flowers" is a dramatization of precisely that critique of contemporary sf. When the narrator later says, "I felt only contempt for my robot story, and would do so however skilfully I wrote it" (*BSF3*, 79), he is giving expression to the contempt that would drive the triumvirate of Aldiss, Ballard, and Moorcock that was, at precisely the time this story was being written, launching the radical rethink of science fiction that was the British New Wave. The somewhat allegorical character of the story is highlighted by the speed with which the narrator's response to his own story darkens from the celebratory to discontent to contempt. The over-familiar science fiction cliché can spoil one's mood remarkably quickly.

The story within a story that the unnamed narrator has just started writing, "Robot with Flowers" is, in truth, not very dissimilar to some of the hackneyed work that Aldiss was still turning out. Novels from *Equator* to *The Dark Light Years* were exactly the sort of thing that Aldiss was, at the same time, railing against, and there is a suggestion also of his early story "T" in this proposed tale. "Robot with Flowers" tells of a war between Earth and an alien world so distant that it takes eighty years to travel between them. An alien battle fleet reaches the solar system and unleashes a weapon that kills about 70 percent of humanity, but not before Earth has dispatched a robot fleet of its own. This fleet carries a weapon so devastating that every alien is killed. When the survivors on Earth learn of this, they send a reconnaissance vessel to learn what their warlike robots are up to now. When this ship returns it brings alarming pictures of "enormous robot cities, and tremendous technological activity," but there's also a picture of "a heavily armed robot, twelve feet high, with its arms laden with flowers" (*BSF3*, 77). The weaponized robots have apparently taken to peaceful pursuits. But this is a misinterpretation: "The robots *have* to destroy all flowers, because flowers exhale oxygen, and oxygen is liable to give the robots rust troubles" (*BSF3*, 77).

Marion damns the story with faint praise, calling it "a decent run-of-the-mill story. Not quite *you*, perhaps" (*BSF3*, 78). In many of the details, however, it is exactly like an Aldiss story: the inevitable war, the size of the robot that by extension belittles humanity, and the importance of misinterpretation are all recurrent features in Aldiss's work. But the problem is that it resembles other science fiction stories also. It is, for instance, "a bit like that Poul Anderson robot story you admired—'Epilogue,' wasn't it?" (*BSF3*, 78). And it also resembles a Harry Harrison story from *War with the Robots*. Harrison is a friend, Anderson is admired, but that doesn't excuse the similarity. By extension, Aldiss is saying, the repetition that is so common in science fiction is a fatal flaw, though what is being echoed is in itself good work. Even if an editor such as Pohl or Moorcock might like the story enough to publish it, Aldiss would still be disappointed by it, but "not just because it's a crib." And a crib, a rip-off as we might now say, could always be spotted because "it lacked emotional tone" (*BSF3*, 78). A copy, we are being told, is evidently inferior because the author is not emotionally invested in its creation.

This is a psychological hinge point, for now the narrator turns to examining his own emotional investment, both in this story and more generally in science fiction: "There was no war in my heart; how could I begin to believe in an interplanetary war with all its imponderables and impossibilities?" (*BSF3*, 79). The author's science fiction to this point had emerged from his personal unhappiness before the arrival of Marion, and therefore it had dealt with dark things: "All fiction was a . . . rationalisation of internal battles," but maybe it was time to "reach out beyond my fortifications and show [my readers] for once a future it might be worth living in" (*BSF3*, 79). This is, of course, a simplification; the complex psychological basis of Aldiss's fiction, which had its roots in war and austerity, among other things, was shaped by far more than his marital status. But as a statement about the New Wave placing greater emphasis on personal insights than generic conventions, it speaks to the heart of the story.

This feels like a conclusion, a statement of intent for the future, but of course, it isn't. The typical ironic twist demands that the story take one more turn, to consider the distinction between fiction, dark or light, optimistic or pessimistic, and reality. The narrator and Marion are preparing to go to a picnic with local friends, and as he gets some beer from the fridge it starts to chug again. "Under ten years old, but you couldn't expect a machine to last for ever. Only in fiction. You could send an animated machine out on a paper spaceship voyage over paper light years and it would never let you down," he says (*BSF3*, 79–80). In the end, the author recognizes that what is most disappointing about his story is that it "seem[s] so far divorced from real life" (*BSF3*, 80).

Marion, who of course does not particularly care for science fiction, challenges this: "We may not have robots yet, but we have a fridge with a mind of its own" (*BSF3*, 80). Aldiss lets this go unquestioned (it's from Marion, and she, like Margaret in *The Twinkling of an Eye*, can do no wrong), but the difference between robots in space and a fridge on its last legs is the critical difference between science fiction and reality. The story ends with the narrator setting himself a challenge: "Why can't I get the fridge into an sf story, and this wonderful sunlight, and you, instead of just a bunch of artless robots?" (*BSF3*, 80). And that, of course, is the story we have just been reading. But can we take Aldiss's word for it that it is "an sf story"? After all, isn't it just the artless robots that make this even tangentially science fiction? And they don't belong in the story but rather are a creature of the story embedded within this fiction. Other than that, what is remotely science-fictional about an author discussing his latest work with his wife, about a couple preparing to set out on a picnic on a beautiful summer day in contemporary Oxford while a cat hunts fish in a pond and a failing fridge chunters away in the background?

Brian Aldiss was a naturally gifted storyteller from a very young age, but as a writer he was often more interested in technical literary experimentation than in plot. As is the way with experiments, some of these succeeded (*Report on Probability A*), while others did not (*The Eighty-Minute Hour*). But I find it interesting how rarely people recognize that "The Girl and the Robot with Flowers" was both his most successful and his most daring literary experiment. This is mostly, I suspect, because the charm and the approachability of the story disguise the fact that it is an experiment. But what Aldiss does in this story is present the idea and the character of science fiction as a topic of debate within what is otherwise a contemporary realist story. That the central character in the story writes sf and talks about sf adds nothing fantastical or unreal to what we are reading. Yet at the same time we emerge from the story with a clear understanding of the critical thinking that lay behind the birth of the British New Wave. Science fiction is presented as repetitive, cannibalizing itself, and the question that underlies the story is whether it is possible to write science fiction that isn't an echo of the familiar. The answer stated within the story is that it is possible, that the fridge and the sunlight we have encountered lie within an sf story. The answer of the story itself, however, the story of the fridge and the sunlight that we have actually read, is not so clear-cut. It is, perhaps, not possible for science fiction to avoid eating itself.

The presentation of this unresolved dilemma within this story is all the evidence we need about what made Brian Aldiss one of the most significant writers of the New Wave.

★ ★ ★

John Carnell, known to his friends as Ted, had edited *New Worlds* and its sister magazine, *Science Fantasy*, since shortly after World War II. His taste was quite conservative, as shown in his favoring of such writers as E. C. Tubb, Kenneth Bulmer, and James White, but he had also been receptive to a new, more challenging group of writers including Ballard and Aldiss. In 1964 Nova Publications sold *New Worlds* and *Science Fantasy* to Roberts & Vintner, and Carnell took the opportunity to move on, concentrating on his own literary agency and launching an original anthology series, *New Writings in SF*, which he edited until his death in 1972. His successor at *Science Fantasy* was Kyril Bonfiglioli, who would be succeeded in 1966 by Harry Harrison and Keith Roberts, who would be in charge of the last five issues of the magazine under its new name, *SF Impulse*. More significant would be his successor at *New Worlds*, for which role Carnell championed Michael Moorcock, only twenty-four years old but already an experienced editor. Moorcock's first issue of *New Worlds* was published in May 1964 (and included Aldiss's story "Never Let Go of My Hand"), and he immediately began to promote the idea that science fiction could, and should, be humane, literate, and relevant to the contemporary world.

This aspiration very quickly led to stories that were experimental in structure. A good example is Aldiss's 1967 "Confluence" (which actually first appeared in *Punch*). This alien phrase book is an early example of something that would recur in many different guises, most famously, perhaps, as *The Meaning of Liff* by Douglas Adams and John Lloyd (1983). Much of it is, inevitably, jokey; for example, one term is defined as "a writer's attitude to fellow writers" (*BSF3*, 183). It is noteworthy that practically all of the definitions are from the male perspective, such as "The new dimensions that take on illusory existence when the body of the loved woman is first revealed" (*BSF3*, 185) and "the smile of a slightly imperfect wife" (*BSF3*, 186). Women seem to have no voice in this language. Other stories began to employ modernist literary techniques such as unreliable narrators and stream-of-consciousness, techniques that had hitherto been almost entirely absent from science fiction. A preference began to emerge for the here and now instead of the distant, fantastic settings of outer space and the far future that tended to characterize more conventional science fiction. This shift enabled a psychological exploration of the conscious and subconscious mind, what Ballard termed "inner space." And for this, Aldiss had the perfect story.

By the late 1950s, from Aldiss's point of view, Britain "was in the grip of no great literary movement" (*ToE*, 269). This is a somewhat dubious claim; by this time the plays and novels of the Angry Young Men (including Aldiss's friend Kingsley Amis) were widely known, along with the poetry of The Movement (including Amis's friend Philip Larkin), and by the early 1960s the working-class dramas often classified as "kitchen sink" had come to dominate the British stage and screen. But the grim, realist aesthetic of all of these literary movements was unlikely to appeal to someone immersed in science fiction and surrealism. In France, however, there were the *nouveau roman* of Alain Robbe-Grillet and Michel Butor and the *nouvelle vague* films of Alain Renais, among others. Aldiss was captivated by "the phenomenon of spiritual isolation" (*ToE*, 270) embodied by these works, which echoed the stasis found in much of his fiction and which, I suspect, reflected his own sense of spiritual isolation, particularly following his separation from Olive and his distance from his children. The sf of the time was filled with space travel and nuclear dread, but he began to think that stillness was "as much worth investigating, as terrifying" (*ToE*, 270), and he began his own version of a *nouveau roman*, or "anti-novel," called *Garden with Figures*.

In *The Twinkling of an Eye* Aldiss makes the bizarre claim that *Garden with Figures* was written to please those who gave him a Hugo for *Hothouse*. Apart from the fact that this first version of the novel that would become *Report on Probability A* didn't feature the watchers from different continua, which means it would be hard to see it at this stage as a work of science fiction, it was actually rejected by Faber a full year before the Hothouse stories won their Hugo Award. Aldiss has also said, "I don't know what a rejection slip looks like" (*BHS*, 39). But *Garden with Figures*, which he finished in 1962, was rejected not only by Faber but also by Robbe-Grillet's publisher in France, by Grove Press in the United States, and by everyone else it was sent to. So he put it aside until Moorcock asked for a contribution and Aldiss sent the novel "with apologies, saying, 'Look, Mike, this is all I've got. I don't think it's very good. No one likes it.' Mike wrote back and said, 'Not only do I like it, but I need it.'"[3] Again Aldiss's memory of the chronology seems open to question, since he implies that Moorcock was begging for contributions right at the start of his editorship. But the issues published at that time were hardly short of contributions from Aldiss, including the special Brian Aldiss issue already discussed.

What we do know is that after Moorcock's enthusiastic acceptance, Aldiss reconsidered his novel and found it rather thin. So he started to expand the story. "The additions I made were . . . the bits in italics about the watchers watching the watchers, and all that," he explained. "I believe I'm right in saying that I also inserted the dominant motif of Holman Hunt's 'Hireling Shepherd.' I don't think that was in the original."[4] These are precisely the aspects of the novel that give it a surreal and science-fictional edge, while emphasizing the sense of stillness and frozen time that ties it to the theme of stasis that is central to such varied works as *Hothouse*, *Earthworks*, *Enemies of the System*, and the Helliconia Trilogy.

The short version of *Report on Probability A* appeared in the March 1967 issue of *New Worlds* alongside Ballard's "The Assassination of John Fitzgerald Kennedy Considered as a Downhill Motor Race" and Christopher Priest's early story "The Ersatz Wine," which makes this entire issue an unequivocal statement of the magazine's espousal of experimental prose. It was only after this that the novel was published by Faber in 1968.

Report on Probability A, at its core, tells the story of three men, G, C, and S, who are each watching the same suburban home. The house is the residence of Mr Mary and his wife. They are always referred to in that formulation, never as Mrs Mary or with a different forename. This is part of the strict, repetitive formality of the language that itself reflects the sterility, the stasis of the story. We learn that the three men were previously employed by Mr Mary; as G reflects, there had been a time when "Mr Mary was paying him a weekly fee" (*RPA*, 11). The letters reflect the former occupations of the men—Gardener, Chauffeur, and Secretary—they are otherwise nameless.

Very late in the novel we learn that Mrs Mary had, some time earlier, had a baby that died. The three men had all been sacked at about that time, and each independently began living in the grounds some two years before the novel opens. What the connection might be, if any, between the death of the baby and the firing of the three men is never revealed, although there is a suggestion that the marriage had started to break down. The couple have separate bedrooms, and once, when C observes them quarreling, Mr Mary is seen to hit his wife, though this incident is treated with the lack of affect typical of the whole book. Are the men intent on guarding Mrs Mary? Are they there in the hope of getting their old jobs back? Are they simply unable to leave the place? Motivation plays no part in the novel; we see what people do described with patient detail, but there is nothing to tell us why they might do it. Much as we do in real life, we see the actions that people undertake without ever really seeing below the surface, without ever glimpsing what might really be going on in their mind. And as the novel demonstrates, a flat, emotionless description of actions can provide no clue as to motive.

The three men knew each other when they worked for Mr Mary, and each is aware of the other two, but they do not interact at any point in the novel. They do connect with others: all three take meals in the small café across the road, and the cook, Vi (one domestic helper that Mr Mary has retained), provides them with food while chastising them for what they are doing. Even Mr Mary and his wife are aware of the observers, though G, for example, is afraid that Mr Mary might spot him. When Mr Mary's wife does speak to G, the exchange seems curiously irrelevant—"When the fishing is poor, they say the price of fish rises" (RPA, 15)—and as they speak, "Mr Mary's wife never entirely stop[s] walking towards the brown side gate; nor [does] she entirely turn her face towards G" (RPA, 16). But we aren't sure how comfortable she is with the watchers. When she sees C through the dining room window, she "move[s] hastily out of sight . . . [and] . . . contort[s] her face and open[s] her mouth" (RPA, 133), and moments later we see Mr Mary peering around the curtains at the same window. "In his right hand he carrie[s] a rifle, grasping it by the barrel" (RPA, 134).

Each of the three watchers lives in a different and otherwise unvisited building on the surprisingly extensive grounds of Mr Mary's home. The former gardener occupies a wooden bungalow that Mr Mary had built as a summer house for his wife, though it seems neither of them visit it, for about two years have passed since G started living there. The former secretary is in a one-time coach house, and C lives in the loft space above the garage. All three outbuildings are shabby: the summer house is leaking and ill-furnished, the coach house boarded up and run-down, and in the garage all four tires of the large black car that C once drove for Mr Mary are flat. When Aldiss and his family lived in a flat at H. H. Aldiss's department store in East Dereham, the complex grounds included a variety of outbuildings such as a garage and engine house, old cottages converted to storage, and a summer house, each of which would have provided the young Brian with a different perspective when he looked back at his home. It is easy to imagine Aldiss remembering these rickety, slightly creepy buildings when working out where to position his three observers.

The focus of the novel is not on the observed but on the observers. Those who are seen are peripheral, of little importance, as shown by the language with which they are described. A page-long description of the face of Mr Mary's wife (*RPA*, 42–43) is so precise as to make her more of an object than a person, but "when S remove[s] the telescope from his eye, she bec[omes] only a vague movement in the lower left-hand window of the house set on a slight rise in the ground beyond the asparagus beds" (*RPA*, 44). As C watches Mr Mary cross the road to the café, he notes that he crosses "in a certain number of strides" (*RPA*, 137), which feels precise but actually tells us nothing. And when Vi is seen through the telescope we are aware only of "a plump woman in a white apron" (*RPA*, 93). These are not recognized, named people but, rather, abstract shapes without clarity or individuality or any real significance in the lives of the observers, as if their entire purpose has nothing to do with what is watched but simply with the act of watching.

When the focus shifts to the watchers themselves, however, and to their small, enclosed, self-made environments, then the detail becomes obsessive and repetitive. The descriptions are notable for being composed largely of negatives: "There was neither frost nor wind that afternoon. The trees in the garden did not stir" (*RPA*, 17); "When he swung his head quickly to the left again, he did not catch anyone looking at him from the window that belonged to Mr Mary's bedroom" (*RPA*, 28). We know more about what is not happening than about what is. And objects are rather pedantically described each time they are mentioned, as if we haven't previously been introduced to them. Thus we are told that G has "a cupboard of unpainted wood," in exactly those words, on pages 13, 14, 18, 19, and so on. And when the space above the garage where C lives is being described, we are told three times in two pages (*RPA*, 122–123) that five cardboard cartons contain his possessions. There is a sense that each time an object is mentioned it is being seen for the first time. Hence C has a niche beside the window where he keeps his telescope, but he keeps putting the telescope on the floor. When he reaches for it in the niche, it is not there, and he has to look around. Then, typically, he sees "on the floor just below the round window, resting with its four sections extended, . . . a brass telescope" (*RPA*, 92–93). It is always "a" telescope, never "the" or "his" telescope, as if it might be a different one every time, as if it has not been seen before. In a sense, these things haven't been seen before, it is always the first moment, in each instant the world is being rediscovered anew. The hands on G's clock have not moved for more than eleven months, and just like that clock, the novel is frozen in time. There is no before, no after; the reason why G, S, and C are not trying to extract meaning from their individual observations is that meaning would imply continuity, and there is no continuity. This is not life, advancing moment by moment, because G, S, and C abandoned such a life when they lost their jobs and settled for the inertia of watching the house and their former employer. Rather, it is like a painting, a still image, a slice across one single moment whose before and after can only be guessed.

This is why the painting *The Hireling Shepherd* by William Holman Hunt is such a potent symbol in this novel. Both G and S possess reproductions of the painting, which was controversial when first exhibited for its illustration of rural sexuality among the peasant class: beside a stream, a barefoot girl has a half-eaten apple on her lap (Eve?) while a shepherd has his arm around her, ostensibly to show her a moth he has caught; meanwhile, behind them, the sheep he is ignoring are wandering away. There is an ambiguity in the picture that seems to interest Aldiss: "On some occasions it seemed to S that she regarded the hireling shepherd with a sort of indolent contempt, on other occasions that her expression was one of lazy complaisance" (*RPA*, 64). The painting tells a story, but because it is a frozen moment of time with no glimpse of what came before or will come after, it is impossible to tell what that story is. He ponders whether another painting of the scene, set perhaps fifteen minutes earlier, might have resolved the ambiguities, for they are "engendered by the fact that it showed only one moment on its timescale"

(*RPA*, 73). But the ambiguities are not to be resolved, for they are surely the point of the painting, and of the novel.

So integral is Holman Hunt's painting to any appreciation of the novel that it is hard to credit Aldiss's claim that it was a late addition. It is easier to accept that the external observers might be a belated addition because in many ways they are not so much part of the story as a way of stressing its theme. We first become aware of these observers when what we have been reading is interrupted by an italicized passage in which Domoladossa and Midlakemela are discussing the report we are reading. Here the world of Mr Mary and his wife is described as Probability A: "We know it is closely related to our continuum, which I like to think of as Certainty X. Nevertheless, even superficially, Probability A reveals certain basic values that differ widely from our own" (*RPA*, 16). We later learn that this manifestation of another continuum, Probability A, is a recent phenomenon: "A week ago, he and all his millions of fellow men were living in a world of apparent uni-probability. Then this other continuum manifested itself" (*RPA*, 38). Later still we learn that Domoladossa is himself being observed by the Distinguishers: "There were four Distinguishers on duty at present, all standing gravely in the open air, gazing at the tall manifestation, on which Domoladossa could be seen at his desk, leafing through the report" (*RPA*, 54). And just as Domoladossa is worrying about how he could possibly judge the moral status of Probability A, the Distinguishers are worrying about the scale of the manifestation: "He may be no bigger than my thumb. He may be as tall as a house" (*RPA*, 55). And the Distinguishers are being observed on a "vast receiving set in a second-storey hall in New York" (*RPA*, 75), though whether this is our New York or not is, of course, unknowable. All of these observers are human, but because they are so disconnected from what they observe they are unable to see the humanity, the reflection of themselves, in what is before them; they are "intellectually fascinated" by what is observed "but not emotionally involved" (*RPA*, 74). Everyone is a voyeur, but what is watched is an object, not a person; there is no connection. The whole novel is filled with people who are emotionally and spiritually disconnected from everyone else.

And there are always more observers unwilling or unable to understand or sympathize with the people they watch. One set of watchers forms a jury listening to a report given by someone known as the Wandering Virgin. They, too, have a version of the Holman Hunt painting, although the painting they describe differs in minor but telling ways from the one in our universe. For instance, their version shows the shepherd carrying a ram's horn, and the girl has a book called *Low Point X*, a book we have already seen on S's shelf. One of the jurymen, the Image Motivator, interprets the painting thus: Victorian painters such as Hunt were "masters of the Unresolved, of the What Next? instant . . . the greatest Victorian pictures represent the imprisonment of beings in a temporal structure that seemed at the time to admit of no escape; so the paintings are cathartic in essence" (*RPA*, 100–101). Again this unresolved psychodrama stands for the unresolved (and undramatic) drama of the novel. In this universe Probability A is called "the Marian Universe" (*RPA*, 101), a reference to Mr Mary and his wife, of course, but together with the appearance of the Wandering Virgin it might also hint at Catholicism. If that is the case, G, S, and C might be avatars of the three wise men paying homage in a world in which the baby Jesus had died. But as a reading of the novel, I suspect that might be a dead end.

The multiple observers are summed up by one watcher, Joe Growleth: "Our robot fly has materialized into a world where it so happens that the first group of inhabitants we come across is studying another world they have discovered—a world in which the inhabitants they watch are studying a report they have obtained from another world." The question Joe ponders is, which of these worlds is real? His Congressman replies, "We don't have to decide what reality is, thank God!" (*RPA*, 96). And the men in New York are in turn being watched by "two young men and a boy who [stand] in an empty warehouse staring at the manifestation in puzzlement" (*RPA*, 125).

The novel is recursive. There is no answer to Joe Growleth's question because there is no reality, because "there were watchers watching them, and they too had watchers, who also had watchers, and so on, and so on, in an almost infinite series" (*RPA*, 153). The "almost" is surely redundant. Meanwhile, "sitting quiet in her own room, the fingertips of one hand resting in her tawny hair, Mr Mary's wife [sits] at her own screen and regard[s] the cycle of universes as night close[s] in" (*RPA*, 153). Her screen is a television, of course, which makes it possible to read this book as a satire on the social disengagement engendered by the spread of television during the late 1950s and early 1960s. Alternatively, this regress of observers might become an expression of

Mrs Mary's despair at the death of her baby. Or maybe Aldiss is simply demonstrating the sterility of modern suburban life. As Colin Greenland notes, "In the first dislocations of *Barefoot in the Head* Charteris notes the spaces between people,"[5] but as we have seen, those spaces were all there already in *Report on Probability A*; in fact, the book is composed entirely of such spaces, therefore linking what Greenland calls the "two polar masterpieces of the new sf."[6] The novel is a bravura demonstration of Aldiss's control of language, but for precisely that reason it gives us no clues as to how to read the book.

Because it gave nothing away, because it resolved nothing, *Report on Probability A* divided readers. James Blish seems to want it both ways, arguing that "though it is the first attempt to adapt the French anti-novel to a science-fictional end, and does not succeed at it, it is so cunningly carpentered that even its failure is definitive."[7] For Philip Strick, the beauty of the novel is that "it challenges all conventional methods of telling a story, by taking them to extremes,"[8] while for Ballard, writing in the *Times*, "This paralysis of the reader's brain unfortunately breaks the one vital link in this or any other chain of perception—that between the book and its reader."[9] Personally, I am prepared to go along with Colin Greenland in considering *Report on Probability A* a masterpiece. I am less sure that I would apply the same description to Aldiss's next novel, *Barefoot in the Head*.

★　★　★

Greenland is right about one thing: the two books are polar opposites. One is controlled, focused, precise, austere; the other is a wild efflorescence of linguistic invention. One sees the world only from the outside, the other only from the inside. One tells us what to see but gives no hint of how to feel; the other shows us how to feel but gives few clues about the reality of what we see. The wonder, indeed, is that the two books come from the same author. But at this point in the late 1960s Aldiss was secure in his new marriage to Margaret and back in regular contact with Clive and Wendy, he was secure financially, and he was secure in his position within the world of science fiction. In 1969, the year after *Report on Probability A* was published and despite the dismay with which that novel was greeted in some of sf's more traditional quarters, the BSFA voted Aldiss the most popular British science fiction writer. In response, Aldiss wrote to Larry Ashmead that the award was ironic: "I'm slowly working away from the field—or rather, more centrally in to what I feel sf should be about."[10] He was trying, in other words, to develop some new idea of what science fiction was and should be, an idea that was not necessarily encompassed by the New Wave but was, at the very least, liberated by that movement. His sense of security allowed him, in *Report on Probability A* and *Barefoot in the Head*, to experiment in trying to identify this new approach, one through its extreme stillness, the other through its extreme restlessness.

The New Wave gave a new freedom to British science fiction writers, a sense that the genre could do more than show competent men proving their manhood in overly familiar spaceports. Brian Aldiss certainly benefited from this freedom, but it is not quite right to describe him as being part of this movement. He was, for a start, somewhat older that the other writers associated with the New Wave. In 1967, when "Just Passing Through," the first of the stories that would be incorporated into *Barefoot in the Head*, was published in *SF Impulse*, he was approaching forty-two and by no means part of the counterculture whose social, political, and cultural ideas did so much to shape the New Wave. He maintained an air of respectability: he was published by Faber, reviewed in the *Times Literary Supplement*, friends with people like Kingsley Amis, and comfortable within the literary establishment of the day, far from the long-haired rebelliousness of the New Wave. At the same time, he was writing such books as *Earthworks* and *Cryptozoic* and editing such anthologies as *Farewell, Fantastic Venus* (1968) with Harry Harrison that represented exactly the sort of garish science fiction normally considered anathema among those who saw themselves as reinventing the genre. He took little part in the communal, often chaotic editorial sessions that Moorcock staged for *New Worlds* and was at odds with most of the people associated with that magazine when it came to things like plot and structure.[11]

Aldiss was an enthusiastic supporter of *New Worlds* and of the New Wave more generally, and when *New Worlds* had financial problems during 1966 he used his contacts within the literary establishment to secure an Arts Council grant that saved the magazine. (In truth, the Literature Panel of the Arts Council had been formed only in January 1966, and with no clear plan for how to support literature was tending to hand out grants to any little magazine that asked.[12] It is unlikely, however, that anyone else in the sf world would have thought of such a source of funding. Moorcock's fulsome praise for Aldiss in the next issue of the magazine could have done little but cement his status within the New Wave pantheon.) Aldiss was, moreover, fully in agreement with Ballard and Moorcock that most British science fiction of the 1950s had been dull and unimaginative. But I'm not sure he was ever convinced that the New Wave was the only, or the right, way forward. It was, however, an opportunity to try different things, to experiment in his writing. Such opportunities don't come along very often, and Aldiss took full advantage of this one.

★ ★ ★

It is hard to imagine a novel more precisely targeted at the *New Worlds* readership of the late 1960s than a story involving drugs and rock music. Yet it is written by someone not of that generation who very likely hadn't tried drugs (Aldiss delights in recording his various transgressions in *The Twinkling of an Eye* but doesn't once mention drugs, and *Super-State* specifically condemns any "reliance on drugs, with their destructive effects on mind and body" [*Su-S*, 85]) and whose familiarity with rock music was limited. Music features a lot in his work but, except for the short novel *Brothers of the Head*, it is almost exclusively classical music and opera, about which he writes quite knowledgeably. We might picture Aldiss as Mr Mary or one of the observers, but we do not picture him, short-haired and besuited, in *Barefoot in the Head*, and we don't even picture him as having much sympathy for this world. This is why I suspect that the story of *Barefoot* was of considerably less importance to its author than the way it allowed him to play with language.

This is not a particularly fresh perception; practically every critical analysis of the book begins with the language. It is, Griffin and Wingrove declare, "the novel in which Aldiss seemed . . . to have broken clean away from sf metaphors in order to deal with existential particulars in terms of wild linguistic experiment."[13] And Richard Mathews declares, "There is a central focus on language, naming, puns, style in this book about schizophrenic landscape perception."[14] For Paul March-Russell the "ebullient wordplay . . . hints at manifold possibilities."[15] The default position that many critics have adopted is that *Barefoot in the Head* was written under the influence of James Joyce. This idea is most persuasively argued by James Blish, one of the few sf critics who seems to have been as familiar with *Finnegans Wake* (1939) as he was with

Barefoot in the Head. Blish states that although *Barefoot in the Head* resembles *Ulysses* (1922) in both structure and narrative, "its texture is much more like that of *FW* [*Finnegans Wake*], even to the echoing of some of *FW*'s most easily recognizable mannerisms (puns that cross over word breaks, chains of long words ending in '-ation,' catalogue sentences) and its unique grammar (which, to the best of my knowledge, no other imitator has ever even recognized, let alone captured)."[16]

Aldiss insisted that *Barefoot in the Head* was not written to echo James Joyce but, rather, was in "the freak-speak of a survivor," though he also wondered whether "it would have been better told in plain language" (*ToE*, 272). This ties in with a comment he made in a 1978 interview. When asked if *Barefoot in the Head* had been translated into a foreign language he replied, perhaps rather ruefully, "It's in a foreign language."[17] Aldiss always loved long, complex, unfamiliar words, from "algolagnia" in *Greybeard* to "enantiodromia," which runs almost like a leitmotif through *Helliconia Summer*, but around those vivid and unexpected words his prose tended to be rather formal and carefully structured, the prose of a writer schooled in the 1930s and learning his trade in the 1950s. The surreal landscapes explored in *Non-Stop* and *Hothouse* are all the more remarkable for the plain, unfussy way in which they are described. Yes, he liked to make words up, usually with a jokey quality, as with the "trappersnappers" and "Tummy-trees" of *Hothouse*, and there were always puns, but these were at the service of the prose rather than in control of it. But *Barefoot in the Head* reversed that order: the novel was a stream-of-consciousness outpouring of puns and wordplay and neologisms within which the formal structures of language were all but lost. It was an attempt to represent in language "a deranged mentality—not one, but a complete continent's—that had already done away with structures of identity and sequence in favour of a vision of teeming chaos."[18] To the 1930s grammarian in Aldiss, it probably did seem like a foreign language. And since he probably knew few if any freak-speaking survivors, the model for this freewheeling language was, however Aldiss might protest, James Joyce. As Colin Greenland put it, Aldiss "did not borrow his new language" from *Finnegans Wake*, "but Joyce was there."[19] Indeed, as Blish insists, the *Finnegans Wake*—type passages "are often more Joyce than they are Aldiss, to no visible purpose."[20] According to Blish, therefore, Aldiss was an acute enough reader to spot some of Joyce's less obvious wordplay in *Finnegans Wake* but not so emotionally engaged, to pick up on Aldiss's argument from "The Girl and the Robot with Flowers," as to make that wordplay his own.

The novel started as a commission from Kyril Bonfiglioli to write a short story for *Science Fantasy*, a travel story with a smattering of science fiction in it, as Aldiss later recalled. That became "Just Passing Through," and it was only after delivering the story that, Aldiss said, "I [began to feel] I had wasted a great opportunity. It was like being on the edge of a spider's web. I could feel a whole something out there vibrating and I didn't quite know what it was."[21] What was vibrating was an idea for an amalgamation of the postwar England Aldiss had returned to in 1947 and the switched-on, tuned-in world of the Swinging Sixties in which he now found himself. "Just Passing Through" was published in the February 1967 issue of *Science Fantasy* (although by this point the magazine had been retitled *SF Impulse* and was edited by Harry Harrison); the other six Acid-Head War stories, as they became known, were published in *New Worlds* between August 1967 and January 1969. Two of them, "Auto-Ancestral Fracture" (December 1967) and "The Serpent of Kundalini" (February 1968), were credited to Brian Aldiss with C. C. Shackleton. Shackleton was one of Aldiss's pseudonyms and the name had disappeared by the time the stories were gathered together as a novel.

Barefoot in the Head opens with the arrival of Colin Charteris in Metz in northeastern France. The name Charteris is self-chosen: "He had dropped his Serbian name to christen himself with the surname of his favourite English writer" (*BfH*, 17). That favorite writer is generally assumed to be the Anglo-Chinese Leslie Charteris, the author of a series of adventure stories written over a period of thirty-five years featuring the debonair criminal-turned-crime fighter Simon Templar, known as the Saint. There is reference to the Saint books within the novel. However, that favorite writer might also be the English writer Hugo Charteris, whose brother-in-law, Ian Fleming, is said to have at least in part based James Bond on him. Hugo Charteris was very popular during the 1950s and '60s, though he has since fallen out of fashion. His characters tended to be alienated, dissatisfied with the world in which they found themselves, viewing contemporary society as either absurd or fit for annihilation; in other words, they were close to Aldiss's own self-image. The newly rechristened Charteris, too, will, over the course of the novel, find the world to be both absurd and suitable for annihilation, while becoming a sort of secular saint. But initially he has the clichéd affect of a hero "walking like a warrior across desert, a pilot over a runway after mission ninety-nine, a cowboy down silent Main Street" (BfH, 12).

Despite the setting and the odd generic name—Hôtel des Invalides—this is hardly the travelogue that Bonfiglioli seems to have anticipated. Rather, the very nonspecificity of the setting seems to be what is important. It is a place of contradictions: "The city was open to the nomad" (BfH, 11), we are told in the first sentence of the novel, yet we are told on the next page, "this city seemed closed to the nomad" (BfH, 12). It is a place where the French hotel owner speaks to Charteris in German, and the girl who speaks in French is not herself French. Identity and place are becoming confused. France had been neutral in the Acid-Head War, but it had not been unaffected, so in this calm-before-the-storm chapter we get a rather gentle foretaste of the breakdown of reality that will become a torrent once Charteris crosses the Channel to Britain. But we are also warned that all of this is a metaphor. The victims of the war are "confined within the tiny republics of their own psyches" (BfH, 19), which makes any conception of external reality a matter of solipsisms that may, or more likely do not, overlap. And Charteris, who provides our viewpoint in this distorted reality, sees "the world . . . purely as a fabrication of time, no matter involved. Matter was an hallucinatory experience: merely a slow-motion perceptual experience of certain time / emotion nodes passing through the brain" (BfH, 18). The novel, in other words, is a phantasmagoria of perceptions with no guarantee that anything is actually perceived. Charteris had worked with the survivors of the Psycho-Chemical Aerosol bombs, and like many such aid workers had himself been affected by the drugs, and so, as he tells us: "I am going psychedelic. That godlike vision must have come from the drug. At least rainbows will flutter in those dark valleys where I shall tread" (BfH, 20).

Most of the drug literature of the late 1960s took a Huxleyan view of the doors of perception, the opening up of new realities, new possibilities. Psychedelia was the ever-present leitmotif of the era, its influence evident in music, design, film, and fashion as well as literature. But Aldiss presents it unfailingly in negative terms: this is a story of disintegration. Thus it can be seen alongside *Non-Stop* and *Hothouse* as yet one more novel of the devolution of mankind—as Charteris tells one of the people working on the film of his life: "My friend, that was a short round we trod, less than two hundred degenerations the flintnapping cavesleepers first opened stareyes and we break down again with twentieth sensory perception of the circuit" (*BfH*, 140)—of people laid low by their human and social failures, of hubris clobbered by nemesis, in Aldiss's phrase. Thus northern Europe (an extension of the socially conservative austerity of postwar Britain) is equated with "constriction, miserliness, conservation, inhibition" (13) and with "images of ruin and deformity everywhere" (*BfH*, 14). This is brought out when Charteris arrives in Dover: "He recollected the England of his imagination. . . . That place was not this" (*BfH*, 34). England, the land that Aldiss hated on his return from the army, is here presented as a dull place, "neither inhabitable nor uninhabitable," a place of dumps and mean buildings and "leprous dwellings," a place "rotting intricate under the creative powers of decay" (*BfH*, 81–82). Britain had been the first country to suffer the PCA bombs, and though their effects may be surreal, dislocating, they are also diminishing: "A curse of alternate inertia had been visited upon the English sexes. Men stood waiting and smoking in little groups, unspeaking; women scurried lonely. In their eyes, he saw the dewy glints of madness" (*BfH*, 34). Everything, social and cultural, that Aldiss found ill and unwelcoming about postwar Britain is here visited on Acid-Head War Britain.

By the late 1960s, when *Barefoot in the Head* was written, Britain had long since emerged from the dull austerity of the postwar world. Color was everywhere in flamboyant clothes, in psychedelic posters and murals, even in the color television, introduced in 1967. Yet the social changes of "Swinging Britain" have no place in this colorless, denatured world with "no flowers or fruit ever on the old entangled damson trees except the dripping mildew where their leaves curdled in brown knots" (*BfH*, 152). The Britain he presents in this novel is closer to the despised country he returned to than to the country he would have seen around him at the time of writing. There is almost a sense of longing for the world in which he was least happy.

As the book goes on, the breakdown of language, signaled by alliteration, portmanteau words, puns, slangy and childish terms, and the odd neologism, increases: the breakdown of the world is heralded by our increasing inability to read the world:

> He paraded with her slowly round the grand room, already partly hyacinth-invaded as they foliaged intricoarsely across the wallpagan, he speaking here and there to the chattering mass of his invitees, all to Angeline maroonly macabre and flowing from the head as part of the mythology of the palapse and from their infested breath and words crawled the crystalagmites she dreamed of dreading in the coral city trees without window or stratum. (*BfH*, 149)

The language, which is intended to be read from the page rather than spoken aloud, therefore acts as a visual representation of the degeneration that Aldiss sees all around him. There is, in other words, a disconnect between the language that we see and the language that we hear. Thus what is central to Charteris's ascent to the status of messiah is his involvement with rock music, the one unavoidable aspect of Swinging Britain that has to be incorporated into the novel. Yet the language in which this musical culture is presented is as resolutely visual as everything else.

The book is punctuated by a number of mostly indifferent poems, often little better than doggerel (this from a writer who would go on to have several books of poetry published from the 1980s onwards)—"And then that night he clasped her tightly / Now she lets him clasp her nightly / Wrongly rightly clasp her nightly" (*BfH*, 26)—and awkward, unmusical "songs." It's as though Aldiss is trying to be hip without quite knowing how. Although he acknowledges Procul Harum and their 1967 hit "A Whiter Shade of Pale" (which incorporates a Bach orchestral suite, thus bringing it closer to his usual musical tastes), he shows little interest in or awareness of the basic structure and rhythm of popular music, or, indeed, in the radical stance that tended to be taken by pop musicians of the time. He has, for instance, a pop group write a song complaining about the introduction of decimal currency: "I do my personal thinking in pounds" (*BfH*, 83). When decimalization did take place in the United Kingdom two years after this book was published, it attracted no such musical protest, mostly because it was a backward-looking conservative issue and pop groups always had more radical things on their mind. Aldiss's rather uncomfortable flirtation with popular culture reads like the work of someone for whom the zeitgeist was always happening somewhere else.

Aldiss was more in touch with the popular culture of the time in his employment of ideas from mysticism. The influence of Charles Berg's *Madkind* seems to have been replaced by George Gurdjieff and his disciple, P. D. Ouspensky, who argued that humans do not possess a unified consciousness and that in order to achieve their full potential they must awaken to a higher state of consciousness, a view that underlay much of the talk about drugs in the late 1960s. The sense of a higher consciousness, and by implication the abandonment of an old consciousness, is something that recurs throughout the novel, in which "the times themselves . . . talk nonsense—but the sort of nonsense that makes us simultaneously very sceptical about the old rules of sanity" (*BfH*, 36). Although the lack of a unified consciousness is reflected structurally in the way that, particularly in the early sections of the novel, we witness a series of encounters by versions of Charteris that break off from the original (whatever that original might be), each encounter proves to be a dead end, and the scene then resets to a new Charteris. These various iterations of Charteris are accompanied by various versions of a young woman who is, for instance, Angelina, whom he meets in the hotel in Metz, and Angeline, the wife of Phil Brasher and who is also sometimes known simply as Angel (an appropriate companion for a Saint).

It is, incidentally, when we read passages that talk of "Boreas taking a firm hold of Angelina to guide her next to him, one great hand under her shirt grappling the life out of her left breast" (*BfH*, 150) that we realize how masculine, how blokeish this novel is. Women are there for sex or to float indistinctly in the orbit of the man; they are not individual, motivated figures with agency of their own. This sexualized worldview may be more apparent in *Barefoot in the Head* because the world itself has been stripped back to basics, but we recognize how frequently this attitude has appeared elsewhere in Aldiss's work.

The disjointed consciousness of Charteris becomes unified in his emergence as a rock messiah in this addled world. In this he is an analogue of that other great messiah figure of 1960s science fiction, Valentine Michael Smith, in Robert Heinlein's *Stranger in a Strange Land* (1961): Aldiss makes a knowing reference to Heinlein with "the heinleiner car" (*BfH*, 187). And like Smith, after his exaltation as a messiah Charteris finds his control over his own life slipping away from him. More and more people become involved in running the cult, organizing the film of Charteris's life that seems to bear little resemblance to real events and arranging the strange pilgrimage sweeping across the roads of Europe toward a vast amphitheater show. To be a messiah is to be in showbiz. And it seems for much of the latter part of the novel that Charteris is following the same route that other messiahs have traveled: toward his own crucifixion. But in the end he slips away, and the last we see of him, he is sitting under a tree on an old bed like an Indian wise man, and when he dies the tree has to be fenced off to protect it from disciples. Aldiss has returned to his beloved East and to the banyan tree beside the River Hoogley.

★ ★ ★

"During the seventies," Griffin and Wingrove argue, "an acute consciousness of artifice emerged in Aldiss's work and a concomitant experimentation with form."[22] It's a strange claim to make, given that a consciousness of artifice and an experimentation with form had been part of Aldiss's writing virtually from the beginning. We see it in the very self-conscious arrangement of stories in *Space, Time and Nathaniel* and in jokey pieces such as "Confluence" and "Confluence Revisited" (1988), as well as "End Game" (1981), which was structured as a palindrome. We also see it inescapably in the linguistic austerity of *Report on Probability A* and what Thomas M. Disch calls the "verbal ingenuities"[23] of *Barefoot in the Head*, the two novels that were central to his engagement with the more experimental aspects of the British New Wave. Yet by the early 1970s the New Wave had begun to recede, and with it the boldest phase of Aldiss's literary experimentation.

The obvious thing about experiments is that they are as liable to fail as they are to succeed, and this is as true of literary experiments as it is of scientific ones. The ambivalence of the responses to the last two novels was enough to suggest that, to some readers, at least, they had not been an overwhelming success. *Report on Probability A*, which, Aldiss believed, would "single-handedly, bring SF into the twentieth century" (*BHS*, 96), instead generated threatening letters from some American readers. In more academic circles the two novels have fared better, though again not without some hesitation. As Paul March-Russell says of *Report on Probability A*: "If . . . Aldiss is proposing an aesthetics of silence, he is doing so by increasing the noise of informational overload."[24] Overall, the poor reception of *Report on Probability A* and *Barefoot in the Head* in the sf community, and the fact that they were largely ignored outside the sf world, made Aldiss "reluctant to return to those chilly waters" (*BHS*, 161). The chilly waters in question are, ostensibly, science fiction, though as we shall see he didn't actually stray far from the genre for very long. We might, more accurately, identify those chilly waters as experimentation.

Aldiss never totally gave up on literary experimentation, but from this point on those experiments were largely confined to his short fiction, particularly the works he called Enigmas. After 1969 he only produced one novel that could unequivocally be described as experimental, and that was one of his least successful works, *The Eighty-Minute Hour*.

Coming in the same year that Aldiss edited the anthology *Space Opera* (1974), perhaps influencing the novel in the same way *Billion Year Spree* influenced *Frankenstein Unbound*, *The Eighty-Minute Hour* was his attempt to write what he called, in a letter to Larry Ashmead, "just a jolly chunk of space opera."[25] It is notable that the more positive responses to the book have picked up on this jolliness, presenting it primarily as a comedy despite the fact, as Richard Mathews notes, that it "doesn't make you laugh out loud."[26] For most readers, this one included, the comedy of the novel is forced, awkward, and unfunny.

The Eighty-Minute Hour was written during what appears to have been a period of strain in his marriage (reading between the lines of his autobiography, such periods happened quite regularly, and Aldiss was usually at fault). Aldiss was traveling around America "talking, drinking, flying, driving," and the novel was "written in spasms" (*ToE*, 299) during that journey. As a result of these circumstances, he noted, "For the first time I seemed at a loss in my writing" (*ToE*, 299). The disjointedness implied by all this comes across in the novel; when all is said and done, the most notable thing about the book is its incoherence.

The novel is crammed with characters, far more than any other comparable work by Aldiss, but these are distinguished mostly by their silly names—Monty Zoomer, Devlin Carnate, Glamis Fevertrees, Choggles Chaplain, Guy Gisbone (clearly a play on Guy of Gisbourne in the Robin Hood stories), and a Croatian lady called Myrtr Tjidvyl (pronounced Merthyr Tydfil)—rather than any attempt at characterization. All of this suggests that Aldiss isn't taking this at all seriously, and we shouldn't, either. The rate at which new characters are introduced suggests also that the story rather got away from him: there is no clear authorial control, no overarching narrative thread, and, barring the daft names, there are no distinct characters that the reader can easily follow. Instead there is a hodgepodge of weird invention that is liable to shoot off in odd directions whenever the author cannot quite decide where his story should take him next.

And these characters seem to appear and disappear in the narrative in unpredictable ways. Some find themselves repeating the same actions endlessly with only minor variations. Some are gone from the text for a hundred pages or so, as if Aldiss had no use for them and simply forgot about them for a while. Some seem to be engaged in world-changing events that uniformly come to nothing, while others travel between realities, each of which they effortlessly mold to their will. It all forms a series of set pieces that never connect into anything like a coherent story.

The novel opens in the aftermath of war. The opening sentence tells us that there are "four things one particularly notices after wars of any respectable size: preparations for the next one, confidence that armed conflict is finished forever, starvation, and feasting" (*EMH*, 1), a line, Aldiss says, that has "frequently been quoted, if only by me" (*EMH*, v). As in *Greybeard*, nuclear warfare has had devastating and unexpected consequences: "The ravaging weapons of war had . . . so torn the fabric of the universe that now strange paths to otherwheres and otherwhens lay open to those who were knowledgeable—or courageous enough to tread those paths of madness" (*EMH*, 11). As the observers in the *Doomwitch* (a reference to the then-recent BBC television series *Doomwatch* [1970–1972]) put it: "The hitherto uninterrupted, ceaseless, *remorseless* flow of time is disrupted" (*EMH*, 34). As a consequence, the world government in this iteration of 1999 starts to receive reports of a Zulu War in South Africa led by Cetawayo, of Russian troops attacking the Ottoman Army, and of Britain invading Afghanistan, events from the late 1870s apparently occurring at the end of the twentieth century. Like *Barefoot in the Head* and *Frankenstein Unbound*, war has therefore damaged the very fabric of reality, in this case opening up connections between universes so that one can drain energy from another. The time turbulences echo other distortions in Aldiss's work, since "several of the reports [mention] that people in the turbulences were stated to be of gigantic stature" (*EMH*, 132). Here again we see variations in size working as indicators of the changes he has created, recalling, among other works, *Hothouse* and *Non-Stop.*

The great power in this version of 1999 is Cap-Comm, a merger of the United States and the Union of Soviet Socialist Republics, Capitalism and Communism, which represents determinism, which "saps the will not to work" and will "make the world like a police state" (*EMH*, 6). Against Cap-Comm is ranged a group called the Dissident Nations whose composition, leadership, and ideology are never exactly clear. But real control in the world seems to be in the hands of a few autocratic individuals, principal among whom are Attica Saigon Smix and the late Auden Chaplain, who was famous for "the legendary patching of mis-applied science with further misapplied science" (*EMH*, 72). Smix, who is in effect the villain of the novel to the extent that anyone can be considered a villain when motives and often actions are so indistinct, feels that "life would be simpler if all the other human beings were killed off" (*EMH*, 107) and represents a "need for the anti-human which has led to the takeover of human affairs by the computer complex" (*EMH*, 6).

Rather than being a jolly space opera, the novel is really a crude parody of the form, littered with jargon yet showing no attempt to make that jargon even appear to relate to anything real. Thus we get a "sunship" whose "ship's transverters dragged the vessel from cupro-space to the ordinary dimensions of the X-World" (*EMH*, 17). In numerous places Aldiss seems to be putting words down for their sound, not their sense, as when space is described as "a zero-infinity nightmare topology, undiminished by distance, unfamiliarised by any proximity" (*EMH*, 18) or the scientific nonsense that has white as a maddening color to run through because "the free play of musculature, the very interplay of elasticity and oxygenation, is impeded by interstices of nul-chromaticity, which lend an a-coeval pseudo-validity to the kinetics of movement" (*EMH*, 176–177). The degraded language of *Barefoot in the Head* is here replaced by a series of buzzwords that look as if they have some sort of scientific meaning but are actually bundled together in combinations that are meaningless. The floor of space feels "warm, worn, hydroptic, apical, pinnate, like the flesh of a vulpine and voluptuous courtesan erotogenically dying" (*EMH*, 19)—"hydroptic" means containing excessive water, "apical" means at the apex, "pinnate" means like a feather, so that this is a whole string of adjectives thrown together without conveying any particularly coherent image. Similarly, the aide Benchiffer's "unction of his own calcareous personality" (*EMH*, 20) is a contradiction, a soothing oil and a chalky personality not normally being united.

What makes this an experimental work, besides the far more careless use of vocabulary than one would normally expect of Brian Aldiss, is, in part, the fact that the novel seems to be being written by one of its characters. The narrator, Durrant, announces the first time he appears on stage: "I want to write a good old-fashioned novel with no more ambition in it than to reflect pleasure and disgust in what I see around me," adding moments later, "I did not intend to write *this* novel. But . . . perhaps that conversation predetermined this book" (*EMH*, 27). The novel thus twists self-referentially on itself, and since the vast majority of the scenes described in the book could not have been witnessed by Durrant, what we are reading is thus an imaginative construct of somebody else's imaginative construct. It's a convenient excuse for the novel's many inconsistencies: it was all made up by someone that Aldiss made up.

What is more interesting in experimental terms is that the space opera is presented as if it is an actual opera. Whereas *Barefoot in the Head* was punctuated by pop songs which, if lacking great lyrics, at least caught something of the zeitgeist; *The Eighty-Minute Hour* periodically breaks into arias, duets, recitative, and the rest of the operatic arsenal. Aldiss was a lot more comfortable in the world of opera than he was in the world of rock'n'roll, so these interludes work better. Thus when four characters suddenly break into song:

QUARTET
Yes, this is the riddle that peasants and commuters
Put to each other in Nineteen Nine Nine
As they dig up their fields or they drive in a line—
As they slump by their holocubes or go to dine out—
Yes, this is the riddle that peasants and commuters
Put to themselves in that terrible moment of doubt—
"Are we compos mentis enough for computers?" (*EMH*, 31)

it doesn't exactly work as dialogue, but, although the scansion needs a little attention and "put to themselves in that terrible moment of doubt" is a very clumsy line, it is closer to song than anything we find in *Barefoot in the Head*.

Presenting space opera as opera is an interesting conceit. It is easy to visualize the story as a series of pompous, garishly dressed characters parading across a stage with a painted backdrop and little sense of place. The operatic format perhaps excuses the silly names and the baroque, episodic plot. But the operatic aspects of the novel only crop up intermittently, and Aldiss really needed to make the space opera work as well as the opera. Instead, there's a carelessness about both aspects of the novel that suggests someone pursuing an idle notion without a great deal of attention. As John Clute remarks, "The reader with true grit will finally come across a few interesting pages, and may feel, in consequence, an absurd gratitude on noting their presence in this distressing text."[27] He was far from alone in this opinion; for David I. Masson, "You have to have a tough constitution, a super-keen memory, and a contempt for reality, to survive[;] . . . the total effect is triviality and emptiness."[28]

★   ★   ★

If *The Eighty-Minute Hour* was less an experiment than a *jeu d'esprit* that was neither as playful nor as spirited as it needed to be, Aldiss's urge to experiment now came out mostly in his short fiction. Sometimes these stories took the form of parodies such as "Commander Calex Killed, Fire and Fury at Edge of World, Scones Perfect" (2003), in which all that is really going for the story is the incongruity of a journey through devastation ending in an English tea room. Despite his gift for comedy, parody never seems to have been Aldiss's strong suit.

He is better when the surreal intrudes into our perceptions of the world, the sense of some deep meaning hovering just beyond our grasp. Thus in "The Plain, the Endless Plain" (1984), for instance, generations of one tribe cross a landscape rendered featureless, a plain so "nondescript that it existed almost as an abstraction" in which "such colours as it possessed were also lost, submerged in a prevailing tawniness" (*RoE*, 254). The lack of color recalls aspects of both *Greybeard* and *Barefoot in the Head*, colorlessness being associated with meaninglessness, with an absence of human control.

In another late story, "How the Gates Opened and Closed" (1995), a story-teller, challenged over the lack of incident in his tales, responds: "What you must learn to enjoy is the lack of event, the silences of a tale" (*CB*, 102). Such silences, which we will catch an echo of in, for instance, *The Malacia Tapestry*, are often found in Aldiss's more successful experiments. Silence allows for the subtle and the surreal, turning the attention inwards, and many of Aldiss's better experimental short stories involve identity. One example is "The Eye Opener" (1995), in which a gigantic head appears mysteriously in the sky and very subtly subverts the masculine perspective of the militaristic power broker who is the narrator.

These are but some examples of the experimentation found in Aldiss's short fiction. But his most common experiments were centered on the use of language and the fragmentation of narrative. For example, "Creatures of Apogee" (1977) works, as *The Eighty-Minute Hour* tried to do, to evoke something completely alien by poetic if often excessive use of language: "Take their great eyes, set in faces pale, evanescent, baroque" (*RoE*, 148), the enjambment of adjectives—pale, evanescent, baroque—that don't seem to belong together an attempt to portray something we don't quite have words for. Yet it presents a familiar pattern in which the central characters, identified only as "he, She, and she" (*RoE*, 147), live lives shaped by the extremes of a long year, which makes this not simply an experiment in language but one of a number of stories that seem to provide a trial run for what would become Helliconia. There is another glimpse of the same notion, for example, in "The Dark Soul of the Night" (1976), again set on a planet with years-long seasons. Like "The Plain, the Endless Plain," it concerns a family group traipsing across a near-featureless landscape that even shares the same color palette, the day "expiring in wreaths of brown, grey and purple" (*BSF3*, 223), their visible world bounded by mists and marked only by crevasses that cross their path. In fact, the journey is over—they reached safety and were rescued—but the viewpoint character, David, cannot escape; he relives and repeats the journey endlessly in his head. As in many of Aldiss's more experimental fictions, the inner and outer worlds are confused; reality is never something we can rely on.

It is not only in the use of language that Aldiss experimented but in the structure of what that language tells us, how we shape what we see or, more telling, how the narrative is shaped for us. Some stories, such as "The Big Question" (1986), might be considered a fragment of experiment rather than an experiment in fragmentation. Clearly he intended this as a technical challenge, writing a story in which every sentence is framed as a question: "Isn't it obvious to us now that the twentieth century and the great part of the century which followed were bristling with certainties—ideological and scientific certainties above all? What but reaction could have followed from such a blind epoch?" (*RoE*, 316). Alas, such a concatenation of questions might convey a sense of uncertainty, a lack of confidence in how we apprehend the world that is typical of Aldiss, but it does not add up to a story.

Aldiss pursued narrative fragmentation more adroitly in his Enigmas. Each of these was a set of three very short stories, often little more than sketches for stories—the set of Enigmas that appeared in *Final Stage* (1974), edited by Edward L. Ferman and Barry N. Malzberg, was given the collective title "Diagrams for Three Enigmatic Stories"—that were linked more by some nebulous sense of mood rather than by anything concrete within the text. As Aldiss described them in an afterword to "Diagrams for Three Enigmatic Stories," the Enigmas are "slightly surreal escapades grouped in threesomes—a form which provides the chance for cross references and certain small alternatives not always available in one story."[29] The first set, "Three Enigmas: The Enigma of Her Voyage; I Ching, Who You?; The Great Chain of Being What?," was published in *New Writings in SF 22* (1973), edited by Kenneth Bulmer, and Aldiss provided an introduction in which he came as close as he could to explaining the idea: "Consider them as paintings, as Tiepolo's engravings crossed with de Chirico's canvases."[30] And he used another artistic metaphor, drawn this time from Shakespeare, when talking about "the assumption which underlies the Enigmas: that the world is a stage on which we, the players, have no adequate means of determining the nature of the drama in which we enact our bit parts."[31] In other words, the fragmentation he pursues in the Enigmas, the sketch of a story allusively linked to the sketch of another story, forms surreal landscapes that make us aware of how little we can reliably know about our world and our place in it. They are extensions of the sort of disconnection we have already found in *Report on Probability A*.

No complete collection of the Enigmas ever materialized, but a number were included in the 1977 collection *Last Orders*. Writing of that collection, and with the Enigmas clearly in mind, Tom Hosty said: "The actual stories, residual narratives for the most part, fade; moods and felicities of imagery linger."[32] While David Wingrove, in *Apertures*, said that in the Enigmas "Aldiss is discussing art and its imitations, and drawing the conclusion that the intellect is insufficient,"[33] the stories "discuss the essence of Free Will and the nature of Predestination" while examining "the effects on Art of cherishing it too much."[34]

CHAPTER 4

HISTORIAN

In Chapter 3 I suggested that there was some doubt about Brian Aldiss's claim that, after the muted and often ambivalent response to *Report on Probability A* and *Barefoot in the Head*, he abandoned science fiction, at least for a while.

The generally accepted form of the story, as laid out, for instance, by Griffin and Wingrove, is that *Barefoot in the Head* was "an exercise with which, temporarily, Aldiss wrote himself out of the genre."[1] Having found himself forced out of science fiction, whether voluntarily or not depending on the source, Aldiss turned to writing two largely autobiographical novels, *The Hand-Reared Boy* (1970) and *A Soldier Erect* (1971), before rediscovering his enthusiasm for science fiction by writing its history, *Billion Year Spree*.

It's a good story, but the facts don't bear it out. And I think, as I argue in this chapter, that behind it lies a deeper ambivalence about Aldiss's relationship with science fiction.

The Hand-Reared Boy is the story of Horatio Stubbs, a child in pre-war Britain whose enjoyment of masturbation eventually leads to sexual initiation with the matron of his boarding school. *A Soldier Erect* continues the story, with Stubbs now part of the Forgotten Army in Burma and cutting a swath through the whores of India. The career of Horatio Stubbs, therefore, closely matches that of his creator (the final part of the trilogy, *A Rude Awakening*, which didn't appear until 1978, takes Stubbs on to Sumatra), and the emphasis on sex, obvious in the innuendo of the titles, matches the interest in what I've called priapic masculinity in Aldiss's life and career.

The first two books in particular enjoyed great commercial and critical success, but their sexual content meant that they were also very controversial. Margaret Aldiss reports that *The Hand-Reared Boy* was rejected by thirteen publishers before finding a home with Weidenfeld and Nicolson.[2] This suggests that it must have been written and submitted to publishers before *Barefoot in the Head* appeared, so it is hardly likely to have been written as a way of abandoning science fiction. Indeed, Aldiss had been intent on writing a mainstream novel immediately after his return from the East, and *Hunter Leaves the Herd*, which he left unfinished in 1947, shares a setting with *A Rude Awakening*, so the idea for these novels may well have been in his mind for some time.

Moreover, there was no obvious abandonment of science fiction. Between *Barefoot in the Head* and *Billion Year Spree*, the period when Aldiss supposedly had left sf behind, three new collections of his short fiction appeared, *Intangibles, Inc.* (1969), *The Moment of Eclipse* (1970), and *The Book of Brian Aldiss* (1972), all three of which contained stories first published in this period. In addition, a revised edition of *Best Science Fiction Stories of Brian W. Aldiss* (1971) came out. Meanwhile, together with Harry Harrison, he edited five volumes in their *Year's Best Science Fiction* series and two volumes of *The Astounding-Analog Reader*. This is less a moving away from science fiction than a retrenchment of his interest in the genre.

In particular, the two volumes of *The Astounding-Analog Reader* testify to a continuing interest in the sort of science fiction influenced by editor John W. Campbell, a sort that was, in political, stylistic and thematic terms, diametrically opposed to everything the New Wave was supposed to represent.

Aldiss would reinforce his admiration for Campbellian science fiction by helping launch the John W. Campbell Memorial Award, which was established in 1972 (the year after Campbell died), and first presented in 1973. Its creation thus belongs precisely in his supposed sabbatical from science fiction. There is a contradiction here, and I suspect that *Billion Year Spree* may have been written, in part, at least, to frame or possibly resolve that contradiction.

★　★　★

Brian Aldiss had been avidly reading science fiction since at least his schooldays. The stories he told in his school dormitories, often salacious if not outright pornographic, would frequently involve robots, aliens. or other characteristically science-fictional devices.

The stories he encountered before the war would have been, typically, the space operas of E. E. "Doc" Smith, a form of fiction that Aldiss described as "Wide Screen Baroque" (*BYS*, 302). After the war, in whatever American magazines were available in the United Kingdom, he most likely would have discovered the hard sf typified by Isaac Asimov, Robert Heinlein, and their like. Such stories are what would have engendered his own interest in science fiction, and the influence of these authors on his early work is obvious.

By the beginning of the 1960s Aldiss was drawing on this knowledge to edit three anthologies: *Penguin Science Fiction* (1961), *More Penguin Science Fiction* (1963), and *Yet More Penguin Science Fiction* (1964). Many if not most of the authors featured in these books were drawn from Campbell's stable. And, despite an avowed aim of promoting the literary acceptance of science fiction—it was in the introduction to *Penguin Science Fiction* that Aldiss first wrote his much-quoted line "Science fiction is no more written for scientists than ghost stories were written for ghosts"[3]—they were very conventional stories. Other than one early story by J. G. Ballard, there is nothing here to suggest the radical rethinking of sf that Aldiss would espouse just a year after the last of the Penguin anthologies appeared.

In a 1962 conversation with C. S. Lewis and Kingsley Amis, Aldiss declared that "one of the attractions of science fiction is that it takes us to unknown places,"[4] places imagined by people "who can write, as well as thinking up engineering ideas."[5] This conversation has the same aim as did the anthologies: to say, in Amis's words, that it was "time more people caught on"[6] to science fiction. Yet if there is indeed a message for the readers of these anthologies, for the listener to this conversation, it is simply that the technological puzzles and competent men of hard sf should be of interest to those who don't normally read science fiction; they do not suggest that the readers of hard sf should be open to other sorts of stories or other ways of telling such stories.

However, at exactly the same time these anthologies were being compiled, Aldiss was meeting with Ballard and Moorcock, and they were shaking their heads over the dullness of British science fiction and the hidebound, conservative character of the genre in general. In an essay published in the same year as Aldiss's conversation with Amis and Lewis, Ballard argued that "it is *inner* space, not outer, that needs to be explored. The only truly alien planet is Earth."[7] In his first editorial for *New Worlds* Moorcock called for fiction that "mirrors exactly the mood of our ad-saturated, Bomb-dominated, power-corrupted times."[8] The three of them were plotting a revolution in science fiction as a result of which the attitudes, the language, the very subject matter of the stories Aldiss was busy anthologizing would be seen to be old fashioned, and in many cases simply irrelevant.

A division was opening up in science fiction, a division that Aldiss himself was, at least in part, responsible for creating. And he was standing resolutely on both sides of the divide.

It was an awkward, untenable position that Aldiss would nonetheless continue to hold throughout the New Wave and beyond. He was spearheading the literary battalions of the New Wave while championing the old; he was celebrating all that was most familiar, most traditional about mid-twentieth-century science fiction while proclaiming that his own work was designed to "bring SF into the twentieth century." (*BHS*, 96). Yet this was the writer who claimed that *Report on Probability A* was designed to please the voters who had given him a Hugo Award for *Hothouse*. It is very possible that he didn't recognize the contradiction implicit in these stances.

The stories he would produce during this supposed absence from science fiction illustrate the contradictory nature of his position. They include "Super-Toys Last All Summer Long" (1969), which would later be the basis of the Stanley Kubrick–Stephen Spielberg film *A.I. Artificial Intelligence* (2001), a humane treatment of an artificial person longing to be fully human whose life is blighted by a failure of communication with the woman he identifies as his mother. It has the literary sophistication of the New Wave, but at its heart is a familiar story of robots identifying as human, which takes us back to the science fiction of Aldiss's youth or to the story embedded in "The Girl and the Robot with Flowers." (Isaac Asimov, for example would produce another take on the same underlying story in "The Bicentennial Man" [1976].) In contrast, "As for Our Fatal Continuity . . ." (1972) was unabashedly part of the more experimental reaches of the New Wave, taking the form of a catalog of surreal, computer-generated artworks by a perhaps insane artist obsessed with the dying words of famous people. The two stories stand as representatives of Aldiss's varied approach to writing at this time: the New Wave added to his arsenal in terms of narrative, structure, and subject, but without removing any of the more traditional and often hackneyed approaches to sf that he had been imbibing since his childhood.

There was a division in science fiction, but Aldiss either didn't see it, didn't want to see it, or had simply decided that it didn't apply to him.

★ ★ ★

How did this lead Aldiss to produce perhaps the most influential book of his career?

I think that Aldiss loved traditional hard sf. It was what he wrote when he started out, and it informed the novels in which exuberance overwhelmed finesse, as in *Bow Down to Nul* or *The Dark Light Years*. And we have seen already how Heinlein had an influence on such varied novels as *Non-Stop* and *Barefoot in the Head*. The ideas of technical literacy, other worlds, and competent heroes, all the virtues of science fiction he had enumerated in his conversation with Lewis and Amis, remained central to his sense of what science fiction should contain.

At the same time, he was deeply immersed in the technical aspects of his craft. Vocabulary, structure, and new ways of telling stories all fascinated him, and the experimental dimensions of the New Wave gave him the freedom to foreground those aspects of his writing. So as much as he loved hard sf, Aldiss was excited by the literary innovations made possible by the New Wave.

And because both the technophile and the modernist were present in his writing, I suspect that Aldiss saw no difference between them. But the readers did. Fans of hard sf saw the New Wave as a betrayal of their genre, while exponents of the New Wave saw hard sf as symptomatic of everything that needed to be swept away. For Aldiss, therefore, the question became how to reconcile the two sides. The answer was history.

This is not as unexpected an answer as it might have appeared at the time. Aldiss's engagement with the stories that had shaped science fiction throughout the twentieth century had been evident in the various anthologies he had edited since 1961. In 1970 he published *The Shape of Further Things: Speculations on Change*, his first volume about science fiction, its debt to the past evident in a title taken from the Wells novel *The Shape of Things to Come* (1933). History, as he perceived it in this book, is not a record of an unchanging past but an engagement with "processes [that] are changing and interacting" (*SFT*, 9). This, of course, lay the groundwork for him to be able to present the New Wave not as a radical discontinuity in the history of science fiction but, rather, as a radical continuity. Thus he can say that, although Moorcock's editorship of *New Worlds* was a revolution with which "a new epoch of sf began in this country," still, "all that happened before . . . should not be forgotten" (*SFT*, 137). The New Wave, therefore, was less a revolution than an evolution; there was no division within science fiction, only necessary and inevitable change, and so he was not straddling two widely separated camps but was simply a part of the natural historic process.

According to that argument, works such as *Hothouse* and *Report on Probability A* were not wildly different but were instead close together on the same spectrum, as Aldiss had always believed. And in that collapsing of the literary distinctions between his various works lay the birth of *Billion Year Spree*.

★   ★   ★

The key to *Billion Year Spree*, or at least what I suspect Aldiss intended to be the key, comes in the final chapter. Having laid out the long story of science fiction, a story that takes us back to Lucian of Samosata, Johannes Kepler, Francis Godwin, Daniel Defoe, and others on to "Doc" Smith and Robert Heinlein, he can finally say that the science fiction of the 1960s, the radical decade that had just passed, "has its inevitable precedents in the sf of the fifties" (*BYS*, 328), which in turn had precedents in the forties, and in the thirties, and in the twenties, and on backwards. This was the climactic argument of the book: that each new decade had introduced changes, developments, or improvements in the character of science fiction but that the genre itself was essentially unchanged. By the time he had reached this point, however, his audience had latched on to other things.

There had been histories of science fiction, or at least historical approaches to aspects of science fiction, before this point. Such works as *Pilgrims Through Space and Time* by J. O. Bailey (1947) and *Voyages to the Moon* by Marjorie Hope Nicolson (1948) had paved the way. But there had been no previous attempt to produce an all-encompassing narrative history of science fiction. And whereas Bailey and Nicolson and their like had been happy to consider Godwin's *Man in the Moone* (1638) or Robert Paltock's *The Life and Adventures of Peter Wilkins* (1751) as science fiction, for Aldiss they were "*not* science fiction or, at the closest, are ur-science fiction" (*BYS*, 89). This was because Aldiss was introducing another innovation in this book, a starting point for science fiction, and with it a strict definition that ruled out any earlier works' being included under the term.

Numerous definitions of science fiction had appeared before this time, from Hugo Gernsback's ("a charming romance intermingled with scientific fact and prophetic vision") to Lester del Rey's ("an attempt to deal rationally with alternate possibilities in a manner which will be entertaining").[9] Most of these, however, had been, or had attempted to be, descriptive. Aldiss's definition, which came right at the start of *Billion Year Spree*, differed in that it was both prescriptive and periodizing:

> Science fiction is the search for a definition of man and his status in the universe which will stand in our advanced but confused state of knowledge (science), and is characteristically cast in the Gothic or post-Gothic mould. (*BYS*, 8)

The first thing to be noted about this definition is that Aldiss didn't actually stick to it. For instance, he insisted that Jonathan Swift's *Gulliver's Travels* (1726) "does not count as science fiction" on the grounds that it was "satirical and/or moral in intention rather than speculative" (*BYS*, 81). The terms "satirical," "moral" or "speculative" have no place in his definition of sf, and indeed the search for "a definition of man and his status" implies a moral or a satirical component of the work in question. After all, much of Aldiss's work had either a satirical aspect (*The Primal Urge, Barefoot in the Head*) or a moral one (*Greybeard*).

But I don't think that Aldiss intended this definition to be taken too seriously: it looked highbrow but didn't actually say very much. What was important in the definition was restricted to the last few words, the reference to "the Gothic or post-Gothic mould," because this phrase effectively excluded the "ur-science fictions" of earlier centuries and confirmed his most important innovation, the identification of Mary Shelley's *Frankenstein* (1818) as the origin of science fiction.

If *The Twinkling of an Eye* is anything to go by, Aldiss arrived at this identification in a rather cavalier manner. While writing *Billion Year Spree* he got irritated by the number of people who variously claimed Verne, Wells, Gernsback, or Campbell as the father of sf, what he calls "this obsessive Freudian quest for a father figure," and in response, "a naughty and fruitful thought came to" him. (*ToE*, 323). His identification of *Frankenstein* as the founding text of science fiction, therefore, arises as much from his discomfort with the various claims that someone was the father of sf as it does from a serious critical engagement with the birth pangs of a genre. If he was to consider himself a science fiction writer, (and once again he is expressing doubts about that status, because he hadn't written an sf novel since "the ill-natured reception of *Probability A* and *Barefoot*" [*ToE*, 323]), then he had to find an ancestor more to his taste than "the jejune outpourings of Gernsback's magazines" (*ToE*, 323).

As I noted earlier, *The Twinkling of an Eye* isn't always the most reliable source of information. The notion that this elevation of *Frankenstein* was the result of no more than a naughty thought might suit Aldiss's impish self-image, but it doesn't really stand up to examination. He devotes a full chapter to *Frankenstein*, more attention than he pays to any other individual work in the entire book, very carefully connecting the novel to the rise of science; he links it to Lyell's *Principles of Geology* (1830–1833), the discovery of fossils, early experiments in electricity and galvanism, and the work of Erasmus Darwin. He makes a telling point when he says: "Symbolically, Frankenstein turns away from alchemy and the past towards science and the future" (*BYS*, 27). In other words, Aldiss very precisely and systematically makes the case that Mary Shelley escapes from the ghost story she had originally set out to write, instead creating an important work in the history of science fiction.

But the identification of *Frankenstein* as the ur-text, the true source from which all science fiction flowed, rests solely on his carefully configured definition.

The insistence on the Gothic mode as a necessary condition eliminates any other potential contender for the title of *fons et origo* of the genre. Aldiss's definition was quickly superseded by others equally unsatisfactory, but somehow the idea that *Frankenstein* was the first sf novel persisted. In fact, you will still find the point being made today although a wealth of histories of science fiction have followed in Aldiss's wake, each identifying a different starting point.

The claim for *Frankenstein* was probably one of the two most lasting effects of the book, the other being his identification of John Wyndham as the "master of the cosy catastrophe" (*BYS*, 335). This has more than a whiff of a leading figure in one generation disdaining the work of the previous generation, and is, of course, on a par with Aldiss's constant insistence that British science fiction had been dull before he and Ballard and the New Wave came along. Yet there seems to have been something visceral, something very personal in the attack. I am not alone in saying that some of Wyndham's catastrophes were very far from cozy, nor am I alone in having then received a postcard from Aldiss demanding: "Why do you hate me so?" Why a defense of Wyndham should be interpreted as hatred of Aldiss opens up questions about Aldiss's sense of self-worth within the arena of British science fiction that are now probably impossible to answer.

Actually, there is a third lasting effect of *Billion Year Spree*: It opened the way for other histories of the genre that continue to appear at regular intervals. All owe a debt to Aldiss. As Mark Adlard said in his review: "It would be difficult to exaggerate the importance of this stupendous book. It is vital, and will continue vital as far ahead as one can see, for any understanding of science fiction."[10] The book won a special award from the British Science Fiction Association, and when, more than a decade later, Aldiss brought in David Wingrove to help him expand and update the book, the resultant *Trillion Year Spree* (1986) added a Hugo Award to his tally. And now Aldiss would be acclaimed as a scholar of science fiction as much as he would be a writer, becoming, for instance, a permanent guest of honor at the International Conference on the Fantastic in the Arts.

★   ★   ★

With *Billion Year Spree* Brian Aldiss had achieved something remarkable: he had remade science fiction in his image. Now, and until subsequent scholarship would start to revise his arguments, *Billion Year Spree* was the touchstone against which our understanding of science fiction was measured. There was a known starting point (with inconvenient earlier works safely segregated as proto-sf), and there was a coherent account of the major milestones along the route from then to now. Above all, Aldiss had unified science fiction, not only incorporating the New Wave into the same body as hard sf, but more broadly, as Adlard put it, "re-connect[ing] that umbilical cord which should connect what we call science fiction to the nurturing body of general culture."[11] As a result, Aldiss had given himself an ancestor worthy of him, emphasizing the importance of the literary path he had pursued while subtly downplaying the work of those with whom he did not wish to be compared, the "brightly coloured pipe dreams" (*BYS*, 189) of Edgar Rice Burroughs and the "cosy catastrophes" of John Wyndham.

What's more, he had given himself ideas for new science fiction novels, novels that would forever associate his name with two of the brightest names in the sf pantheon, the authors on whom he had lavished the most attention and most praise in *Billion Year Spree*: Shelley and Wells. Aldiss had written "The Saliva Tree" as an homage to Wells, one among numerous echoes of Wells in his work, but it was very distinct from anything that Wells himself had written. Now, however, Aldiss took *Frankenstein* and *The Island of Doctor Moreau* (1896) and, later, Bram Stoker's *Dracula* (1897) and inserted his own characters and plot. The original work was thus twisted, distorted, re-presented, so that the original story existed only on the sidelines while, center stage, the main ingredients of the original would be reused to tell an entirely new story, one that was generally not compatible with what Shelley, Wells, or Stoker had first written.

Such "parasitic novels," as Andrew M. Butler calls them, were not new, of course.[12] Tom Stoppard had revisited Shakespeare's *Hamlet* in his absurdist play *Rosencrantz and Guildenstern are Dead* (1966), and after Aldiss, *Frankenstein* in particular would be reimagined innumerable times, from *The Memoirs of Elizabeth Frankenstein* (1995) by Theodore Roszak to *The Casebook of Victor Frankenstein* (2008) by Peter Ackroyd. But Aldiss's first venture in this vein, *Frankenstein Unbound*, was something new both for him and for British science fiction.

The novel appeared at almost the same time as *Billion Year Spree*, emphasizing the link between them and suggesting that Aldiss was writing the novel about Frankenstein as he was writing the chapter about *Frankenstein*. This interconnection is made explicit when the protagonist, Joseph Bodenland (since *Boden* means "land" in German, this is a curious sort of tautonym), meets Mary Shelley and tells her, "*Frankenstein* was regarded by the twenty-first century as the first novel of the Scientific Revolution and, incidentally, as the first novel of science-fiction" (*FU*, 47). Since that idea had been proposed for the first time only weeks earlier as he was writing *Billion Year Spree*, this was a rather bold statement. But it allows the novel to reinforce the message of the history, and Aldiss had never lacked for boldness when it came to assessing his own pronouncements.

As in *Greybeard*, the action of the novel is set in play by the unintended consequences of a weapon of war, in this case "impact-raids" (*FU*, 7), the use of nuclear weapons above the atmosphere that has resulted in a breakdown in the structure of space and time. War is, once again, equated with madness. Bodenland concludes that "we never had as secure a grasp on reality as we imagine" (13), but here the breakdown, the failure to grasp reality, is not only mental but also physical as people suddenly and without warning find themselves in a different time.

Thus, fewer than twenty pages into the novel (it is quite a short book), Bodenland is abruptly transported from Texas in August 2020 to the outskirts of Geneva at the beginning of the nineteenth century. The first person he encounters there proves to be Victor Frankenstein. Bodenland, who is clearly very familiar with the story because he recognizes the name of Justine Moritz, a serving girl accused of murder, "felt [him]self in the presence of myth and, by association, *accepted [him]self as mythical!*" (*FU*, 28). Bodenland is following Frankenstein through a typically Gothic storm when he first sees the Creature: "In most respects it was human in shape, but gigantic in stature, and there seemed nothing of the human being in the way it suddenly paced forward from the trees" (*FU*, 30). The size of Frankenstein's Creature, the very origin of science fiction in Aldiss's eyes, thus serves to reduce in stature the merely human, which is in itself a trope in Aldiss's science fiction. The awkwardness of this situation is revealed when Joseph, planning to confront Frankenstein, asks himself: "Supposing that this encounter revealed *my* unreality rather than his?" (*FU*, 41).

We have, therefore, one of Aldiss's fictional creations encountering one of Shelley's fictional creations and pondering whether either is real or whether both are in some way mythical. The questions about reality that are thus raised are further confused by a curious interlude just after Bodenland's first encounter with Victor Frankenstein. A very convenient timeslip abruptly shifts Bodenland from May 1816 to August, and he sets out to find Byron and Shelley at the Villa Diodati. This, surely, is Aldiss being a fanboy, particularly when Shelley enters the room and Bodenland finds himself "flushing . . . with the agonizing exhilaration of confronting the author of *Frankenstein, or The Modern Prometheus*" (*FU*, 57). When she does talk to him about the origins of the story, they turn out to be little more than a list of influences: ideas from Shelley and Byron, Polidori's ghost story competition, Erasmus Darwin's *Zoonomia* (1794), Coleridge's "Rime of the Ancient Mariner" (1798), Horace Walpole's *Castle of Otranto* (1764), the work of Mrs. Radcliffe, and Godwin's *Caleb Williams* (1794); it reads like an off-cut from *Billion Year Spree*. And Joseph similarly seems to be quoting from the history when he responds by talking impersonally about the future reception of the novel: its fame rests on "its power of allegory . . . in which Frankenstein, standing for science in general, wishes to remould the world for the better, and instead leaves it a worse place than he finds it" (77). Bodenland plans to use Mary's fiction as a guide to the real world he is in: "If I could borrow a copy of Mary's book I could map [the route of Frankenstein's Creature], ambush, and kill it!" (67). How, if the Creature remains alive in the novel, that novel might provide a guide to killing it is a question that neither Bodenland nor Aldiss considers. Moreover, this is August 1816; Mary has told her ghost story, but it is a long way from being the novel that would be published in 1818. There can, therefore, be no book that might act as such a guide, though we might ponder how much of that eventual novel is Shelley's and how much is down to what she has been told by Aldiss's alter ego, Bodenland. He does tell her that there is a Victor Frankenstein living in Geneva at that moment, but does so only as he is leaving her, and no meeting between author and creation is engineered. The story of the writing of *Frankenstein* and the reimagined story of the book are presented as two distinct and mainly unconnected tales.

As Griffin and Wingrove note, the characters of Shelley and Byron "do strike one as literary caricatures of their originals,"[13] but the more problematic figure here is surely Mary Shelley. Aldiss combines the eager fanboy with the priapic masculinity that had been central to his two previous novels. The first thing that Bodenland does is have sex with Mary, as if her real worth is seen as sexual rather than literary. At this moment a character who is formally identified as Joseph or as Bodenland throughout the rest of the novel suddenly becomes the more familiar Joe. For this one scene, if nowhere else, Joe is, as Patrick McLeod puts it, "a vicarious wish-fulfilment for Aldiss"[14] who can, through his creation, prove himself to be Mary's perfect lover, more ideal even than Percy Shelley. (That Percy Shelley is unworthy of her is shown by the belief that Aldiss ascribes to him, that "it's Man that has to put Nature right, you know, and not vice versa" [*FU*, 62], which is the exact opposite of the position taken by Aldiss in his other novels.) In Nicholas Ruddick's account, from the union of Mary Shelley and the Brian Aldiss substitute, Joe Bodenland, "springs science fiction, a form of literature that shares the thoughtful and radical qualities of its parents and that alone can properly confront the cultural predicament of the twentieth century."[15] If Mary Shelley is the mother of science fiction, then Brian Aldiss has made himself the father.

There is, of course, the thickness of a piece of paper between Mary and Aldiss/Bodenland, one a real person rendered fictional, one a fictional character standing in for a real person, and they do recognize this disconnect: "We do not exist in the same world!" Mary tells Bodenland, while for Joseph, "we were mere phantoms in the world, or so we saw it, and scarcely less than phantoms to each other" (*FU*, 74). But though this brief exchange directly addresses the difference between the real and the fictional that seems to underlie the novel, the question is not answered and is instantly forgotten. Bodenland's belated wondering if "there might be a 2020 in which I existed merely as a character in a novel about Frankenstein and Mary" (*FU*, 140) abandons the question in favor of simple recursiveness.

Immediately after this dalliance, another convenient timeslip shifts Bodenland back to the point where he had encountered Frankenstein and his Creature, and Mary Shelley will not further intrude upon the story that she wrote. Instead Bodenland, a twenty-first-century American, and Frankenstein, a nineteenth-century European, will simply accept that the world they jointly inhabit is the sole and unquestioned reality, and the reader is assumed to accept the same thing.

Aldiss manages to hand-wave a skimpy explanation for the timeslips that readily sweep Bodenland to whenever the author wants him to be without having any effect on anyone else: "The grave time-ruptures of my own age . . . were sending their ripples backwards" (FU, 81). But Aldiss is remarkably careless with everything to do with time in this novel; the timeslips serve the purpose of letting Aldiss meet Mary Shelley and write his own version of Frankenstein, but they are never central to the story. For instance, when Bodenland is in prison in Geneva, he writes a letter to Mary asking for her help, though this is a full month before they meet, so Mary could have no knowledge of the author and no such letter is mentioned by Mary when they do meet.

Bodenland gets out of jail thanks to another convenient timeslip, one that shifts him to midwinter, when a flood facilitates his escape. Freezing in the wilderness, he is helped by the Creature, then meets up with Franken-stein and is taken to his secret laboratory. In the laboratory, having drugged Frankenstein, he finds the Creature's bride and realizes that it is the head, at least, of Justine Moritz. After the Creature and his bride have fled the tower, Frankenstein starts rambling—"a phantasmagoria of flesh and flesh remade, of vegetation intervening—humans are just turnips" (FU, 138)—in a way that oddly recalls Hothouse. And then Bodenland quotes the line "an eternal return such as Ouspenski postulates" (FU, 139), which, of course, echoes Barefoot in the Head. The novel ends with a long chase across a frozen world, time and place unknown, leading to a tower that may be a city and that may mark the end of time. Here Bodenland kills the Creature and his bride, but not before the Creature tells him, "In trying to destroy what you cannot understand, you destroy yourself!" (FU, 155). Bodenland is left nowhere and with no purpose, diminished as are all of Aldiss's characters by his violent response to whatever is new or different.

Personally, I feel that Frankenstein Unbound is a slight, superficial work, but it was widely hailed at the time of its publication. In his long review of the novel, for instance, Ian Watson acclaimed Aldiss as "the resurrector of Mary Shelley's novel" who had performed "one of the most dynamic acts of transtemporal editing ever undertaken" in producing a novel that was "bet-ter conceived and better written" than the original.[16] In other words, Aldiss has, transtemporally, proved himself to be the only begetter of the work that he claimed to be the only begetter of science fiction. For Mark Adlard, "The appearance of [*Billion Year Spree* and *Frankenstein Unbound*] together . . . [has] . . . delivered two perfectly aimed kicks, muscular and elegant, to indicate the direction in which science fiction is going to proceed."[17] It was the sort of near-ecstatic response that Aldiss had been waiting for. It wouldn't last; in *Foundation* 130, two issues after the death of Aldiss had been announced, there was a special section of four essays dealing with Mary Shelley's *Frankenstein* and its literary descendants. Not one of these essays so much as mentioned Aldiss or *Frankenstein Unbound*. But for the moment, Brian Aldiss was back where he wanted to be.

★　★　★

One of the things that makes me dubious about the claim that Aldiss had abandoned science fiction before *Billion Year Spree* put him back on track is the fact that, as he was writing that and *Frankenstein Unbound*, he was also working on *Moreau's Other Island*, finishing it in 1974. Writing two science fiction novels and a history of the genre at roughly the same time suggests someone rather more engaged with sf than the stories would have us believe. *Moreau's Other Island* would not appear for another six years, however,.

It is not exactly clear what the problem was, but Michael Collings tells us that Aldiss "was not fully satisfied and withheld [*Moreau's Other Island*] for some years, until outside pressures caused him to publish it."[18] It may be that Aldiss thought his use of thalidomide in the book was too raw a wound at the time, or perhaps he simply felt that two novels in a row that revisited major works by other well-known authors was too much. As for what the outside pressures were that caused him to publish it in 1980 (when thalidomide was no less raw a wound), we may never know. Whatever the reasons the manuscript languished for six years among Aldiss's papers at the Bodleian Library, Oxford, though, I can't help feeling that *Moreau's Other Island* is a stronger and more coherent work than *Frankenstein Unbound*, if only because we do not meet H. G. Wells but are instead presented with an updated sequel to *The Island of Doctor Moreau*.

In *Billion Year Spree*, Aldiss describes *The Island of Doctor Moreau* as "Wells' best book" (an arguable claim, though it illustrates Aldiss's affection for the novel) and compares it to "Prospero's island . . . peopled by Calibans" (*BYS*,

137). It is this, the island of Calibans, that is the focus of Aldiss's updating, but it is not just Beast-People who take on the role of the "freckled whelp hagborn—not honour'd with / A human shape"[19]—every character in Aldiss's novel is physically or morally deformed. Collings seems somewhat surprised that "in the world Aldiss portrays, there is no one to trust. Everyone is flawed, deformed physically or psychically; all are more Beast than Human,"[20] yet that is perfectly in keeping with the soured view of humanity we have witnessed in *The Dark Light Years*, *Earthworks*, and elsewhere. Indeed, in its portrayal of the psychic and moral ruin that accompanies humanity's embrace of war and diminishment of others, it stands almost as the archetypal Brian Aldiss novel.

War is, of course, inescapable. The novel begins with "a global war which threatens to lay waste much of the land area," and even in the remotest part of the Pacific Ocean there are "symptoms of pain" (*MOI*, 2). Although the whole novel takes place on an island seemingly untouched by war, the conflict infects and makes monstrous everything human that we encounter. Roberts, the narrator, is the only survivor of the crash of a space shuttle, echoing Wells's original novel, in which Prendick, the narrator, is the only survivor of a wreck. But whereas Prendick is an honest, scientifically literate reporter with whom we side morally and emotionally in all that follows, Roberts is no innocent, and his moral stature is steadily diminished throughout the novel.

Like Prendick, Roberts is unwelcome on the island that he eventually reaches. Prendick is rescued by the alcoholic doctor Montgomery and the Beast-Person M'Ling; here Roberts is rescued by the alcoholic Hans Maastricht and the Beast-Person George. But Aldiss uses the initial encounter to emphasize that there is little difference between human and beast. George has "a snout-like nose, wrinkled in a sneer like a hyena's, and two almost lidless eyes" (*MOI*, 9), whereas Maastricht is "also a great hulking brute. His face [is] fat and pasty; it [bears] a besotted, sullen expression" such that Roberts is "as disconcerted as by George's savage stare" (*MOI*, 10). In Wells the animals are made into a sort of debased humanity, striving and failing to find something better than themselves; in Aldiss, the humans themselves are debased.

As is often the case in Aldiss, this debasement is indicated by size. Maastricht is large and brutish, but the Moreau figure, the Master, Dart, is even more monstrous, "at least three metres high, impossibly tall for a human"

(*MOI*, 20). This greatness is nothing but show, the result of a robotic exo-skeleton; the real Dart, when eventually we see him, is "cut down to size. . . . He ha[s] no legs" (*MOI*, 28) and uses a mechanized wheelchair. Dart, it turns out, is a bitter, angry man who was a thalidomide child, born with no limbs. When first introduced in the late 1950s, thalidomide had been sold as a cure for morning sickness that was perfectly safe during pregnancy, but it soon became clear that it caused severe birth defects, and it was withdrawn from sale in 1961. By the early 1970s, when Aldiss was writing this novel, the surviving thalidomide children were reaching their teenage years, prompt-ing a renewed awareness of and sympathy for the victims. Aldiss's use of the deformities of thalidomide as a physical representation of Dart's moral deformities is, therefore, to say the least, far from typical of the period. Dart was rendered monstrous by the interventions of science before he was born, and it has made him monstrous in himself.

But, as Dart points out, "There's a war going on all round the world, which you're part of and I'm not. Who's fighting that war, ask yourself! Not freaks like me, Mr Roberts, no, but normals like you! War's your idea! Wiping out's your idea" (*MOI*, 79). Dart is a monster, like Moreau inflicting unspeakable cruelties on the animal people of the island, but for Aldiss war will always remain the greater evil. It is not, however, as distant from the island as Dart, in his godlike detachment, or Roberts in his apparent innocence might like to believe. Roberts discovers that everything on Moreau Island is financed by the U.S. government, prompting him to ask, "Do you think the war is sufficient excuse for the cruelty and misery inflicted on the creatures here? Aren't we supposed to be fighting against just such hellish injury to life and spirit here?" (*MOI*, 102). In fact, Roberts is an under-secretary of state, his own department is funding Dart's work, and the paperwork would have crossed his desk: "In that file lived Moreau's other island, a doppelganger of the real island, a tidy little utopia docketed into paragraphs and subheads" (*MOI*, 138). Roberts is himself complicit in the horrors he finds on the island, though for him, as a bureaucrat, they were just neatly labeled files rather than the brutal and messy reality he encounters. Aldiss, as a soldier, had the typical soldier's contempt for those who stay safely at home directing a sanitized version of the war without ever experiencing the bloody violence on the ground. From that perspective, Roberts is every bit as guilty as Dart.

And for all Dart's protestations, the work he is doing is directly implicated in the war. In the labs Roberts finds a creature he had not encountered before: "It stood under one and a half metres high and was disproportionately thick of body[;] . . . the overall effect of the creature was of a malignant gnome" (*MOI*, 139). It speaks perfect English. Victor Frankenstein had failed to educate the tabula rasa that was his Creature; Dart, like Moreau before him, had gone further than Frankenstein by teaching his creations to speak. This creature is, therefore, a reverse of Frankenstein's: small and fluent rather than large and uneducated. But the link between the two (and between the two Aldiss novels) is specific. Dart's work is "the culmination of the Frankenstein process . . . [in which] . . . the natural order would be entirely supplanted by the unnatural" (*MOI*,147). The creatures, SRSRs, members of the Stand-by Replacement Sub Race, have been designed to replace a humanity wiped out by the inevitable nuclear war. And in this small creature we see, yet again, the diminishment of humanity already encountered in *Non-Stop* and *Hothouse*.

The thematic concentration on war in this novel, what Dart calls "the perfect human excuse to exercise power, personal power as well as national" (*MOI*, 65), stands in place of the issue of colonialism that underlies Wells's original, which is suffused with fear of the other and disgust at what the white races have done to them: "The island is . . . an imperial space outside society where the colonizer can do anything they wish without fear of retribution from society."[21] Questions of colonialism and race do play a small part in Aldiss's novel, as, for instance, when Maastricht dies and Dart says: "I've known Hans for years. He had coloured blood in him. I always said booze would kill him" (*MOI*, 78). Yes, Maastricht was drunk, but Roberts confirms that the concrete of the dockside collapsed, causing the crane that Maastricht was driving to tumble into the harbor. Neither his race nor the drink had anything to do with Maastricht's death. But in a novel concerned with the more general diminishment of all humanity, Dart's remark shows that a man who likes to be known as the Master and whose use of prosthetics makes him appear to be taller and greater than anyone else does literally look down on other humans as much as he does on his creatures.

Moreau's Other Island mirrors the plot of *The Island of Doctor Moreau* quite closely, so it inevitably builds to a climax in which the Beast-People rise up against their human creators. In Wells's novel, without the constant torturous intervention of their maker, the Beast-People revert to their animal nature, giving the novel a tragic fall. In Aldiss's, however, there is a more triumphant sense that Dart's interventions are longer-lasting. As Roberts concludes, "They had moved closer to man. I had moved closer to them" (*MOI*, 158). The revolt has actually made them more human, while at the same time increasing the humanity of Roberts.

Although it was more coherent and had a more powerful impact than *Frankenstein Unbound*, *Moreau's Other Island* was rather less well received. Several critics talked of it in terms of what Emma Tennant called "a good yarn in the old style,"[22] while Steev Higgins, for one, linking this novel to the "cardboard sets" of its predecessor, *Enemies of the System*, worried that "Aldiss may be growing more concerned with the message over the medium."[23] For once, less-than-ecstatic reviews did not seem to put Aldiss off.

★ ★ ★

The third and final part of this loose trilogy of recursive science fiction, *Dracula Unbound*, was clearly intended as a direct sequel to *Frankenstein Unbound*.

In the late 1980s, Roger Corman made a film version of *Frankenstein Unbound* starring John Hurt, Raul Julia, and Bridget Fonda playing Mary Shelley. Released in 1990, it was the first film to be made from Aldiss's work, and it was not a success. During filming, Aldiss had suggested a sequel to Corman, *Dracula Unbound*. When *Frankenstein Unbound* failed, Corman decided not to go ahead with the sequel, claiming that it would be too expensive to film. *Dracula Unbound* appeared instead as a novel in 1991, and it was full of the sort of rapid shifts, spectacle, and sketchy characters that suggest something intended to be a movie.

Bram Stoker's *Dracula*, hardly mentioned in *Billion Year Spree*, is given much more attention in *Trillion Year Spree*, where it is compared to *Frankenstein* as a "diseased creation myth" (*TYS*, 53). It is notable that all three of the novels that Aldiss has chosen to revisit have this quality in common, as if the remaking of life is central to his notion about what should constitute science fiction. *Dracula* is, Aldiss decides, "the great Victorian novel about VD, for which vampirism stands in as Stoker's metaphor" (*TYS*, 179). This insistence that the novel is about sex and the fear of sex, a relatively new approach to Stoker's work at the time though not as totally unknown as Aldiss claims, obviously plays to Aldiss's own fascination with sex, so it is a little surprising that sex is almost entirely absent from *Dracula Unbound*.

Dracula Unbound is presented as a direct sequel to *Frankenstein Unbound*, with Joseph Bodenland again serving as our viewpoint character. Yet Aldiss is even more careless with chronology in this novel than he was in its predecessor. *Frankenstein Unbound* opens with a letter dated August 2020; *Dracula Unbound* opens in turn with a letter dated August 1999, yet at one point the archaeologist, Clift, refers to Bodenland's "association with Victor Frankenstein and Mary Shelley and all that" (*DU*, 48), though that association came twenty-one years *after* the events of this novel. Here, Bodenland and his wife Mina are in a mature relationship that is undergoing some stress, and as the novel opens Bodenland is about to miss his son's wedding day. This would suggest that by the time *Frankenstein Unbound* opens, Bodenland would be in his sixties, which is obviously not the case, and everything indicates that Bodenland and Mina are in a fresh and relatively new relationship at that point, and their children are small.

In this universe, Bodenland Corporation (which did not exist in *Frankenstein Unbound*, and which is elsewhere called Bodenland Enterprises, a carelessness with the name that suggests that Aldiss wasn't really paying full attention to this novel) has invented inertial disposal, in which things such as nuclear waste are frozen in time, becoming "suddenly stationary with regard to universal time-decay" (*DU*, 18). This opens up the prospect of movement through time, despite Bodenland's insistence that "the inertial disposal process is far from being a time machine. It is almost the reverse" (*DU*, 18). It is perhaps redundant to note that such a system might have counteracted or prevented the timeslips that would, twenty years later, set the events of *Frankenstein Unbound* in motion.

The sense of time being out of joint is further emphasized by the archaeological discovery in the American West of a human skeleton in Cretaceous rock dating to "over sixty million years before mankind in its most primitive form walked the earth" (*DU*, 22). Associated with this discovery is a phenomenon that is christened the "Ghost Train" (an apposite name, given that it turns out to be "the train of the Undead" [*DU*, 70]), an object that resembles a train moving at high speed across the landscape but not connecting with it or interacting with it in any way. Only by using Bodenland's inertial device, effectively taking themselves outside time, are Joe and Clift able to board the ghost train. The ghost train has been created at the behest of a powerful demon figure known as Dracula, who intends to use it to conquer the world.

That this Dracula is monstrous is clear enough, but we are never exactly sure what he is. At one point Dracula proclaims to the vampire Bella, "For all our strengths, we remain forever slaves to the human imagination" (*DU*, 125). Yet we have also been told that these creatures come from a time before humanity and therefore, presumably, the human imagination, appeared on Earth. And they inhabit a place outside time, which makes them inevitably more powerful than the humans they seem to fear. The only thing we can be sure of is that this Dracula does not equate to Bram Stoker's creation. But when Bodenland arrives in Victorian England the first thing he does is seek out Stoker, immediately telling him things about his novel (which hasn't been written yet). When we recall how wary Bodenland was of what he could say to Byron, Shelley, and Mary Shelley, it is evident that, broad as *Frankenstein Unbound* was, it was considerably subtler than this novel.

There are subtleties, even beauties, in the writing that one might expect of Aldiss, for instance, the way Mina, skydiving in 1999 and experiencing a sense of freedom—"the zing of high altitude could wash away even memories. . . . The hollowness she felt encroaching on her life could not reach her here" (*DU*, 69)—is juxtaposed with Bodenland after Clift has been killed in the ghost train. He feels "utterly detached from his own body. The conscious part of him float[s], as a goldfish might watch from the bowl the activities in the room to which it was confined" (*DU*, 69). And yet the story feels delineated by very broad strokes, as if the patient build-up of detail from the Helliconia books of a few years earlier for instance, has here been swept away by an impatient rush to get everything done with as quickly, as luridly, and as violently as possible.

Thus, although Aldiss claimed that he "tried not to take too many liberties with Bram Stoker" (*DU*, 201), that is exactly what he seems to have done; certainly, the faithfulness to Mary Shelley in the earlier book is absent here. Stoker is even more of a caricature than are Byron and Shelley in the earlier novel, and Aldiss has changed everything from Stoker's home (relocating him from Chelsea to Aldiss's home outside Oxford) to his literary legacy (implying that *Dracula* was his only or first novel, when in fact he had already published four novels and a collection of stories, plus some nonfiction, including a book about the United States which makes his seeming ignorance of Bodenland's homeland seem most unlikely). And when Stoker is in effect pressganged into joining Bodenland's adventure he really has very little to do, as if Aldiss wanted to bring him face to face with his most famous creation but then had no idea what further part Stoker should play in the story.

Not that Aldiss seems to have cared all that much about the story. It is filled with cliché: Vampires cannot face the cross and are unable to endure direct sunlight, and Aldiss does nothing fresh with them. Already, for instance, in Polanski's 1967 film *Dance of the Vampires*, a Jewish vampire had been unaffected by the Christian cross, but Aldiss doesn't seem to have thought about such a joke or its more serious implications. He adds in to the mix the sort of time travel paradoxes that we have encountered far too many times in too many stories. And he makes Dracula so powerful—he "had the ability, in common with a disease of the brain, to erase engrams and deface memory" (*DU*, 164)—that he can ensure victory only by playing fast and loose with the logic of his own story. Bodenland takes over a time machine, the ghost train, and by smartly moving back and forth in time he is able in the last few pages to right every wrong and finish off the baddies.

It is a careless, over-hasty, car crash of a novel called by more generous reviewers "a cheerful shambling rush of a book,"[24] while a more acerbic assessment by John Clute has him "diddl[ing] a yarn of the old genre, a finger aside his nose."[25] Aldiss would not perpetrate another of these quasi-historical mash-ups.

★   ★   ★

In 1973, the year of *Billion Year Spree* and of *Frankenstein Unbound*, Aldiss's career changed in other, perhaps more subtle ways. It was the year in which the first of his Enigmas appeared in *New Writings in SF*, and it was also the year in which Damon Knight's *Orbit 12* featured four linked stories by Aldiss: "Serpent Burning on an Altar," "Woman in Sunlight with Mandoline," "The Young Soldier's Horoscope," and "Castle Scene with Penitents." At the time there was no suggestion that these stories were intended to form part of a novel, but in 1976, expanded, extensively revised, and retitled ("Serpent

Burning on an Alter" became "A Feast Unearned," "Woman in Sunlight with Mandoline" became "Woman with Mandoline in Sunlight," "The Young Soldier's Horoscope" became "A Young Soldier's Horoscope," and "Castle Scene with Penitents" became "Castle Interior with Penitents"), they were incorporated in *The Malacia Tapestry*.

This is the only thoroughgoing fantasy novel that Brian Aldiss wrote, and is generally recognized as one of his finest literary works. But this "deliberate fantasia of anachronism, an ahistorical pot-pourri,"[26] as David Pringle describes it, is also his most intense engagement with history. This is a world in which time has come to a stop. Things are forever on the verge of happening but never actually happen. Changes are rumored, but as the novel ends, everything has reset to precisely the way it was as the novel opened. It is a world in which stasis is institutionalized, recalling in that respect the static worlds of *Hothouse* and *Report on Probability A*. History has developed to this point but can go no further. It is, I suspect, a view of history that Aldiss had to formalize in *The Malacia Tapestry* before he could go on to explore the repetitions of Helliconia.

Malacia is a conflation of times, a place of triremes and tricorn hats, with names drawn from across Europe such as de Lambant and Kemperer, so that it calls to mind the atemporal placelessness of M. John Harrison's Viriconium, introduced in *The Pastel City* (1971). And like Viriconium, it is a place of imposed stasis: "The immemorial duty of the Supreme Council was to protect Malacia from change" (*MT*, 17). Like the stopped clock of *Report on Probability A*, this is a place of frozen time and consequently a place where nothing can happen. And later we learn of the "Original Curse" as a result of which "time had congealed about [the] city. (*MT*, 230).

It is forever threatened by the armies of the Turks, but an actual attack never comes. It is on the cusp of a technological revolution: an immigrant from the north has developed a form of photography that he is trying to fashion into something resembling cinema, but such technology is not allowed to be developed. That same immigrant is introducing socialist ideas, but here the social classes are rigidly separated, and though our bohemian protagonist, Perian de Chirolo, may dream of crossing such barriers, he is, in the end, never able to do so.

But Malacia is out of time in other ways, too, for it is not part of actual human history. This is a world in which one family of dinosaurs attained intelligence and eventually developed a civilization (a distorted echo, perhaps, of "The Under-Privileged"); as Perian de Chirolo's father, in a rambling and disconnected monologue, tells us, it was "*homo saurus*, meaning us . . . our kind began cold-blooded" (*MT*, 146). The characters look, sound, and behave exactly like humans. I suspect that for long passages both author and readers forget that they are not human, as when de Chirolo encounters "slaves—mostly black women" (*MT*, 211) at an aristocratic party. Then something happens to remind us of their saurian ancestry, as when these same aristocrats set out after "tyrant-greave or devil-jaw" (*Tyrannosaurus rex*?) on what is known as an "ancestral hunt" (*MT*, 221), in other words, hunting their own ancestors.

And yet the saurian nature of the inhabitants of Malacia matters not one jot. After all, the novel was inspired by and is illustrated with etchings by Gianbattista Tiepolo, pictures that are incorporated as set pieces within the text and provide the chapter titles. Aldiss had long admired the work of Tiepolo and his contemporary Giovanni Battista Piranesi. In *The Shape of Further Things* he had compared the light *Scherzi* of Tiepolo with the dark *Carceri* (Prisons) of Piranesi: "One is Ariel, one Caliban" (*SFT*, 102). But in his typically gloomy view of the state of the world, he concluded that "the future offers none of the lightness and magic of Tiepolo; we are heading instead for one of Piranesi's prisons!" (*SFT*, 172). It is, therefore, interesting, and perhaps deliberately perverse, that Aldiss chose Tiepolo as the source for Malacia while making this world as much a prison as an etching by Piranesi. And although Tiepolo's baroque renderings of Venetian life capture the style and mood of Malacia, they are very human. What matters is not the nature of the characters but how they behave, and in particular, how they negotiate their way through the complex, static society of their city-state.

Our viewpoint character, de Chirolo, is an out-of-work actor who is hired by Bengtsohn in connection with his invention of the "zahnoscope": "I have developed here a process whereby a judicious mixture of silver iodine will secure on a slide of glass an image of whatever is placed before the zahnoscope. A second process involving oils of lavender and heated mercury fixes the image permanently on the glass. This is painting without hands" (*MT*, 26). De Chirolo, together with his friend and fellow actor de Lambent, the aristocratic Armida Hoytola, and the seamstress Letitia, are to pose for a series of such photographs that together tell a melodramatic romantic tale. It is a familiar tale of sexual betrayal, because all dramas are old and familiar, with prescribed lines, actions, and costumes. Bengtsohn has nonetheless chosen to stage it in modern dress, and it is this novelty as much as the newness of the technology that is considered outlandish. Hoytola, Armida's father, tells de Chirolo that Bengtsohn's zahnoscope drama should look to history: "Set a few millennia ago, among people of proper standing, the story acquires dignity, one judges" (*MT*, 85). The past is ever present in Malacia, and nothing can be judged except in comparison to history.

In the process of filming, de Chirolo falls in love with Armida, whose social status puts her beyond his reach although he dreams of being accepted into the aristocracy. Like any number of Aldiss characters, de Chirolo is a philanderer, trying, for instance, to seduce the hard-working seamstress—"not that [he] really cared about her" (*MT*, 79)—in the hope of persuading her to make a fancy shirt for him for free. As the astrologer, Seemly Moleskin, tells him: "Though you may think yourself the most flexible of men, yet you are held frozen in an attitude which will undo you" (*MT*, 80). The characters are thus no more capable of change than are their times: Letitia will be forever poor but honest, Armida will remain a spoiled rich girl who seduces members of the lower orders for her pleasure, and de Chirolo will end as he began, a philandering actor of limited range (when he boasts about his acting prowess, Armida replies: "Have you yet attempted to impersonate a modest person?" [*MT*, 174]). One of the religious men who haunt the novel says of this: "In the continuing war between Good and Evil, every man is little more than cannon-fodder. All we can do is decide into which cannons we should allow ourselves to be thrust" (*MT*, 244–245), but it would seem the choice is already made.

When de Chirolo is persuaded to take an experimental balloon trip (for which he sits astride a horse that is tethered to the balloon), he looks out across the "city-state as a whole, working like an open watch. [He] saw every part depending on every other, ticking away the millennia in a perfectly arranged manner" (*MT*, 102). He sees this, as every citizen of Malacia would see it, as a sign of continuity, everything in its allotted place, everything working because it is all a piece in a fixed pattern. Bengtsohn, the stranger, would, on the other hand, see it as a sign that everyone has an equal part to play. Bengtsohn's socialism is what must doom him because it threatens to bring change to a place that is incapable of change, though the novel is replete with images that suggest its necessity. The city is in an impossible situation.

The novel constantly introduces us to fine craftspeople—Letitia and her family, creating fine linens and shirts, and Bledlore, who creates exquisite glasswork—yet these craftspeople live in poverty, the quality of their work "scarcely recognized except by a few cognoscenti" (*MT*, 114), among whom de Chirolo and his friends inevitably number themselves. Yet it is an age of great wealth, though the wealth is concentrated in the hands of a few noble families. As de Lambant says, "What a decadent age we live in" (*MT*, 114). De Chirolo and his friends move through this world complaining about the cost of things, trying to get things cheaply or for free, perennially broke and on a quest for drink and sex. They epitomize the dissipation of the age. The title of the novel comes from a passage in which de Chirolo, de Lambant, Armida, and Bedalar are talking about the decadence of their society, and Bedalar imagines that "one day like today, things might run down and never move again, so that we and everything would hang there like a tapestry in the air for ever more" (*MT*, 123). The image captures Malacia, which has as de Chirolo puts it, a "suspended quality" (*MT*, 123) about it. De Lambant prefers to consider it a comfortable age with "no major questions struggling for answer, no cold winds howling in from the dim religious north, and not too many headless corpses in the sewers" (*MT*, 124). This is where Aldiss's inescapable fascination with war comes in, for Armida counters that there are always wars, and they "could almost be said to constitute life" (*MT*, 124). The stasis of Malacia is both a curse and a benefit, valued because "lack of change implies peace" (*MT*, 290) but damaging because nothing can change; everything ends precisely as it began. There is no history in Malacia because history is all there is.

At one point *The Malacia Tapestry* was intended to be the first volume in a trilogy. Indeed, in 1979 *Foundation* 17 reported that a second volume, *The Igara Testament*, was well under way. But neither that promised novel nor the untitled third part of the trilogy ever appeared. In all probability such sequels would have proved impossible because within the state of Malacia all that would be possible would be repetition. But the sense of eternal return, explored on a relatively small scale in *The Malacia Tapestry*, would lay the groundwork for a much larger exploration of the theme in what was certainly the most grandiose project Brian Aldiss ever undertook.

CHAPTER 5

SCIENTIST

There is an extraordinary passage in *Bury My Heart at W. H. Smith's* in which Brian Aldiss lists his credentials as a member of the British literary establishment: "I have served on the Arts Council Literature Panel, have been chairman of the Society of Authors' Management Committee, have taken my turn as a Booker Prize judge" (*BHS*, 96); had the book appeared a little later he would certainly have added being elected a Fellow of the Royal Society of Literature in 1990 and being awarded the OBE in 2005. But, he insists, it would be a mistake to consider him a member of the establishment because he had "a liking for science as a path to understanding" (*BHS*, 96).

Why an interest in science should be regarded as in any way an obstacle to being an establishment figure is not immediately clear. There have, after all, been more than a few members of the literary establishment (however we might choose to define that nebulous term) who have had an interest in science, from H. G. Wells to Ian McEwan. But it is obvious that *science* was a totemic word for Aldiss. Without having studied science beyond school, he retained an interest in the topic and read quite widely. In *The Twinkling of an Eye*, for instance, he records how having recently learned about Heisenberg's Uncertainty Principle colored his viewing of *L'Année dernière à Marienbad* by Alain Resnais (1961), which in turn shaped the thinking that led him to *Report on Probability A*. This is presumably another reason why he considered the novel, even in its earliest incarnation, a work of science fiction.

Science is what made him who he was, it defines him as secular and rationalist, though religion plays a prominent and at times problematic role in his writing. In earlier works, religion is generally regarded dubiously. In *Non-Stop*, religious routine is a way in which Marapper avoids actually doing anything, while in *The Primal Urge*, Jimmy feels that a "good old pagan idea" (*PU*, 140) is preferable to Christian theory. And when, in *Greybeard*, Charley talks of the Lord's will, Jeff replies, "After all He's done to us this last fifty years . . . I'm surprised you're still on speaking terms with Him" (*GB*, 21). I think this doubt is probably close to what Aldiss himself felt at the time: that religion is an unnecessary restraint on humanity's natural instincts and behaviors. Yet though the tone of voice in these early novels constantly suggests that religion is wrong, that man should follow science rather than belief, there is still a sympathy with believers, as when Charley decides that "there had to be something higher than man if all creation was not a mockery" (*GB*, 134).

But in later works that perception was modified as the sympathy for believers began to outweigh the antagonism towards the belief system. Thus, among the numerous religious figures that populate *The Malacia Tapestry*, performing sacrifices and telling fortunes, some, such as the astrologer Phillibus Parterre, who contends that "our kind originated from goats and the precursors of goats" (*MT*, 158), are treated as charlatans and figures of fun in the way Jingadangelow is in *Greybeard*. But others, such as the astrologer Seemly Moleskin appear to see their static society more clearly than anyone else. In *Frankenstein Unbound*, Victor Frankenstein dreams of being able "to deliver into man's hands some of those powers which had hitherto been ascribed to a snivelling and fictitious God!" (*FU*, 42). Yet when Bodenland discovers the second creature, he says, "I saw that all my previous beliefs in progress were built on shifting sand. How often, in my past life, had I claimed that one of the great benefits the nineteenth century had conferred on the West had been science's liberation of thought and feeling from organized religion" (FU, 120). But now, in the creature, he sees that the triumph of science was a triumph of big business and government over the individual, incurring the loss of the human spirit, which religion celebrates

The change from a straightforwardly secular view of science and religion to a more nuanced perspective comes around the time of *Barefoot in the Head*. It was the 1960s, the period when the counterculture of drugs and rock music, the very society featured in the novel, was in search of some spiritual, though not necessarily religious, meaning, and Aldiss gave them a secular messiah in the shape of Colin Charteris. And we find in later novels such as *Helliconia Spring* other characters who play a similar but not so explicit messianic role.

Once, the scientific worldview, the natural environment within which the story took place, had been unquestioned. Whether it was robots attempting to think for themselves in "Who Can Replace a Man?," an astronaut returning from Mars and finding himself displaced in time by 3.3077 minutes in "Man in His Time" (1965), or galactic debris inspiring schisms, crusades, and sacrifices in "Heresies of the Huge God" (1966), it was never a question of whether these actions were possible. The scientific ideas around which the fictions turned might be realistic, unlikely, or absurd, but they were there to be accepted for the sake of the story. But now Aldiss began to call on science as a prop, a justification. He would summon authority figures as if to say this is all real, it is carefully worked out, it is trustworthy, not some wild science fiction invention.

These differing worldviews can be illustrated by two novels of the late 1970s. Aldiss's rather clumsy satire of communism, *Enemies of the System*, pits a religiously based society against an apparently secular one, while his odd fable *Brothers of the Head* uses science as a justification rather than science as a subject.

★ ★ ★

In the mid-1970s Aldiss was at a conference in Posnan, Poland, at which one of the academics from the Eastern bloc said: "Certainly no writer in the West would dare to write a story in which Communism had conquered the world" (EoS, iv). The short novel *Enemies of the System* was Aldiss's immediate response. We might question how well he met the terms of the challenge, however, for in *Enemies of the System*, communist mastery of the galaxy is at best a pyrrhic victory.

The novel opens with fifty-two of the "elite of the system" (*EoS*, 1) leaving, as an official reward for their loyalty, for a vacation on the wilderness planet Lysenka II. Aldiss emphasizes their drabness, their lack of individuality. Male or female, they wear clothes "so subdued in colour and material, as to resemble a uniform" (*EoS*, 1), while their conversation is stilted because character and humanity have been leached from them. As one of the tourists says, echoing official slogans in a way that robs the statement of any individuality, "Pleasure is stipulated as one of the factors of our vacation, and so compatibility is part of the guarantee. Don't you find compatibility a positive quality, a constructive quality?" (*EoS*, 3). The planet they visit is described not as being suitable for life but rather as "suitable for the establishment of law and enlightenment" (*EoS*, 5). These are not characters; they are mouthpieces for an absolutist system in which humanity has no part. Yet in their unthinking conformity to the Soviet idea they see themselves as "fully in command of their world" (*EoS*, 13), though this is equated with their being "standard products of the System, without minds of our own" (*EoS*, 15).

Their untamed holiday world is named for Trofim Lysenko, the Soviet biologist who opposed genetics and proposed the idea of environmentally acquired inheritance and who was responsible for geneticists' being branded "enemies of the people" under Stalin. The novel will, in its way, dramatize this notion. The form of communism that holds sway is known as "Biocom," now celebrating its one millionth anniversary, an absurd sweep of time in which, to illustrate Aldiss's perception of communism, humanity has advanced not one iota; as one of the tourists remarks, "In a million years, we have in fact achieved less than *sapiens* achieved in a century or so" (*EoS*, 87). Like *Hothouse* and *The Malacia Tapestry*, among others, this is a world of stasis, outside time because it is unchanging. For instance, although Lysenka II was discovered more than a million years earlier, it has been only ten years since a base was established there, and nothing has been done to render the planet habitable. Thus, when the tourist bus crashes, "everything wait[s]. Movement [hangs] suspended in the damp, leathery air" (*EoS*, 26).

Aldiss's view of communism is distinctly Orwellian, and as in *Nineteen Eighty-Four* (1949), central to the portrayal of the system is control of language and therefore of thought. The six tourists whose misadventures are at the core of the novel are constantly coming up against things they are not allowed to say, and therefore not allowed to think. Thus when communications go down they are initially told that the failure is due to "a strike at Satellite Control in Peace City" (*EoS*,10), which might imply that the regime is not working to the benefit of all. But when the characters are rescued at the end of the novel, they are firmly told: "There was no strike. . . . Merely a little technical problem, now disposed of" (*EoS*, 98), the use of the word "disposed" hinting, perhaps, at the brutality of the regime. And the creatures that attack the tourists after the bus crash are not native to the planet, which is still at a carboniferous stage in its evolution; instead, the creatures are devolved humans descended from those who crashed there more than a million years earlier. But when one relatively free-thinking member of the group, Vul Dulcifer, points this out, he is reprimanded by the tour leader, Constanza: "Utopianist Dulcifer, I hereby give you notice that you will be reported for deviationism" and for discussing "classified information before someone who is not a member of the elite" (*EoS*, 39). The person who should not hear this "classified information" is Constanza herself, who is thus policing what she allows herself to hear and, therefore, to think.

Already a key contrast is being laid out in the novel. On one hand the humans within the communist regime are static, unchanging: For a million years they have remained exactly the same. On the other hand, the humans who crashed onto a planet unsuited to sustaining human life have, over the course of a million years, devolved into something bestial. Devolution is, of course, something we have seen repeatedly in Aldiss's work, and the beastlike humans recall *Moreau's Other Island*, which had been written at this point but not published. Aldiss, in other words, plundered his own work to present two extremes, but what is most interesting about *Enemies of the System* comes in between these extremes.

The six central characters leave their fellow tourists by the wrecked bus and set off through hostile territory to try to find help. They are quickly captured by a group of humans who have not devolved. To the six, their captors are not *Homo uniformis* and so are less than human, but what we should notice is that they have retained their humanity, against the odds, by maintaining a sense of community and through religion. The six are held in a cage inside a massive cave system that is the heart of an elaborately structured community. They see individuals fulfilling particular social roles, those who guard the cave system, for instance, and those who prepare food. They also witness communal entertainment and communal worship. Earlier in his career, Aldiss would have presented such religious observance as a sign of weakness within the society, but now it is clearly a sign of strength, what has held the people together and kept them human.

In a novel in which failure of communication is an inescapable metaphor, it is inevitable that the communists are unable to comprehend the people that they see as primitive. As the degeneration of the beings they find on Lysenka II is explained in linguistic terms—"How did these people become animal? . . . [T]hey lost the one basic art which makes us *homo uniformis* and which made them human, the art of language" (*EoS*, 70)—so reliance on accepted forms and slogans is what defines them as *Homo uniformis* and so makes them part of the system. But this is also what prevents them from understanding the humanity of their captors, indeed, what prevents them from being fully human themselves. One of the strictures of the system, expressed more than once in this short novel, is "Never think what cannot be said" (*EoS*, 72). This is a stricture against speculation, which is why the system is so static; but in their captivity, the visitors must speculate in order to understand what is happening and thus perhaps escape. But always there is a conflict between the need to speculate and the restrictions that have governed every aspect of their lives. This central failure of communication is highlighted when the leader of the captors waves a shard of mirror in front of Sygiek and the others offer wildly divergent interpretations of what it might mean:

> "He is asking you to mate with him," said Takeido, and sniggered.
>
> "Maybe he had a daughter like you once," suggested Burek.
>
> "He is commenting on facial similarities between our species and his," said Kordan.
>
> "He is asking you to see that our kind and his are much alike," said Dulcifer, "and that you are much prettier than he is."
>
> "He is going to cut your eyes out," said Constanza. (*EoS*, 83)

Even Dulcifer, who comes closest to being the sympathetic, rational figure we are meant to identify with, fails to recognize that the captors and the captives are not merely "much alike" but are the same. Aldiss does not once take us inside the mind of the captors, so the meaning of the mirror is never revealed, though we might perhaps assume it is something along the lines of "know thyself!" Adherence to Biocom is a form of madness in line with Berg's *Madkind*, an inability to see reality if it differs in any way from what the system tells them to believe. So the captives do not understand anything that their captors do, they fail to recognize the cave in which they are held as a fragment of the crashed spaceship in which their captors arrived on the planet, and they cannot see the religious practices as anything other than a direct threat.

When, at the climax of the novel, a rescue party bursts violently into the cave, only the reader feels any sadness that this small fragment of humanity that has survived for a million years should be thus snuffed out. All the six characters care about is their return to the hidebound world of the system. But their brief exposure to something outside the system renders them unsuitable for life within it. The moment the visitors are rescued, they are denounced by their tour guide, Constanza, and all are arrested as enemies of the system.

Enemies of the System is a skimpy novel that repeats familiar, well-worn arguments about communism without in any way providing flesh for the characters, solidity for the setting, or any advance on the work of Zamiatin, Huxley, or Orwell. Despite the claim of Aldiss's perennial apologist, David Wingrove, that it "will doubtless stand the test of time far better than any of Aldiss' previous works,"[1] one cannot help agreeing with Brian Stableford that this is a hollow novel in which "the same old nightmares are on parade again, looking well-drilled but rather haggard, and the ritual indictments are made."[2]

★　★　★

If *Enemies of the System* suggests that religion is better at sustaining humanity than a communism that is very specifically science based (Biocom), the novella *Brothers of the Head* uses science to justify the most extravagant aspects of this fable.

Brothers of the Head was originally published as part of a new illustrated series from Pierrot Publishing. In this instance the illustrations were by Ian Pollock. In his introduction to the 2012 reprint of the text only, Aldiss claims that this was the first book from Pierrot, but a book by Harry Harrison appeared earlier. Aldiss also claims that every copy of his book was sold: "They sold immediately, but nevertheless Philip [Dunn, the publisher; Aldiss doesn't give the surname] went broke" (*BoH*, x). Pierrot, however, continued publishing books for three years after *Brothers of the Head* appeared before finally going out of business.

Aldiss says that the idea for the story came to him in a nightmare at the end of a holiday on the north coast of Norfolk. He dreamed of conjoined twins with a third head growing on one of the twins. He is quick and careful to claim scientific credibility for this image: "Looking up the reality of their deformity, I found there was a medical term for it: *diprosopus tetrotus*; a defect in human babies causing them to be born with two heads" (*BoH*, ix). In fact, *diprosopus* is an exceptionally rare condition in which certain facial features are duplicated; in the most extreme form, *tetrotus*, the baby would have four eyes, four ears, and some doubling of the pharynx, all on one head, and the two faces would act simultaneously. Two heads on one body would appear to be conjoined twins, but then, the two conditions seem to overlap to such an extent that it is not always clear where one ends and the other begins. But Aldiss had a medical term for his conflation of the two conditions that he inflicted on the unfortunate brothers Tom and Barry Howe.

The twins represent, in one body, humanity divided against itself, the perpetual state of war that Aldiss has consistently shown to be his acidic view of modern life. Our first glimpse of them is of two boys "fighting each other steadily with a machine-like hatred" (*BoH*, 8). They are separate, at war; it is only as they run away that we see that they are "inseparably joined in the middle" (*BoH*, 9). They are almost cartoonishly set up as opposites: Tom, who cries, "I'm the normal one!" (*BoH*, 52), is fair and rational; Barry has black hair, is given to irrational, violent anger, and has "a deformity, a second head, growing from his left shoulder" (*BoH*, 8). This extra head, silent and inert for most of the novella, appears to belong to "an old man; its features . . . withered, its hair grey" (*BoH*, 33), though the appearance of age in this instance does not equate with wisdom. But then, no one in this world is wise.

The twins are raised, with their sister Roberta, on L'Estrange Head, a remote and barely accessible bird sanctuary on the Norfolk coast where Albert Howe, their father, is the warden. As in "The Saliva Tree" and "North

Scarning," Aldiss makes the Norfolk landscape suggestive of something eerie and unsettling. In our first glimpse of the boys fighting, "isolation [lent] a supernatural quality to their violence" (*BoH*, 8); later, when they retreat to L'Estrange Head once more, their violence again is reflected in the landscape as their quarrels are linked to birds and animals dying: "Our little lagoons and ditches were sick, our lake choked; their waters had turned the colour of gherkins, thickened by algae" (*BoH*, 60). The link between the sickness of the landscape and the sickness of the brothers—another echo of Wells, this time recalling *The Croquet Player* (1936)—is made explicit when Roberta says, "Never before had I felt the desolation as hostile" and moments later adds, "For the first time in my life, I was scared of my own brothers" (*BoH*, 61–62).

Tom and Barry have only one talent: singing. But it is enough to have them taken up by a music producer, who pairs them with a group called The Noise that has recently lost its lead singer and promotes them as a novelty act under the name The Bang-Bang. Their first song, "Two-Way Romeo"—"We're two in one and all in all / Shoot double-barrelled wherewithal" (*BoH*, 20)— proves to be controversial. The issue of whether "deformed people [should] be allowed to flaunt their sexuality" was enough to "keep the pot of virtuous sentiment, seasoned with prurient interest, a-boiling for a long time" (*BoH*, 21). The Bang-Bang inevitably become a massive rock sensation.

One interesting question about *Brothers of the Head* is how much it relates to *Barefoot in the Head*. The titles echo each other, of course, and both involve rock music; they are the only two books Aldiss wrote that do so. And there is something reminiscent of Charteris when we are told that the twins have "a blind urge to be exploited" and "wanted the world to know of them" (*BoH*, 36), as if the two desires are the same and inseparable. But then, when we learn that one of The Bang-Bang's songs is called "Year by Year the Evil Gains" (*BoH*, 45), which is the overall title of the set of Enigmas published in *New Writings in SF 27*, and another song is called "Probability A" (*BoH*, 47), it seems that Aldiss is gaily throwing in all sorts of references to his own work. So any consonance between *Barefoot in the Head* and *Brothers of the Head* may be intentional but of little real significance.

A notable difference between the two books is that the songs quoted in *Brothers of the Head* work rhythmically and lyrically better than do those in *Barefoot in the Head*. When the novella was adapted as a film (directed by Keith

Fulton and Louis Pepe, released 2005), however, The Bang-Bang became a punk outfit, and the romanticism of Aldiss's lyrics—"Where dark starlight grows on bushes / And eyes house laughing kookaburra birds" (*BoH*, 97)—didn't suit the raucous aesthetic of the movie, so we still haven't heard whether they really work musically. Yet since Aldiss devotes a chapter in the novella to the manager, Zak Bedderwick, analyzing the lyrics of the songs, something that never happened in *Barefoot in the Head* (for David Wingrove, the "astute, analytical insights" make it "at once more accessible and more immediately expressive than *Barefoot in the Head*"),[3] it would seem that in *Brothers of the Head* more thought went into the words.

But the enmity between the two brothers is inescapable—"They were too close. They were always a crowd" (*BoH*, 31)—and their musical career inevitably implodes. They make a physical as well as a metaphorical return to obscurity at L'Estrange Head, where they become "a mad animal fighting itself to death. . . . They had become feral" (*BoH*, 59). They are indeed fighting to the death, because the endless conflict causes Barry to have a seizure. The twins are too closely conjoined to be able to separate the dead body from the living, so Barry's body is animated with an artificial heart though he is braindead. But in the absence of Barry's control, the nameless secondary head starts to come to life, only to continue the feud. When Tom cries out in the night, Roberta recalls, "Barry's arm was across Tom's throat. It was withdrawn as I entered, slithering quickly under the sheet" (*BoH*, 72–73). The serpentine arm has an echo of the supernatural quality of our first glimpse of the battling twins. When the extra head finally awakens, practically its first words are: "Now I am escaping. . . . The two wicked ones who imprisoned me will be punished" (*BoH*, 86). Of course, the newly vivified head can exact its revenge only at the cost of its own brief life.

Brothers of the Head is a slight book, more lyrical and more tightly constructed than *Enemies of the System*, but overly obvious in its metaphors. Taken together, the two novels have an air of treading water through the late 1970s. But then, Aldiss's most ambitious works were shortly to appear.

★ ★ ★

In 1978, with the appearance of *A Rude Awakening*, Brian Aldiss brought his Horatio Stubbs trilogy to a belated conclusion. But he was already setting about a new sequence of mainstream novels, the Squire Quartet, the first volume of which, *Life in the West*, was published in 1980. The book was one of Aldiss's most successful novels. Anthony Burgess saw the story of mid-life crisis, a failing marriage, and the dissolution of a great family name as "emblematic of [the situation of] the West in an age of recession and doubt."[4] That is certainly how Aldiss wanted the novel to be read, though I tend to agree with John Clute that it "never really worked as a tract for the times."[5] More accurately, I think, we see in the acerbic, blustering character of Thomas Squire a portrait of the author adrift in a world he feels at odds with. But then, Aldiss had been at odds with the world ever since he returned from the East in 1947. In that respect, it is interesting that the final part of the quartet, and arguably the last major novel that Aldiss wrote, was called *Somewhere East of Life*, which, as Clute puts it, "tells us that there is nothing more to say."[6]

Aldiss seems to have sensed that with *Life in the West* he had not hit the nail as squarely on the head as he had intended. In a letter to his son Clive that serves as a preface to the first part of his other major sequence of the 1980s, he says that he was dissatisfied with the partial success of *Life in the West*, in which he sought to "depict something of the malaise sweeping the world." The Helliconia Trilogy started out as a more oblique approach to the same issue, but as he consulted a variety of scientists about his setting, "invention took over from allegory" (*HSp*, 5), even though the further he got from his original conception the more Helliconia seemed "relevant to our century" (*HSp*, 5).

As the three novels that make up the Helliconia Trilogy advance, the scenes—set first aboard the Earth Observation Station Avernus and in later volumes on Earth—grow longer, more dramatic, and more complex. It is as though these passages are making explicit the allegorical aspects of the work that might otherwise be lost amid the novels' density.

★ ★ ★

The sense that science is to be used as a justification for flights of fancy, as in *Brothers of the Head*, and that religion has an important part to play in holding cultures and communities together, as in *Enemies of the System*, are both present in the Helliconia Trilogy.

The important role, for good or ill, played by religion in shaping and sustaining Helliconian society is something we will see throughout the trilogy, from the religion of Akha in the caverns of Pannoval at the start of *Helliconia Spring* to the great wheel of Khanabhar at the end of *Helliconia Winter*. The use of science, or more accurately of scientists, to justify the novels' inventions is made explicit in the acknowledgements that close the first and the last volumes in the sequence. Here Aldiss specifically thanks Professor Tom Shippey (philology), Dr. J. M. Roberts (history), Desmond Morris (anthropology), Dr. B. E. Juel-Jensen (pathology), Dr. Jack Cohen (biology), Dr. Peter Cattermole (geology and climactics), and Professor Iain Nicolson (cosmology and astronomy). In *Helliconia Spring* Aldiss declares that "the great globe itself, yea, all which it inherit, is largely their work" (*HSp*, 559). In the final volume he rows back a bit on the suggestion that Helliconia is largely their creation, thanking them instead for "invaluable preliminary discussions" (*HW*, 285), but there is still the implication that the trilogy is as much a work of science as of science fiction. Perhaps only in declaring such a rational basis for his invention could Aldiss feel secure in presenting Helliconia, as he told Clive, as "a stage of the kind of drama in which we are embroiled in our century" (*HSp*, 5).

Nevertheless, the idea of a world in which seasons last for centuries did not spring fully armed from the minds of a handful of consulting scientists. Its origins can be traced back through the long history of Aldiss's science fiction. In part, of course, it is one more iteration of the world in stasis that we have seen already in *Non-Stop* and *Hothouse*, in *Report on Probability A* and *The Malacia Tapestry*. But he had also been trying out the notion of overly long seasons for almost a decade in his short stories. In "The Dark Soul of the Night," for example, a family group is desperately seeking safety after being shipwrecked on a large planet whose eccentric orbit means that "the long winter was setting in, a winter that would mean the death of every living thing. Spring would not come again for another six or so Earth-years" (*BSF3*, 223). A year later, in "Creatures of Apogee," Aldiss again experimented with the notion of a world that was "a slave to its lethargic orbit; for in the course of one year, from the heats of perihelion to the cools of apogee and back again, not only lives but generations and whole civilisations underwent the cycle of birth and decay" (*RoE*, 149). As the sun grows steadily closer and hotter, the beings of apogee contemplate a time not too far off when the oceans surrounding their decadent palace will boil away, and other very different creatures would inherit the world: "In their own tongues, with their own gestures, they would obey their own deities" (*RoE*, 159).

The common factor in these stories, which are clearly trial runs for the ideas that would underlie the Helliconia Trilogy, is that, on such a world, the change of the seasons would be devastating. And the inhabitants of such a world must be aware of what is approaching, whether the deadly cold of winter or the deadly heat of summer. Not only can no winter child expect to live so long as to see the return of autumn, nor a summer child expect to know another spring, but the intervening season can bring only death. If you understand the turning of the year without ever being able to experience it, how would that affect the way you view your environment and your society? How would it shape the beliefs you hold?

These are big questions, and it would take a big book to attempt an answer to them. The resultant Helliconia Trilogy was easily the longest and most ambitious single work of Brian Aldiss's career. For comparison, the three books combined are about thirteen times the length of *Enemies of the System*. It was a major project; the question is, how well did it succeed?

*   *   *

The trilogy begins and ends with a blank screen. As *Helliconia Spring* opens, a snowstorm has "filled the world with howling energy, transforming it to a grey-white darkness" (*HSp*, 11), and as *Helliconia Winter* ends, "the wind [takes] the sound and smother[s] it in the weight of falling snow" (*HW*, 281). The world is colorless, without shape, without form. We have seen before, in *Greybeard, Barefoot in the Head,* and "The Dark Soul of the Night," that a monochrome world betokens the failure of humanity's dominion over nature, and that is more savagely, more brutally the case here. Human civilization will, in time, make a mark on the white screen, and over the centuries that civilization will grow, become richer, more elaborate, more colorful. But no matter how technologically advanced it becomes, all will eventually be wiped away and the screen left blank once more. All that humanity might achieve counts for nothing in the grand scheme of things.

What's more, the whiteout in the opening and closing pages marks the turn of the year, the completion of the circle. All will happen again. The individuals involved will be different, but spring will come, civilizations will ilse again, there will be more wars, more conflicts, and then winter will arrive once more and all will be wiped out. For all the perennial changes that are played out across Helliconia, this world is as static in its way as the ship in *Non-Stop* or the city-state of Malacia. Change amounts to nothing, because nothing lasts.

Cyclical imagery recurs throughout the trilogy, including the way the sequence ends with Luterin riding alone into the snow in despair at human society and begins with Yuli emerging from the snow desperate for human society. Yuli is approaching manhood—"seven years old, virtually a grown man" (*HSp*, 11)—and on a hunting expedition with his father when his father is captured by phagors. Phagors are the monstrous creatures that haunt the trilogy. They have two long, sharp horns on their heads (hence the other name by which they are known, "ancipital," which means "double-edged") and horned, three-toed feet. They are taller than a human but fairly human in shape, although "inside their barrel bodies they carried their intestines above their lungs . . . their limbs were jointed in a different way from a man's" (*HSp*, 177), and their body temperature is lower than a man's, so they are better fitted for the winter climate. They are intelligent and can speak Olonets, the common language of Helliconia, but they are fierce and dangerous warriors. In general, they are ascendant during the winter years and enslave humans; humans are ascendant in the summer years and enslave the phagors. There are other humanoid and intelligent races on Helliconia, but the humans and phagors are at the top of the evolutionary chain, though the importance of the connection between the two races is something that only becomes obvious in later volumes.

As is so often the case with Aldiss, unless the intent is comic or ironic (for instance, in "T" or "Who Can Replace a Man?"), we do not see things from the perspective of the antagonist or the non-human. Thus, later in *Helliconia Spring* we watch a phagor war party gathering and setting out on a seemingly interminable journey to attack a human city, but we are never really given insight into their intent or motivation. Even when we come to understand their importance to the survival of humanity on Helliconia, they remain the monstrous, the incomprehensible and implacable enemy. When Yuli recognizes, therefore, that there is no chance of rescuing his father, he has no choice but to flee from the territory of the phagors. He ends up in the city of Pannoval, built in massive caverns under a mountain.

Pannoval is presumably not the only human community to have survived since the previous great year, but it is the only one we hear about. Its survival should make it a repository of knowledge from earlier times, so that when the spring returns humanity might re-emerge better prepared for what might come. But that doesn't happen. Any such knowledge has become ritualized within the offices of the autocratic religion that rules the city. In *Helliconia Summer*, therefore, we are aware of Pannoval as a revered religious center, somewhat like the Vatican in being the headquarters of one of the world's most powerful and conservative churches, but it is emphatically not a source of knowledge from the past. Thus, as with the surviving fragment of humanity living in a cavern in *Enemies of the System*, religion here has played a vital role in human survival on Helliconia, but the concentration on belief instead of knowledge means it has done nothing to advance humanity.

In Pannoval, Yuli realizes that the best way to survive is to join the all-powerful priesthood. For a while he becomes a true believer in the religion of Akha, but as he starts to witness the power and the cruelty of the priesthood, including the use of torture reminiscent of the Spanish Inquisition, so he is increasingly alienated from their rule. Finally, he is able to escape, along with the woman he will eventually marry and two prisoners he has rescued from the cells of the priesthood. When they emerge beyond the mountains, they find a people with "no arts to relieve the monotony of their hard life" (*HSp*, 124), and so Yuli starts to create a society. The ambivalence of Aldiss's attitude toward religion is perhaps expressed in his description of Yuli's purpose as he "became at last a real priest, and tried to instill in the people a feeling for their own spiritual vitality" (*HSp*, 124).

The story of Yuli and of Pannoval is little more than a preamble to the novel. The story now jumps forward several generations and shifts its focus to Embruddock, a community founded by Yuli's descendants. In *Helliconia Summer* this will be one of the great cities of the world, but for now it is still small and rough. After leaving the lakeside village where they started, they have taken over what they think of as the ruins of an old town consisting of stone buildings, but in fact, as we learn (though they do not), it is a palace from a former age, with a grandeur that is not only faded but can no longer be comprehended. As with the enclosed, priest-ridden community of Pannoval, we are again being told that the past survives, but not knowledge of the past. At one point, images in one of the ruins will be examined but not understood, although from our perspective they reveal much about the nature of Helliconia.

But then, because we are always watching Helliconia from the outside, we always have privileged information that is not known to any of the characters. That information comes primarily from Avernus. Earth Observation Station Avernus, home to "some five thousand men, women, children, and androids" (*HSp*, 143), has been observing the system for more than one great year and in particular is watching events on the planet Helliconia. Again, therefore, there is knowledge of what happened before the last great winter, but that knowledge is never referred to, never disclosed. It is enough for us to know that each great winter wipes the slate clean and that, though humans survive, their civilization does not but must start again from scratch come the spring. In the second and third volumes the passages relating to Avernus, and through Avernus to Earth, grow steadily longer and more complex until they act as a counterpoint to events on Helliconia. But in the spring, with human civilization barely getting started, there is nothing to counter, so in *Helliconia Spring* these passages are brief, impersonal, widely spaced (the first mention of Avernus, for instance, is on page 142, the second on page 181), and largely confined to providing the sort of factual information needed for the reader to understand the situation on Helliconia. Thus it is that we learn that Helliconia is in orbit around Batalix (Star B), which is in a binary system with Freyr (Star A), and though Helliconia is "almost six hundred times as distant from Freyr as Earth is from its primary" (*HSp*, 181), that distance is closing, hence the steady change in the climate on the planet. Helliconia has a year of 480 days in which it orbits Batalix, but there is a great year of 1,825 Helliconian years (2,592 Earth years) in which Batalix and its planets orbit Freyr.

The story that we watch through the lens of Avernus is basically a dynastic saga involving rivals for the throne, murder, usurpation, enemy attacks, and plague, the sort of dramas that might be played out in any dark-age setting. But while center stage is occupied by large characters engaged in violent and romantic actions—the brothers Nahkri and Klils, who seize power though "Klils had no sense and Nahkri no wisdom" (*HSp*, 203) and the hunter Aoz Roon, who killed the brothers and seized power in turn because he "understood—or thought he did—what was good for the tribe" (*HSp*, 205)—our focus has to be on the ever-changing background. Here we see snow melting over a longer period each year, rivers starting to run free of ice, more land becoming available for agriculture, and trees that have been bare for longer than anyone can remember suddenly producing seed. In particular, we see the human, social, and physical changes wrought by these vast environmental transformations.

The most obvious physical change is brought about by Bone Fever, a pandemic that strikes with the approach of the great spring and that kills perhaps half of humanity, leaving the survivors thinner, less stocky. In *Helliconia Winter* the characters suffer a variant of the same disease, the "Fat Death," which in turn kills almost half of humanity and renders the survivors shorter and fatter. The physiological changes brought on by these diseases, of course, better equip people for the environmental changes that are coming: "The virus destroyed. But it was a life-giving destruction" (*HW*, 126), we are told. The idea of a life-giving destruction seems somehow typical of Aldiss. Only at the very end of *Helliconia Winter* do we learn that both Bone Fever and the Fat Death are the result of "a tick which travelled from phagors to mankind carrying the plagues necessary to mankind's survival in the extreme seasons" (*HW*, 279–280). This is knowledge that has been passed on from one great year to the next, but it is ignored and hidden for political and religious reasons.

The central character in the latter part of *Helliconia Spring* is Laintal Ay, a direct descendant of Yuli, who acts as a witness to rather than a participant in the dramas that are played out and who is therefore an observer of the social changes that come with the environmental changes. As he recovers from Bone Fever he muses on "how much was owed to women" (*HSp*, 498). This makes explicit one of the curiosities of this novel: the more powerful, the more transformative characters tend to be women. With the exception of *Greybeard* and some portions of *Hothouse*, this is not normally true of Aldiss's work. When we are told that women are traditionally "our source of labour when the hunters are in the field" (*HSp*, 397), we might normally expect that statement to reflect the author's own attitude. Certainly, women in the majority of his novels are there to be lust objects, scolds, or companions, rather than major players in shaping the world. And in the two subsequent Helliconia novels, women tend to be demoted to those more familiar roles.

But here, women are at the forefront of the intellectual renaissance that is happening in Embruddock.

Central to this renaissance is the independent-minded Shay Tal, who initiates an "academy" (the name, I'm sure, is meant to resonate with those of the ancient Greeks, suggesting the first movement from barbarism to civilization). As the weather changes, Shay Tal sees how newly emerging grains can be used to make better bread, and when the phagor war party appears she conceives a plan to defeat them. Her academy is ignored and denigrated by the men because it is about ideas rather than practicalities—"Have you no certainty for me," Aoz Roon demands, "No certainty in this damned uncertain world?" (*HSp*, 266)—a challenge later answered by Shay Tal's acolyte Vry, the astronomer. Vry can predict the next eclipse because "the universe is not random. It is a machine. Therefore one can know its movements," a statement that is characterized as "deeply revolutionary" (*HSp*, 456). Shay Tal's influence is shown also when Oyre tells Laintal Ay that she loves him but will not be his woman, because, she says, "If I become your possession, I become nothing." Instead, "by remaining independent like Shay Tal, perhaps I can achieve something" (*HSp*, 358).

Typically, Aldiss is at best ambivalent about human evolution. His books, colored by his wartime experiences and by the failing society he returned to in 1947, commonly show civilization in decline, humanity facing its own failure to maintain a good, peaceful life. From *Non-Stop* and *Hothouse* to *Barefoot in the Head* and *Moreau's Other Island*, society fails. *Helliconia Spring* is one of the very few works that is designed to show society and civilization growing, though by the end of the trilogy it has cyclically risen and fallen once more. But even in the first volume, which in a single lifetime takes us from a crude hunter-gatherer, pre-medieval society to a far more sophisticated, luxuriant, early modern one, the advance of civilization is not an unalloyed good. The steady environmental improvement brings consequent ills, and the social order is more easily broken down than built up, so that, following the failure of Dathka's coup, Vry can exclaim: "Human beings are such messes. We were better when the snow contained us, frozen, when we had no . . . hope!" (*HSp*, 533). This may be one of Aldiss's best books, but it is, for all its superficial signs of advancement, a pessimistic book.

The Helliconia Trilogy was clearly intended to be Aldiss's masterwork, a huge saga spanning centuries that encompassed sweeping environmental and societal change. And he wrote at a length commensurate with that ambition: *Helliconia Spring* was far and away his longest novel to date. It would win both the BSFA Award and the John W. Campbell Memorial Award, and it was widely and often enthusiastically reviewed. Indeed, it was better received than any of his fictions since the 1960s, although the critics were, as ever, divided. For Thomas Clareson it was "perhaps the most audacious venture of the year,"[7] though Mary Gentle worried that the book overdoes its allegorical ambitions, and the characters "represent so much . . . [that they] . . . have hardly time to be simply human."[8] And one critic attacked the novel so savagely—writing that "the epic material wanders, aimless and discouraged"[9]—that it provoked howls of outrage from Aldiss's usual supporters, Brian Griffin and Harry Harrison. The question was, of course, how well Aldiss could sustain the ambition, the audacity, if you will, across the next two volumes.

★ ★ ★

Helliconia Summer, which is even longer than its predecessor, appeared just a year later. It is not a direct sequel: centuries have passed, and the focus of the novel has shifted from the descendants of Yuli in Embruddock to the rival state of Borlien and its king, JandolAnganol. And the role of Avernus in the narrative has changed, as well.

In the first book it was implied that the virus which brings about Bone Fever and the Fat Death means that anyone who visited Helliconia from Avernus would inevitably die. That still seems to be the case but no longer seems to be an obstacle. In *Helliconia Spring* we learned that other than transmitting film of life on Helliconia back to Earth, film that takes centuries to arrive, the small cluster of humans aboard Avernus is completely cut off from home. They cannot return, they cannot be relieved; travel to Avernus was always a one-way trip. But there was a suggestion, conveyed by the impersonal way in which everything about Avernus was discussed in the first volume, that the dedicated scientists who make up its population are so devoted to their quest for knowledge about the system of Batalix and Freyr that they are fully reconciled to this state of affairs. That, however, is no longer the case. Now they are described almost as prisoners; their dedication to the study of Helliconia "was not of their choosing. They had no alternative" (*HSu*, 68), and "many aboard [Avernus] felt that their lives remained artificial lives, without the zest of reality" (*HSu*, 112). Meanwhile, Earth itself has come to be no more than a myth: "Earth was not accessible like Helliconia. . . . [It] had become a sort of ideal—a projection of the inner lives of those aboard" (*HSu*, 179).

This is a recipe for discontent and disorder, which duly come. Avernus, in this respect, comes to resemble the breakdown of civilization that took place aboard the similarly isolated generation starship in *Non-Stop*. The leader of a rebellion that took place before the novel opens had been punished by being "sent down to his death on the surface of Helliconia" (*HSu*, 113). But this execution, rather than instilling fear in the population, had actually excited envy. The hunger to escape the artifice and the restrictions of life on board Avernus is so great that once every ten years a lottery is held, the winner receiving the chance to go down to Helliconia and certain death. It says something of the peculiar conditions aboard Avernus that the drawing is wildly popular.

One notable difference between *Helliconia Spring* and *Helliconia Summer* is that, in the former, those aboard Avernus are all nameless, faceless scientists, the observers, not the observed; in the latter we start to learn the names of people on Avernus. They are no longer impersonal roles but are characters engaged in the action. One is "Billy Xiao Pin . . . a typical representative of Avernian society" (*HSu*, 68), who happens to be the most recent winner of the lottery. He dies eventually, of course, but only after traveling extensively and passing on information that may lead to the growth of scientific knowledge on Helliconia. After Billy's death, his watch is stolen by the no-good son of the trader Muntras, who has taken him in, but the son is in turn killed and the watch discovered by the inquisitive shopkeeper, CaraBansity. The watch shows not only the Helliconian date and time but also a date and time that are meaningless to the people of Borlien, prompting CaraBansity to say of it: "Where are the craftsmen now who could manufacture such a jewel?" (*HSu*, 29). The watch is seen as a survival from a golden age in the previous great year, raising the prospect of further technological development.

One thing worth noting: Bone Fever, which enables winter people to survive the summer, is the hinge point of *Helliconia Spring*. The Fat Death, which enables summer people to survive the winter, is the hinge point of *Helliconia Winter*. But there is no such plague in *Helliconia Summer*, so Billy's death from a form of the plague helps provide the connecting fabric that ties the first and last volumes together. At the same time, the cause of his death and the mysterious watch also illuminate the intense ignorance of the true state of the world that is the abiding theme of the trilogy.

There is technological innovation independent of anything that may come inadvertently from Avernus. For instance, in one battle JandolAnganol is defeated by the barely human Driats because the Driats have access to firearms. It is misleading to try to compare the development of Helliconia too closely with that of Earth, but in this, at least, Helliconia is roughly equivalent to Europe in the early modern period. (Though there is no comparable advance in astronomical observation and knowledge; no one on Helliconia is looking up at Avernus as Avernus is looking down on them.) As with *Helliconia Spring*, the bulk of the novel is given over to dynastic struggles: wars, intrigues, and betrayals. At the heart of the novel is JandolAnganol, who is not the brightest of rulers (the similarity of his name to that of Jingadangelow in *Greybeard* is perhaps not simply coincidence), and his wife, the beautiful Queen MyrdemInggala. Unlike *Helliconia Spring*, in which independent and strong-minded women spearhead the intellectual and cultural development that the novel traces, here MyrdemInggala is the only significant female character.

There is a moment of seeming magic associated with the queen, as there had been with Shay Tal. In spring, Shay Tal is present when invading phagors start to cross a lake that abruptly freezes around them, trapping and killing them all. In summer, MyrdemInggala is present when the remnants of a Sibornalese invasion fleet are first stopped by a mass of dolphins and then crushed by sea monsters. Though there are scientific explanations for both that are connected to the changing seasons, there is still an air of the extraordinary and the convenient about these incidents. But whereas Shay Tal's standing is enhanced by the occurrence she witnesses, the central thread of *Helliconia Summer* concerns MyrdemInggala's loss of status.

For dynastic reasons, JandolAnganol is persuaded to set aside his wife in order to enter into an alliance by marriage with the ruling house of Embruddock. This, we realize, if JandolAnganol does not, is part of a plot by other powers to further undermine Borlien, which has already been weakened by its loss to the Driats. In these books neither Brian Aldiss nor, indeed, the observers aboard Avernus tend to pay much attention to the most powerful states on Helliconia. In spring, Embruddock is basically struggling to stay afloat and is noticeably inferior to neighboring states, while in summer Borlien is already in decline as the novel opens. But then, that's only to be expected; Aldiss never was particularly interested in political power, but rather sees decline and failure as the inevitable fate of all.

What I'm saying, of course, is that the novel fits into the broad pattern of Aldiss's work in two ways. First, the environment tends to be hostile; second, humanity tends toward violence and depravity. This is summed up when the old trader Muntras witnesses a group of phagors being killed: "Over his lifetime, he considered, his fellow human beings had grown nastier, more spiteful, less forgiving. Maybe it was the weather" (*HSu*, 236). One of the persistent features of the trilogy is the way global survival patterns in the extreme environment are described. Thus as the hottest part of the long summer approaches, volcanic eruptions are triggered that throw acidic dust layers into the atmosphere that "double Helliconia's albedo, reflecting the increasing heat of Freyr away from the surface" (*HSu*, 488). The forest fires generated were "the end of the world for many frightened creatures. To a more detached view, it was a sign of the world's determination to save itself and its freight of organic life" (*HSu*, 489). Every step in the preservation of life is accompanied by destruction.

One of the characteristics of Aldiss's writing from the start of his career has been his employment of strange and unusual words. We see it, for instance, in his rather freewheeling neologisms such as "pervertebrae" in *The Primal Urge* and in much of *Barefoot in the Head*, as well as his use of words like "ancipital" to describe the phagors. There are times, it must be said, when such unfamiliar words seem to be chosen more for their sound than for their sense. For instance, of the several non-human races on Helliconia the Madis, who are just achieving sapience, are described, curiously but consistently, as "protognostic," a word that, the dictionary tells us, applies to the Hellenistic origins of the Christian heresy of Gnosticism. I'm not sure how the word is being applied here (perhaps Aldiss was thinking of "prognathism," which refers to a protruding lower jaw), but we are told, for example, about their "protognostic innocence, which reminded those who looked on them of animal faces or the faces of flowers" (*HSu*, 91). This hardly seems to relate to the dictionary definition of "protognostic." Yet along these less-traveled by-ways of vocabulary, Aldiss happens upon a word towards the end of the novel, "enantiodromia," which encompasses so neatly the entire structure of the book that he repeats it several times in the novel's closing chapters and revisits it in *Helliconia Winter*. A principle of Jungian thought, it refers to the way one thing turns into its opposite, both as a governing principle of natural cycles and in psychological terms. The trilogy encompasses such transformations on the macroscopic level—the way the world is changed by the extreme seasons of the great year—but also in terms of plot and character. The story is full of sudden reversals: The Sibornalese invasion fleet is devastated en route and finally is rendered meaningless by a simple deception. The king of Embruddock tries to bring down his rival, JandolAnganol, only to be killed and have his capital devastated. The academic presentation about the history of the phagors shows them to be the original inhabitants of Helliconia and the source of human religious worship, only for this revelation to spark a riot and denunciations of heresy.

This enantiodromia invariably moves from good to bad, just as, aboard Avernus, as Thomas Clareson puts it, "belief is gone; only despair remains."[10] Even under the bright sun of high summer, the pessimism of *Helliconia Spring* is sustained.

★　★　★

The Helliconia novels continued to be well received. Clareson called *Helliconia Summer* "one of the most notable recent works of science fiction,"[11] while Peter Caracciolo simply regarded the trilogy as "Brian Aldiss's masterpiece,"[12] a view I'm sure Aldiss would have agreed with since that was clearly his purpose. And like the first volume, *Helliconia Winter* would go on to win a BSFA Award. Yet there is a sense of a change of pace in this volume.

I think the first two volumes of the trilogy got away from him; their rather ponderous length makes them somewhat otiose. As Mary Gentle said: *Helliconia Spring* "has the disadvantage of moving so slowly that at some points it just stops."[13] The final volume makes the whole thing tighter, more controlled, more carefully structured. Writing of the early 1990s, the time of the Squire Quartet and *Dracula Unbound* and just a little after *Helliconia Winter*, Aldiss says: "I could tell my writing was improving: my sales figures kept getting worse" (*ToE*, 445). Those sales figures might have been falling not because the writing was better (there is little from this period that matches the literary qualities of *Greybeard* or *Report on Probability A* or the linguistic efflorescence of *Barefoot in the Head*) but because it was becoming more self-indulgent, the storytelling more clogged. But it is interesting to wonder whether the first two Helliconia novels had failed to perform to the stellar level that Aldiss anticipated. Thus, while *Helliconia Summer* followed so quickly on the heels of *Helliconia Spring* that the two books must have been written very close together in one extended creative effort, there was suddenly a two-year gap before *Helliconia Winter* appeared. It was time enough, perhaps, to reconsider the response to the first two books and reflect that reconsideration in the final volume.

Whatever the reason, *Helliconia Winter* is a considerably shorter book than its predecessors, comes with a map that Aldiss had not considered necessary before, and spells out details that he had previously allowed to emerge slowly and often obliquely. Thus, the novel begins with a lengthy and detailed account of the various nations of Helliconia, telling us that the phagors, the ancipitals, were "its elder race," detailing the nature of the system, and relating that "now Helliconia was poised on the brink of the winter of another Great Year. Darkness, cold, silence, waited in the centuries ahead" (*HW*, 17). This is the sort of authorial interjection that Aldiss hadn't felt called on to make in either of the preceding volumes. The long explanation of what led to the establishment of Avernus (*HW*, 96–103), absent from earlier volumes, suggests that this might almost be considered a standalone novel. The story is more focused, the cast smaller, and there is a lot more background information. Aldiss directly tells us several things that he only implied in the first two volumes. It's as if he is trying to make it more reader-friendly than they were. The heart of the story is Luterin, son of the Keeper of Khanabhar, where the Great Wheel, the holiest site on Helliconia, is situated. Luterin goes into the army, is heroic in a war against Campannlat, and then escapes the massacre of the returning army ordered by the Oligarch. With a slave called Toress Lahl, whom he captured after killing her husband in the war and with whom he slowly falls in love, he makes his way back to Khanabhar. Along the way he survives the Fat Death and recognizes that it has fit him for the coming long winter. He discovers the treachery of his father (which is also what had previously led to the death of his brother), kills his father, and escapes by entering the Great Wheel, a massive ring of stone cells with only one entrance and exit; the prisoners spend years pulling a chain to turn the wheel until their cell is once again aligned with the exit. This is the only one of the three books with a single clearly identifiable protagonist who is on stage throughout the novel.

The story, therefore, is less one of dynastic intrigue than a straightforward *bildungsroman* telling how one man slowly discovers the facts about his world. Largely concentrating on one perspective rather than shifting viewpoints tells us more about the experience of being in the world, even if we know less about the complex politics of the world.

And while the focus of the parts of the story set on Helliconia have shifted, so has the focus of the parts of the story set elsewhere. Just as Helliconia is collapsing into winter, so Avernus is dying, its original eight families reduced first to six, and now to two. They are so divorced from Earth, which they can never know, that "the families [have] fallen victim to a sort of neurasthenia of the senses and [have] lost touch with reality" (*HW*, 75). Avernus feels more than ever like the ship in *Non Stop*: "The attenuation of the spirit had been embraced" (*HW*, 76). Avernus became a battleground of violence and sexual perversions: "The Avernus, haven of technology, temple of all that was positive and enquiring in mankind's intellect, was reduced to a tumbling arena, in which savages ran from ambush at intervals to break each other's skulls" (*HW*, 77). Moreover, "not only did individuals not know each other: they were now strangers to themselves" (*HW*, 174). Detachment from home once again becomes a detachment from self, which in turn generates war. It reflects the sour, pessimistic view that is a commonplace in Aldiss's work: both Avernus and Helliconia are doomed in the inescapable nature of things.

The passages about Avernus, which were very brief interventions in *Helliconia Spring*, then longer and with named characters in *Helliconia Summer*, become brief again and without any named characters as the space station dissolves into anarchy. Meanwhile, attention shifts to Earth. Barely mentioned in the first two books except as a place so distant and inaccessible that it is on the order of a thousand years after the event that the broadcasts from Helliconia are received, Earth here becomes a more significant player in the story. The odd aside is replaced by page upon page of narrative; the future history of Earth is described broadly but with a lot of significant detail, a story of wars, disease, and catastrophe leading eventually to a hypercapitalist dictator-ship which "made a small percentage on every lungful of oxygen breathed," while those who had escaped to other planets were "free to found their own petty nations and ruin their own lives their own way" (HW, 102). By the end of the book there are named characters on Earth, and at times it feels as if Helliconia has stopped being the subject of the novel and is little more than a metaphor that illustrates the central concern of this far-future Earth.

This is not exactly a positive view of humanity's future, but then there is no such positive view anywhere in Aldiss's work. Perhaps inevitably, nuclear war destroys human civilization, though Earth survives under a new ice age. The war is blamed on religion: "Mankind had grown up and forgotten Gaia . . . had invented its own gods . . . had enslaved itself, in hate as much as love" (HW, 136). James Lovelock's Gaia hypothesis had fascinated Aldiss ever since he first heard about it. Earlier novels such as *Hothouse* and *Greybeard* showed how receptive he would be to Lovelock's ideas, and the Gaia hypothesis would appear in one form or another in much of his work. But the Helliconia Trilogy was very specifically a representation of Gaia. In the planet of Hellico-nia he had a place whose monumental seasonal and environmental changes were Lovelock's self-regulating system writ large. Here that central concern is made explicit, Earth entering a nuclear winter just as Helliconia enters its own devastating winter. And the villain of the piece is, seemingly, religion.

In *Helliconia Summer* the observers on Avernus had declared that religion is "a primitive obsession, an illness, an opiate for those who could not think straight" (HSu, 449). And in a typical passage in *Helliconia Winter*, Odim, speak-ing of the time he lived in Uskutoshk, says, "I behaved like an Uskuti. I believed like an Uskuti. I conformed. [But having left that place] I find that I have absolutely no belief in God. At his passing, I felt a weight lifting" (HW, 130). This suggests that religion is socially conditioned, a consequence of where and in what society one lives. But it is the organized church of Sibornel that becomes the focus of opposition to the increasingly authoritarian rule of the Oligarch. The Oligarch has been responsible for the massacre of a Sibornalese army and has embarked on a program of genocide against all phagors, despite knowing from a surviving religious document that it is the phagors that carry the virus that ensures the survival of humanity through the centuries of the great winter. In other words, killing off the phagors would also kill off humanity. The enemy of humanity is therefore political, a populist hatred of the other, rather than religious. Indeed, religion has been responsible for the survival of information from previous great years (though we have seen in earlier volumes how little of that information is actually disseminated).

This picture is somewhat confused when we discover that the Oligarch is also Luterin's father, the Keeper of Khanabhar, and hence an important religious figure. But when the Oligarch says that "God is mankind's greatest lie—a buffer against the bleak truths of the world" (*HW*, 242), echoing the views of Avernus from *Helliconia Summer*, we may get the impression that his sin is less to do with religion than with hypocrisy.

And there is another curious quasi-religious device that runs through the trilogy and that confuses the picture even more: "pauk." Pauk allows the people of Helliconia to communicate directly with their dead, referred to as "gossies" or "fessups." The nature of this state, and the character of the gossies, is different in each of the three volumes. Whereas, in spring, the gossies had been "creatures of hatred, bewailing their failed lives, pouring scorn on the living, [by summer] all anyone gets is sweetness and consolation" (*HSu*, 158). There is a suggestion that this is wish fulfillment, some sort of fantasy, yet when MyrdemInggala goes into pauk, she learns the location of someone that in reality she doesn't know. Yet she also questions "whether the phantom [is] not in her head, whether there could be survival for anyone after death . . . [but] pauk was her consolation" (*HSu*, 451). In the first two volumes people saw multiple layers of ancestors in pauk, but in the third volume this changes again. Now the visitor sees only the gossie of the most recently deceased ancestor, who in turn goes to speak to earlier generations, and here the gossies are neutral and helpful. In *Helliconia Winter*, which is full of explanations for what was taken for granted in the earlier volumes, Aldiss attempts a seemingly rational account for pauk: the survivors of Earth's nuclear winter have learned empathy—"It became a dominant feature, with survival characteristics" (*HW*, 138)—and because they retain their transmissions from Helliconia (at this point watching the events from spring), they find a way to beam empathy to the Helliconian gossies in time for the nature of pauk to change during summer and winter. As an explanation, this is noticeably feeble. It doesn't account for how MyrdemInggala might learn something she had not previously known, nor does it give us any notion of what the gossies might be if they are not actually the Helliconian dead. But I suspect that by the time he was writing *Helliconia Winter*, Aldiss realized how awkward pauk was for the allegorical purpose he envisaged for the sequence.

It is possible that pauk was originally conceived as a metaphor for Gaia, a personification of an almost geological awareness. In *Helliconia Spring* there is always a sense of descending through layers of earth and rock before the encounter with the gossie, one of several chthonic aspects to that novel, from the descent into Pannoval at its start to Laintal Ay's encounter with the protognostics toward the end. But the more pauk becomes a means of conveying both information and mood, the less it works as an expression of Gaia. Yet however pauk was conceived, the fact of being able to talk to the dead provides a substantial grounding for religious belief, which tends to undermine the unease about religion that Aldiss repeats throughout the sequence. Certainly, there is no indication that Aldiss ever seriously worked out how something like pauk might affect the religious character of Helliconia. And by the time *Helliconia Winter* appeared, when the trilogy has become more explicitly about Earth, the suggestion that pauk represents an emotional link between Helliconia and its watchers on Earth tends to suggest that Aldiss was stuck with something that didn't really belong in the evolving metaphorical structure of his creation.

And if Helliconia is a metaphor for Earth, as the novel ends with the inevitable return of winter, a white, blank, inhospitable world, then the message is that the future Earth we have watched being assailed by catastrophe, struggling to recover, then being struck by another catastrophe, must just as inevitably repeat this cycle. In David Langford's words, the trilogy offers "two escape routes from cyclic history: enlightenment and extinction."[14] But the Aldiss we have followed from *Non-Stop* to *Enemies of the System* has never displayed much faith in enlightenment. The Helliconia Trilogy is a somber work that, even at its most colorful, never quite escapes the sense of human failure and decline that underlines everything Aldiss wrote. If it is not exactly the masterpiece it aspired to be, the trilogy is still one of the most ambitious and most impressive works of his career. In terms of his science fiction, at least, it was a high-water mark.

CHaPTeR 6

UTOPIAN

When *Helliconia Winter* appeared in 1985, it marked the exact midpoint of Brian Aldiss's career. His first book, *The Brightfount Diaries*, came out in 1955; his last, *The Complete Short Stories: The 1960s*, was published in four volumes in 2015. It was also, though nobody at the time could have anticipated this, his last book-length work of science fiction to attract and merit serious critical attention.

Why this might be is not altogether clear. Perhaps, after the years-long effort of producing something of the scale and ambition of the Helliconia Trilogy, he was drained. The trilogy had won awards, but had perhaps not been quite the commercial and critical success that Aldiss believed it deserved to be. Perhaps he felt that his career was better served if he moved in another direction. He was now successful and secure, one of the very few contemporary science fiction writers recognized and applauded outside the tiny bubble of the sf community. In 1981 he had been invited onto the jury of the Booker Prize, the first and so far only writer primarily known for science fiction to have been thus approached. It was the year that Salman Rushdie won for *Midnight's Children*, though Aldiss wanted the prize to go to *The White Hotel* by D. M. Thomas.

Aldiss's major creative effort after finishing the Helliconia Trilogy was to return to the series of mainstream novels that would become known as the Squire Quartet, although the Squire family would play little more than a peripheral role in it. Yet these novels do, at a distance, illuminate something of Aldiss's shifting relationship with science fiction.

Like so much of Aldiss's mainstream fiction, *Forgotten Life* (1988), the second book in the sequence and the first to appear after the Helliconia Trilogy, plunders Aldiss's own life. In particular, like such varied works as *Non-Stop* and *A Soldier Erect*, it draws yet again on what is obviously the most significant experience of his life, his time with the Forgotten Army in Burma. The central figure, the tellingly named Clement Winter, is going through the effects of his recently deceased brother Joseph. Joseph was the brother everyone looked down on, but as Clem reads his papers a picture emerges of a vigorous, questing spirit who served in Burma and then in Sumatra, wrote books about the East that didn't sell and pornography based on his own seemingly endless amorous adventures, and in the end discovers the peace he had always sought. As a self-portrait it is, of course, exactly how Aldiss would want to be seen. By comparison, Clem, outwardly the more successful brother, is seen to have a dull, sterile life trapped in a joyless marriage and unable to respond when offered his own chance at redemption. It is, as John Clute rightly notes, the "summa of Aldiss's best self as a writer,"[1] while in my own review I pointed out the echo of his best science fiction in the concentration on emotionally empty characters who "are trapped by their own inaction[;] decay results from an inability to adapt to change, entropy is of our own making."[2]

Amid all of this is a very cruel portrait of Clem's wife, Sarah, who writes safe and reassuring science fiction under the name Green Mouth, a name that is surely indicative of the contempt with which Aldiss regards both her and her profession. It is an excellent novel, one of the best he wrote, but its overall message is that the time Aldiss spent in Burma and his various priapic adventures both before and during his two marriages are what was important and gave his life savor, while science fiction is associated with a dull and empty life.

Empty characters and failed lives are even more apparent in *Remembrance Day* (1993), in which the lost lives of the three central characters are brought together in the curiously low-key climax of an IRA bombing. I said at the time that "as he grows older, Aldiss seems to fall more and more out of love with life and this is the most negative and dispiriting book he has written,"[3] though in fact there was more to come along those lines.

The drumbeat of unhappiness and the failure to find meaning in life were still there when Aldiss came to write the last volume of the quartet, *Somewhere East of Life* (1994). Now, though, he seemed to be a little more reconciled to science fiction than he had been in *Forgotten Life*. Indeed, the novel can itself be read, at least marginally, as science fiction. It is, for a start, explicitly linked to *Barefoot in the Head*, which had originally borne the subtitle *A European Fantasia*, although it was dropped from later editions. *Somewhere East of Life* is subtitled *Another European Fantasia*, as if we are meant to read it as a continuation of or at least a response to that earlier novel. In fact, little if any of *Barefoot in the Head* is to be found in *Somewhere East of Life*. The way in which mental and linguistic derangement is used to suggest the moral and physical derangement of war, the whole point of *Barefoot in the Head* finds no echo here. The fragmentary grasp on meaning is replaced by fragmentary memory.

The central character, Roy Burnell, has had ten years of his memories stolen, leaving him with no more than a partial and wildly distorted awareness of a world that is in a process of dramatic change. As he tries to track those memories down through various post-Soviet republics, the holes in his memory are clearly representative of the holes in reality caused by the collapse of the Soviet Union.

In this novel Aldiss is trying to make sense of a world that no longer makes sense on his terms. As John Clute perceives, the novel "says nothing new. Or, more accurately, it tells us that there is nothing new to say."[4] But I think this perception applies not only to this novel but more broadly to Aldiss himself as he approached the end of the twentieth century. The world as he understood it, the world he explored in novel after excoriating novel, was shaped by World War II and by his contempt for the political order that emerged from that war. That was the shape that lay beneath diminished humans fighting in a spaceship in *Non-Stop*, LSD perverting our very notion of reality in *Barefoot in the Head*, or the successive rise and fall of humanity described in the Helliconia Trilogy.

But the death of Joseph Winter suggested that the Forgotten Army was now just a thing of the past, while in *Somewhere East of Life* we learn that those who forget the past are condemned not to repeat it, as George Santayana would have it, but rather to live in a different past. The instruments that Aldiss had used, with varying degrees of success, to confront and condemn the world could not be so readily employed as the world changed. And I think that over the final thirty years of his career Aldiss would increasingly find that he had little new to say about this new reality.

★ ★ ★

There was, in fact, a fifth Squire novel, though it is not generally recognized as such and is never included among what we should perhaps call the Squire Quintet.

The reasons for this are various: the four novels that make up the quartet are among the most assured and successful pieces of writing that Aldiss produced; the fifth was not. The four novels of the quartet are, despite the occasional science-fictional device, intentionally mainstream both in their affect and in the way they are presented; the fifth was not. And the fifth novel came the better part of a decade after *Somewhere East of Life*, long enough to have severed any obvious connection with what came before.

The novel in question, *Super-State* (2002), is nowhere presented as being part of the Squire sequence, but among the huge cast of characters we encounter Ann, Francine, and Jane Squire. And when we learn that the Squire family home, Pippet Hall in Norfolk, is now in danger from rising sea levels because of global warming such that in the foreseeable future the hall and its surroundings "would be swept away—and with them something valuable of English history" (*Su-S*, 24), there is a clear implication that, as in the earlier novels, the Squires are meant to be somehow representative of Englishness. *Englishness* was a very potent term as far as Aldiss was concerned; his autobiography, *The Twinkling of an Eye*, which had appeared just three years earlier, was subtitled *My Life as an Englishman*.

Of course, other than in the first volume, *Life in the West*, the Squires are never much more than supporting players in the novels, and the same is true here. Given the restless way the focus of the novel shifts among the characters, however, it is hard to tell who, if anyone, is meant to be anything other than a supporting player. Just as *Somewhere East of Life* deliberately recalls *Barefoot in the Head*, *Super-State* seems to be almost a rewrite of *The Eighty-Minute Hour*, but without the operatic interludes. Most noticeably, it has the same huge cast and the same propensity for giving many of them silly names such as Amygdella Haze, Dr Barnard Cleeping, and Barbara Barbicandy.

Like *The Eighty-Minute Hour*, *Super-State* begins with a gathering of super-rich people on a private estate, with individuals appearing very briefly before the focus shifts to someone else. We learn little of them other than the fact that they are vapid and self-centered, and everything comes down to their privilege. Like *The Eighty-Minute Hour*, it is a very particular perspective on a future where things are nothing more than an indulgence for the wealthy: "I love plenty of plenty, don't you?" says the especially vapid novelist Rose Baywater. "It's so utterly nice" (*Su-S*, 7). This opening party is the wedding of Victor de Bourcey, son of the president of the European Union, to the restaurateur Esme Brackentoth. But Esme has been detained while opening a new restaurant at the summit of Mount Everest and has sent an android to take her place. Later she is kidnapped by terrorists wanting to get at her new husband's father, yet her reluctant kidnapper turns out to be a young refugee, Karim, and the two fall in love. The story of the hardship and privations that Karim suffered on his way from Iran to Ireland—"a great myth of endurance and protest against the tyrannies of the world" (*Su-S*, 129)—is told in a matter-of-fact, unemotional way that rather calls to mind both *Report on Probability A* and *HARM* (though I wouldn't think to link those two in any other way).

The opening scene reaches its climax when, in contrast to the sort of contempt for nature indicated by Esme's restaurant on Mount Everest, nature turns against the privileged. A tremendous storm builds in the mountains around the setting for the party, thereby putting a herd of wild horses to flight which then stampedes through the bubble of privilege. Such intimations of human endeavor being shattered by the wildness of nature, and the social world thus being diminished, tie this novel to *Hothouse*, *Greybeard*, and Helliconia. The global warming thread and the kidnap thread mingle when the collapse of an ice cliff in Greenland sends a tsunami across the Atlantic toward the west coasts of Britain and Ireland, and where Esme and Karim are killed.

The profusion of plot strands which, as in *The Eighty-Minute Hour*, never quite resolve into a coherent whole, includes the story of a spaceship called the *Roddenberry*—"a tiny needle in the lethal immaculacy of space" (*Su-S*, 96)—that is approaching Jupiter. Beneath the ice of Europa, the *Roddenberry's* crew finds a fish-like being weighing thirty-two grams that it christens Eucarya. But the discovery that we are not alone in the universe has no great effect, other than providing extra stimulation for the EU's war against Tebarou.

Tebarou is a small Muslim state in Asia (we learn very late in the book that it has a border with Laos, which perhaps makes Tebarou roughly equivalent to Aldiss's old stalking ground, Burma) that is in an alliance with Africa, where, we are told, "the deterioration of climate . . . has meant a mass invasion—or attempted invasion—of our shores by the luckless and unskilled" (*Su-S*, 28). Prefiguring the refugee crisis that we have seen over the course of the past few years, and seen exclusively from the perspective of the privileged denizens of the European super-state, this "invasion" has apparently been averted by the use of the military, but it provides sufficient motivation for the European powers to launch their own invasion of a sovereign state. It is no surprise that the few glimpses we have of this war show that things do not go well for the invaders.

In yet another plot strand, we are introduced to the INSANATICS, a protest group that interrupts the ambients (the novel's version of the Internet) with anti-war messages. The first of these echoes a typical Aldiss refrain that takes us back to Charles Berg and *Madkind*: "If war is declared, it is proof once more that mankind is mad" (*Su-S*, 32), and again, "There is no way in which we can ever become humanely rational" (*Su-S*, 33). As Daniel Potts, one of the novel's mouthpieces for Aldiss, says in a long lecture: "I have no doubt that, with the dawn of true wisdom, such matters as war, conquest, retribution would not be allowed admittance into our considerations" (*Su-S*, 89). The INSANATICS ascribe this insanity to the fact that more and more people are moving "away from nature. They thereby starve themselves of the intimations of nature, weather and the seasons" (*Su-S*, 34). The novel thus brings together all of the concerns that had dominated Aldiss's thinking since at least his time in the army about the madness of war, the failure of governments, and the way nature overwhelms humanity.

To this extent, therefore, *Super-State* belongs with the novels of the Squire Quartet, broadly addressing Aldiss's various discontents with the state of the world, his sense that the insanity of the world is a reflection of the insanity of those who, by means of wealth or power run the world. But this has been a consistent theme in his work since his earliest stories; there is nothing new to say because the world itself is nothing new. The trouble is that Aldiss says this less coherently here than in any of his novels, mainstream or science fiction, since *The Eighty-Minute Hour*. And like that earlier novel, this book is filled with too many characters pursuing too many strands of plot, characters who are distinguished by their names but not by anything that amounts to individuality or personality. As one character remarks, among the fleeting glimpses of largely uninteresting betrayals and adulteries: "What misery there was in the fucking world . . . You had to fight . . . to take what pleasure you could, just as you struggled to keep yourself warm against the metaphysical cold" (*Su-S*, 135). But this book is more interested in the metaphysical cold than in the fight or in those doing the fighting; it is a schema for a novel rather than a novel.

★ ★ ★

As with the other Squire books, *Super-State* is ostensibly about the present, but its gaze is unflinchingly on the past. Joseph Winter's time in Burma is more full of life than Clem's dull present; Roy Burnell's lost memories of ten years ago do more to define him than anything in his present life. And in their deliberate echoes of *Barefoot in the Head* and *The Eighty-Minute Hour*, both *Somewhere East of Life* and *Super-State* direct us back to Aldiss's writing of a quarter of a century earlier.

But this heavy emphasis on the past is a characteristic of nearly all of Aldiss's work in the twenty years or so after Helliconia. His looking backward at his own work in *Somewhere East of Life* and *Super-State*, for instance, is also there in his first full-length work of science fiction to appear after Helliconia. Variously called *The Year Before Yesterday* in the United States and *Cracken at Critical* in the United Kingdom, this was an updating of two very early works, the novella "Equator" (also published as *Vanguard from Alpha*), which first appeared in *New Worlds* in 1958, and the novelette "The Impossible Smile," which was first published under the pseudonym Jael Cracken in *Science Fantasy* in 1965. These are crude, formulaic works of the sort that he himself would describe as hokum, "sheerly appalling vintage science fiction"[5] as Gwyneth Jones puts it, and it is interesting that after the serious effort of the Helliconia Trilogy Aldiss should return to such highly colored works.

The two stories are interpolated into a linking narrative called "The Mannerheim Symphony," and the narrator of that story refers to them as "the world of trash" (*CaC*, 18). Although Aldiss makes considerable changes to the stories, particularly to "Equator," he does nothing to diminish their crudities. "Equator," for instance, sees the World Government of the original changed to "Company Earth," a corporatizing that subtly changes the dynamic of the story. Those who ask to visit the Rosk ship in the original are "politely refused admittance, and provided with acceptable explanations" (*EQ*, 11); in the revised version they are "fobbed off with a varying stream of excuses. Rancour [begins] to enter the fragile relationship" (*CaC*, 114). And he introduces a long aside about Gaia that was nowhere in the original, understandably so because James Lovelock was ten years or more from formulating his hypothesis when Aldiss first wrote the novella. Yet the story of a chisel-jawed heroic spaceman, mysterious aliens, and duplicitous Earth agents remains a garish and unconvincing adventure.

"The Impossible Smile" is an alternate history featuring secret agents battling the Germans, who have won World War II. It is, like "Equator," overloaded with coincidences, desperate escapes, and people behaving uncharacteristically to ensure that the hero is not killed. At the core of the story the telepathic hero, Wyvern, is linked to a supercomputer on the Moon as part of a Nazi plot, but he instantly forms an alliance with the computer that effectively gives him near superpowers. It is twenty-year-old hokum, and Aldiss clearly relishes its clichés.

The encompassing material, "The Mannerheim Symphony," also has an alternate history setting in which Churchill was assassinated before World War II and Germany is now ascendant, which rather undermines the embedded story, "The Impossible Smile." It is not clear why, in a world controlled by the Nazis, anyone would think to write a "maybe-myth" (in the novel's coinage for science fiction) about Germany's winning. But Aldiss was not obviously concerned with such logical niceties. Despite Jon Wallace's rather grand claim that *Cracken at Critical* puts generic science fiction into "a more complex framework, and examin[es it] with a modern, more critical eye,"[6] I suspect that this was Aldiss's attempt to cut loose from the complexities of Helliconia and turn back to a simpler form of science fiction in which he didn't have to think about it too much.

"The Mannerheim Symphony" begins with an unnamed composer walking home after the triumphant debut of his second symphony. As I have noted elsewhere, Aldiss here writes of classical music with much more warmth and confidence—"the dark exultant strains of my last movement, which had expanded as never before the sombre chords of my tonal palette" (*CaC*, 8)—than he ever displays in writing about pop or rock music. The elated composer is musing on a comment by Sibelius that music is the bridge between "the everyday world of appearances and the magic world of the inner life" (*CaC*, 7), so when he stumbles on the body of a murdered girl, "it [is] difficult at first to determine whether the dead girl was from the world of appearances or the world of inner life" (*CaC*, 7). The sense of movement between worlds, between appearance and reality, so heavily prefigured here never really materializes in the book.

The dead girl, for instance, is all appearance but no substance. Aldiss seems to have taken his reversion to an old form of science fiction as an opportunity to abandon the competent independent women who sometimes appeared, for instance, in Helliconia, in favor of the object of sexual desire. When the composer discovers the girl's body he is more concerned with what is revealed by her nakedness than he is with the fact of her death or the thought of her suffering. Later, it is revealed that he had recently had an affair with the girl, but at first he seems not to recognize her, presumably too interested in her naked body to notice her face or to feel any human connection with her. It is only after he learns her name that he thinks to cover her face.

But the girl is nothing more than an object, a device to set the plot moving. She had visited his house just before her death; did the composer's wife recognize her or know of the affair? The girl is apparently an American agent working against the Nazi government, though whether and to what extent the composer might be involved is unclear. And she is carrying the two trashy paperbacks, the "maybe-myths," that both we and the composer will read during the course of the novel. *Cracken at Critical* is little more than a means of directing us back to those early Aldiss stories, which are repeatedly described as trashy yet in which Aldiss was so invested that he went to the trouble of revising them and including them here.

★   ★   ★

Autobiographical elements had appeared not only in Aldiss's mainstream fiction from *The Hand-Reared Boy* onwards but also, rather more disguised, in science fiction novels such as *Non-Stop* and *Cryptozoic*. Inevitably, perhaps, this led to more overt autobiographical writing, beginning with "Magic and Bare Boards," which first appeared in 1974 as part of the Profession of Science Fiction series published in *Foundation* before being reprinted as Aldiss's contribution to *Hell's Cartographers*, a collection of short personal histories of science fiction writers that he co-edited with Harry Harrison.

But Aldiss's exploration of his personal history began in earnest with *Bury My Heart at W. H. Smith's*, which is really a collection of anecdotes about his life as a writer. He was always a good raconteur. For those who remember him, often the first thing that comes to mind is listening to his endless tales, often salacious, always gossipy, about his encounters with other science fiction writers. Such tale telling, "the tale of a mask that cannot keep a secret,"[7] as John Clute puts it, is what *Bury My Heart at W. H. Smith's* is all about. The stories are entertaining and well polished, but so they should be, having been told many times, and I suspect it was becoming difficult to tell the difference between the life and the stories told about that life.

That certainly became the case when, a few years later, Aldiss finally produced his autobiography, *The Twinkling of an Eye: My Life as an Englishman*, one of the longest and to a degree one of the best books he wrote. As a memoir it is not totally reliable, and it contains enough errors of fact to raise doubts in the reader. But what is interesting is where the focus of the story lies.

The first half of the book is divided fairly evenly between Aldiss's childhood and his wartime experiences. The ways in which he talks about these two formative stages, however, are completely different. As might be evident from all we have seen so far of both the life and the fiction, the account of his childhood is full of alienation, exclusion, and abandonment. By contrast, his description of army life is full of camaraderie, a feeling of belonging that he had not felt before then. Despite the dangers inherent in stalking an unseen enemy through dense jungle, the sense that comes across time and time again is one of happiness. It was perhaps the happiest time of his life, and it was in a setting in which everything, the color, the heat, the vegetation, was unlike anything he had ever known before. The experience of being at war, the contempt of the common soldier for those in command, and the landscape that defined this experience all appear repeatedly in his fictions, but they are always transmuted (for instance, into the densely overgrown passages of the ship in *Non-Stop*). It is as if the unhappiness of childhood was something he had to express directly in order to try to get it out of his system, while the happiness associated with his time in the East gave his imagination free rein to play with ideas and images.

When Aldiss returns to Britain in the midst of postwar austerity the sense of companionship is lost and the disengagement of his childhood is re-established. The book's subtitle seems ironic, because although he has precise and surprisingly conservative views concerning what Englishness (not, you note, Britishness) means, at the same time he is like an exile in his own land, as though, Gary Wolfe suggests, "he's watching his past the way the figures in *Report on Probability A* look at each other."[8] It is an astute observation. After his intense engagement with his army comrades in Burma, once he returns to Britain Aldiss always feels as though he is on the outside looking in. This perhaps explains the disconnected, almost voyeuristic feeling that one gets throughout his career, from the earliest work such as "Outside" to *Greybeard*, *Report on Probability A*, and *Helliconia Winter*. Brian Aldiss was raised in what Clute calls "the Land of Ago,"[9] a land that, as a child, he was denied, and that was, in the postwar settlement, lost. The "melancholy harshness"[10] (another Clutean term) apparent in so much of Aldiss's best work is here made flesh in his sense of his own life.

Other than these two formative periods, what is central to the book is not writing, or later hard-drinking friendships with such people as Harry Harrison and Kingsley Amis that sometimes feel like an attempt to recapture the masculine camaraderie of the army, but sex. From his sexual initiation at the hands of the matron at his last school (an incident that is repeated in *The Hand-Reared Boy*), his sense of self-worth seems to have been inextricably linked to what I have called priapic masculinity, the sexual adventuring that shaped his life. He recounts the many prostitutes he visited during his time in the army in India, Sumatra, and Hong Kong. After the breakup of his first marriage, he regrets the temporary loss of contact with his children that resulted but not the affairs that caused it. And the later parts of the autobiography are a constant hymn of praise to the wonders of his second wife, Margaret, but you don't have to be an expert at reading between the lines to notice the quarrels and periods of estrangement that seem to have resulted from extramarital relationships. There were times when one suspects, as I have suggested, that Aldiss saw himself as H. G. Wells, with Margaret taking on the role of Jane, except that I imagine Margaret was rather less willing to overlook Aldiss's sexual adventures than Jane was Wells's.

The Twinkling of an Eye seems to have been a long time in development. It would have been finished by 1997, because it contains no mention of the sudden death of Margaret Aldiss that year. But he followed the autobiography quickly with a supplementary volume constructed mostly from the diaries that both had kept during the latter stages of her cancer. *When the Feast Is Finished* (1999) is not a book that Margaret Aldiss would have welcomed. In a review that is, in large part, personal memoir, Colin Greenland notes that "personal attention was something she was inclined to deflect."[11] That is not something that could be said of Aldiss, and he confessed in the book that he was "sustained by the drama of it" until after her funeral, when "the real emptiness entered."[12]

However much his sexual attention might have wandered during their marriage, something went out of Aldiss's life and his writing when Margaret died. She had been his most consistent bibliographer; her original 1962 work, *Item Forty-Three*, had grown over the years into a 360-page annotated bibliography and guide, *The Work of Brian W. Aldiss* (1992). She had kept his papers and his finances in order, and as "The Girl and the Robot with Flowers" shows, she had been the sounding board who exerted a quiet influence on his writing.

★   ★   ★

The first novel to appear after Margaret's death shows the want of that influence. It is also the only novel he wrote that is credited as a collaboration, as though Aldiss felt the need for an extra voice overseeing the composition. In a letter to *Foundation* he notes that Margaret was dying as he wrote the novel: "I would never have completed the book without my necessary collaboration with Roger Penrose, to whom I owed and owe a great debt."[13]

His collaborator on *White Mars*, Sir Roger Penrose, was Rouse Ball Professor of Mathematics at the University of Oxford. The pair met when Aldiss sold his house to Penrose. It is not clear what Penrose's contribution to the novel was; it may be that he started out simply advising Aldiss on some of the scientific ideas mentioned in the book, much like the numerous scientific advisors who helped with Helliconia. The bulk of the novel seems to be entirely Aldiss's conception and creation, and Penrose has no other work of fiction to his name.

Like much else that Aldiss was writing during the 1990s and early 2000s, it is a book that references the past. The full title, *White Mars: Or, The Mind Set Free, A 21st-Century Utopia*, plays with the 1914 novel by Wells, *The World Set Free*, which posited the idea of nuclear weapons, and possibly also his late work of nonfiction, *Mind at the End of Its Tether* (1945), which presented the idea of humanity being replaced by a more advanced species of being. These two books are among the more pessimistic of Wells's works. *White Mars* is also an obvious rejoinder to the Mars Trilogy of Kim Stanley Robinson—*Red Mars* (1992), *Green Mars* (1993), and *Blue Mars* (1996)—which explored the political and practical issues surrounding the terraforming of that planet (coincidentally, Aldiss's appeal to Antarctica as the model for a White Mars anticipates Robinson's own *Antarctica*, which appeared later that year). Aldiss acknowledges Robinson by naming a street in his Martian community K. S. Robinson Avenue. In keeping with the way Aldiss has referenced other science fiction figures throughout his career, other streets are named for Konstantin Tsiolkovski and Ben Bova.

The idea of a White Mars was prefigured in January 1997 in a pamphlet that Aldiss distributed at Green College, Oxford (which later merged with Templeton College to form Green Templeton College, one of the newest graduate colleges at Oxford, specializing in subjects relating to welfare and environmental well-being). He wrote the pamphlet in his position as president of the Association for the Protection and Integrity of an Unspoilt Mars (APIUM), an organization that he founded, may well have been the sole member of, and which disappeared very quickly. The association's position, as laid out in this pamphlet, which is reproduced as an appendix to the novel, supported manned expeditions to Mars but opposed any idea of terraforming. "Mars must become a UN protectorate, and be treated as a 'planet for science,' much as the Antarctic has been preserved—at least to a great extent—as unspoilt white wilderness. We are for a WHITE MARS!" (*WM*, 323). This pamphlet is clearly the inspiration for the book, which is a polemical expansion of the ideas in the pamphlet. This is obvious from the opening scenes of the novel, featuring a special UN debate in which various arguments are voiced for and against the idea of terraforming Mars. The persuasive argument is the one against terraforming: "This arrival of a crew of men and women on the Red Planet must have nothing to do with conquest" (*WM*, 9). It was time to overthrow the old colonialist ethos: "The planet Mars is a sacrosanct environment and must be treated as such" (*WM*, 9); it must be preserved for science. The first astronauts on Mars say as much when they declare that "to try to alter—to terraform—this ancient place would be wrong. A terrible mistake. Not just for Mars. For us. For all mankind" (*WM*, 16). The pro-terraforming arguments are perfunctory, and the APIUM argument is given at length—this is as much propaganda as fiction.

It is not only the fact that it is a collaboration that marks *White Mars* as an oddity in Aldiss's career; it is also the only book he wrote as an overt utopia. This would seem to be antithetical to everything Aldiss believed, since his work consistently argued that war was inevitable, that humanity was inherently destructive, and that nature would win out over whatever passed for civilization. There are hints of utopian ideas in earlier novels, but they are always undermined. *The Primal Urge* presents a vision of complete sexual liberation, something that Aldiss himself would have welcomed, but human behavior is such that it leads to disorder. The citizens of the communist state in *Enemies of the System* address each other as Utopian; they have been conditioned to believe that their society is indeed a utopia but in reality it is morally and creatively dead. The same applies to *The Malacia Tapestry*, which concerns another society that has reached a state of complete inertia. As one of the characters says in *Super-State*: "We live in what our grandparents would have called a material utopia; yet misery plays as large a part in human life as ever" (*Su-S*, 86). There is, in Aldiss's view, no place within the human character for the perfections of a utopia. As he put it in *Billion Year Spree*: "The trouble with utopias is that they are too orderly. They rule out the irrational in man, and the irrational is the great discovery of the last hundred years" (*BYS*, 75–76). That he should still turn toward the idea of a utopia at this point is, therefore, intriguing. Was it an accident of timing, the need to present something positive at what would have been, for him, an emotional low ebb? Or was it that the blank slate of a White Mars would be more powerfully argued if it was suggested that this might provide a setting for a better society?

Whichever it might have been, the presentation of a utopia in this novel is surprisingly conventional. Until the time of Wells, a utopia was invariably a static society that had been created at some distant point in the past by one great and far-sighted personality such as Thomas More's King Utopus. With *A Modern Utopia* (1905) Wells upended that notion, making a utopia a process, not a destination. Aldiss and Penrose follow Wells in making the Martian utopia a process, writing "I . . . came to see utopia as a condition of becoming, a glow in the distance, a journey for which human limitations precluded an end" (*WM*, 260), but they follow More in making it a process initiated and guided by one man, in this case Tom Jefferies. And as is often the case in such worlds, people seem to behave unbelievably wisely and skillfully when it comes to operating their utopia. Thus, when Jefferies sets his utopian plans in motion with a questionnaire sent to everyone on Mars, "91 per cent of the domes' inhabitants" (*WM*, 53) answer, an unbelievably high response rate for any survey. And, of course, Jefferies is conveniently able to call on "the assistance of able organisers" (*WM*, 53). When you're a wise leader establishing a utopia, it is clear that everything works better than it does in reality. It is usual for those who believe in logic to assume that everyone else will be swayed by a logical argument—the benefits of longevity are spelled out as the opportunity to "achieve true rationality and experience the pleasures of untroubled intellect" (*WM*, 278)—and that is a common aspect of top-down utopias such as this.

Travel to and from Mars is under the control of an outfit called EUPACUS (EU, Pacific Rim, and US). When a massive fraud is discovered all flights to and from Mars are stopped, and the repercussions of the fraud rapidly lead to the meltdown of the entire world economy. Earth is here treated with the sort of sour disdain that is typical of Aldiss's more general view of human society:

> To gratify its desire for profit and then more profit, capitalism had required economies of abundance, plus economies of scarcity into whose markets its entrepreneurs could infiltrate. Now, under this guiding but predatory spirit, there existed

only the voracious developed world and a few bankrupt states, mainly in Africa and Central Asia . . . Prisons filled. Stomachs went empty. (*WM*, 39).

The result of this economic collapse is the isolation of Mars, and it is this that allows the great Tom Jefferies to plan his "constitution for utopia" (*WM*, 51).

White Mars allows no more room for "the irrational in man" than do any of the other utopias that Aldiss disdained in *Billion Year Spree*. Thus every obstacle to the perfection of society can be easily overcome by common sense and the application of logic. When, for instance, Jefferies's meeting is interrupted by masked men fighting on behalf of the overthrown EUPACUS, they are easily overcome by the mob, and then Jefferies addresses them with a few well-chosen words that instantly convert the leader of the masked men to his cause. And we get largely unsubstantiated statements such as this: "Were it not for our anthropocentrism, we would long ago have established a law, observed by all, against the pollution of the oceans, the desecration of the land, and the destruction of the ozone layer" (*WM*, 64). A nice thought, but greed and selfishness are more likely villains here than anthropocentrism, and when has any law been observed by all?

Throughout the bulk of the novel there is a sense that if something seems logical, then everyone will, of course, go along with it. The persistent problem with utopias is referred to—"the mutuality required for a just society implie[s] that we must hope to improve the individual" (*WM*, 114)—without ever really being addressed. Thus, we are told that "the provocations of racism" had been removed because "we were all in the same boat, rather than in many jostling boats" (*WM*, 115). But racism tends to be a particular problem when everyone is in the same boat and looking for excuses to exclude some from access to the limited resources. Everyone wants to do the right and decent thing, assuming there might ever be agreement as to what the right and decent thing actually is, and so anyone who "reject[s] everything offered them in the way of enlightenment" (*WM*, 122) is described as a malcontent, whereas "people are surprisingly willing to assist when they see a worthwhile enterprise" (*WM*, 232). And it is assumed that common sense is actually common, that "like all good radical plans for mankind's happiness, it contains nothing that most sensible people don't already know" (*WM*, 222). And, naturally, every issue that confronts the nascent utopia, such as crime or discontent, arises in series rather than at the same time and is unrelated to everything else, allowing it to be solved in isolation before switching attention to the next issue in line. Aldiss's utopia works only because he goes directly against every sour and disdainful view of humanity he had espoused in all of his previous novels.

Of course, as easily as the problems of racism might be solved by the application of rational thought, this doesn't preclude a remarkably old-fashioned view of the role of women in this brave new society. Thus, we are told by Aldiss's mouthpiece in the novel that "the centre of 'family life' [is] the woman who must bring forth a new generation, and both she and her children [need] such protection as a male could give" (*WM*, 65). And at one point Cang Hai, Jefferies's daughter, escapes an attempted rape by masturbating the man instead and is later praised for evading rape "as any woman might have done, had she [a] cool enough head" (*WM*, 238). As we saw in relation to *Cracken at Critical*, any temporary sense of independence that women might have achieved in, for instance, *Helliconia Spring* is lost the moment Aldiss reverts to an older form of science fiction.

At some point Aldiss realizes that this unproblematic stroll toward this utopia requires something in the way of plot, which is where the scientific community comes in. The scientific base is separate from the settlement where most of the story takes place, and the scientists have little or no interest in the social and political changes that Jefferies is setting in motion. The scientific idea that runs through the novel (presumably the aspect provided by Penrose) is the search for the Higgs boson. At the time this novel was written, the Large Hadron Collider had been planned but not built, and the Higgs boson was no more than a theoretical assumption. The novel assumes that the LHC failed to find the Higgs boson but instead found a "smudge" roughly where the boson should be. Further smudges were subsequently discovered in a seemingly regular pattern that says something profound about the nature of reality. The search for these smudges is being conducted on Mars at the same time as the experiment in utopianism. All of this, however, is wrapped up in scientific and pseudo-scientific lectures of such tedium that it is difficult to make out anything dramatic in this new search.

Now, tongue-like protuberances start to be noticed around the scientific base, and one of the scientists claims: "Olympus Mons is not a geological object. Olympus Mons is a sentient being of a unique kind" (*WM*, 186). It is, in short, a huge and apparently intelligent barnacle. The thing, Olympus, also called Chimborazo, is assumed to be a composite being made up of all life on Mars, which came together in this form as a way of surviving in the planet's harsh environment. The thing therefore serves as a metaphor for the experiment in utopianism, in which humanity is coming together in co-operative form as "a new step forward in human consciousness, represented by the word 'utopian'" (*WM*, 198). But following this first contact with a massive and intelligent alien life form, Chimborazo first becomes an object of wonder to distract the humans from whichever petty problem has arisen to interrupt their inevitable advance towards their utopia and then a possible *deus ex machina* to allow everything to turn out right.

White Mars is marred by its atrocious sexual politics, its naiveté about the practicalities of establishing a utopia, and the sense that the author of Aldiss's previous books couldn't possibly believe a word of this. On top of that, it is dull. (K. V. Bailey, always a generous reviewer, considered the novel an "odd hybrid" whose "page after page [of] dialogue and discussion" was "familiar stock of the utopian genre."[14]) Aldiss wrote some very good books and some very bad books in his time, but none of them have ever been so remorselessly dull as this one. The characters are without character, plot is entirely absent, and the writing is uniform, monotonous. There is nothing here to engage the eye or the mind. Aldiss always had a love of long and obscure words, which litter his books. They often seem awkward, with characters using a vocabulary that they are unlikely to possess. But here there's a clumsiness to it, also. In one typical exchange late in the novel we get: "'you will turn us yet into a pack of coenobitic monks,' Crispin said, in his usual jocular fashion" (*WM*, 302). There are more familiar words to be used in casual conversation (*coenobitic* refers to a community of monks), and there is nothing jocular about either the remark or the phrasing. For all that the idea of a White Mars seems to have exercised Aldiss (two years later he further explored the underlying ideas in a story called "A Whiter Mars: A Socratic Dialogue of Times to Come," which he included in his 2001 collection *Supertoys Last All Summer Long and Other Stories of Future Time*), this is a novel to which he seems to have devoted little in the way of attention or interest.

Despite this, and I think that to some degree Aldiss must have been aware that it is an awkward, rather clumsy novel, he was very protective of it. When, in 2005, Elizabeth Leane published a paper in *Foundation* exploring the way *White Mars* "conducts its own playful dialogue with the discourse of popular science books, while engaging seriously with issues of science policy,"[15] on the whole a very positive take on the novel, Aldiss complained that she did not discuss "the logical utopian nature of aspects of the Martian landscape" or recognize that the book "is an intricately constructed polemic."[16] Aside from the fact that such considerations would have been beyond the purview of Leane's paper, this response, unusual even for Aldiss, who could be very touchy at times, seems oddly defensive. The fact that he references his wife's death in the letter suggests that the personal circumstances in which the book was written meant that it had to be cushioned from anything he might conceive as criticism, though Aldiss the critic would have been quick to disavow such a response in others.

★　★　★

With the new century, a change occurred in Aldiss's publishing history. To that point almost all of his work had been published by prestigious names such as Faber, Cape, HarperCollins, and Gollancz. But of the eighteen books that appeared between 2001 and the end of his life, eight were published by The Friday Project, an enterprise set up exclusively to publish or bring back into print the works of Brian Aldiss. (The Friday Project died when Aldiss did; subsequent volumes of *The Complete Short Stories* covering the 1970s, 1980s, and 1990s were advertised but never appeared.) Six others were brought out by small or specialist presses, including a collection of essays, *An Exile on Planet Earth* (2012), that was published by the Bodleian Library to coincide with the deposit of the Brian Aldiss archive at that library. Only the remaining four books were brought out by the sorts of publishers with which he was more normally associated, including a collection (*Supertoys Last All Summer Long*) and a novel (*Super-State*) from Orbit, a mainstream novel (*Affairs at Hampden Ferrers*, 2004) from Little, Brown, and another science fiction novel (*HARM*, 2007) from Ballantine in New York. One can only conclude that his work was no longer attracting the sales figures or the critical attention it had once done.

Yet, while his novels might have gone off the boil, his short story writing continued unabated. Throughout the 1990s and early 2000s, Aldiss was producing stories at pretty much the same rate he had been doing since the 1970s, and a number of these were being included in Best of the Year anthologies and being shortlisted for awards. True, some of these were extracts from the novels he was writing or at least companion pieces to those novels. Two of the best stories from the early 1990s, for instance, "FOAM" (1991) and "Friendship Bridge" (1993), were associated with his mainstream novel *Somewhere East of Life*, though the stories themselves first appeared in the anthologies *New Worlds 1* and *New Worlds 3*, both edited by David Garnett, thus demonstrating the generic instability of that novel. And the late stories in, say, *Cultural Breaks* (2005) often display both the urge to literary experimentation and the impish sense of humor that have been familiar in Aldiss's work throughout his career. "Tarzan of the Alps" (2004) is, for instance, the tender story of how the misinterpretation of an old movie steers a couple through the misfortunes of life in a remote part of South America.

There was still a sense of the New Wave writer in the way Aldiss combined what he elsewhere called the "wide-screen baroque" of space opera with surrealism in stories such as "Aboard the *Beatitude*" (2002), in which entire civilizations are cavalierly consumed as fuel for a starship on the hunt for a criminal galaxy. Such stories are not necessarily among his best works. Aldiss published more than four hundred stories in his career, and his restlessness, his love of experiment, the way his sensibilities ricocheted back and forth between the most conservative science fiction and the wildest surrealism, always edged with a cynical humor, meant that reading any of his collections necessitated, as I said in my review of *Cultural Breaks*, "negotiating occasional pieces that dissipate in inconsequentiality or fizz in bravura but somehow unsatisfactory surreality in order to savour the gems."[17] But that is even more reason to celebrate the occasional gems that Aldiss continued to produce into his ninth decade.

★　★　★

The thing about stories like "Tarzan of the Alps" and "Aboard the *Beatitude*" is that Aldiss was very consciously taking a familiar story or type of story and finding something new in it. It was something he had been doing for his whole career in works as varied as *Non-Stop*, *Frankenstein Unbound*, and *White Mars*. It was there in the way he plundered his own past in *Forgotten Life*, *Cracken at Critical*, and *Super-State*. It was becoming such a consistent feature of his work that it seems to have been an almost unthinking device, but whereas, in a story of half a dozen pages or so it could still be carried off with a certain élan, it was becoming more difficult at novel length. Aldiss's sour disapproval of all that we are, which had been a part of his mental make-up since the moment he arrived back in Britain in 1947, was becoming too much to bear. It would result in what was probably his most bitter account of the wretchedness of what passes for human civilization, *HARM*. But before that there were other novels, not generally well-received and in some cases barely noticed, pointing the way.

The four novels that followed *Super-State* seem to form, more by accident, I suspect, than by design, two pairs of two. *The Cretan Teat* (2002), in which a Byzantine icon becomes the focus of a bawdy account of the collapse of civilization, marries together two familiar Aldiss interests, sex and the downfall of humankind, without quite getting the tonal balance right. His next novel, *Affairs at Hampden Ferrers*, also seems tonally off-key. It is set in a small Oxfordshire village where miracles start to happen. This is the sort of romantic comedy that seems totally unnatural for Brian Aldiss.

As *The Cretan Teat* turns to a more distant past than usual in Aldiss, so does *Jocasta: Wife and Mother* (2005), which reinterprets the familiar Greek myth of Oedipus. Aldiss insists that Jocasta must have been aware that the stranger she married was in fact her own son. In this reinterpretation of the myth, therefore, the mother/wife shares in the guilt of her son/husband: she could have stopped what fate had in store but chose not to. Thus revisiting the "interior lives and reasons, fallible memories, and . . . motives, obvious or ulterior"[18] of these actors in the primal myth, Aldiss reconfigures the Oedipus Complex for a different age.

And while *Affairs at Hampden Ferrers* played with the archetypal characteristics of an English rural fantasia, so *Sanity and the Lady* (2005) presents an equally commonplace literary device, the country house drama. Here the family and associates of Sir Edgar Laurence, gathered at his grand home by the sea, experience alien visitations that cause them all to behave abnormally. Like Jocasta before them, the characters find themselves engaged in long internal dialogues as they attempt to determine who they are, but whereas Jocasta's growing self-knowledge is played out as tragedy, here it is comedy. For John Clute, these novels are the genuine outpouring of old age, "an old man's . . . denatured rumination on the nature of art and consciousness."[19] But the disappointments of a life that didn't meet expectations, turned outward into a more generalized disgust at everything in the world that was mankind's doing, had been with Aldiss since he left the army. It was there in his earliest fictions. These novels were denatured because he was saying what he had said before, and by turning to types of story that did not suit his style of writing, he was still failing to find a new way of saying the old things.

★　★　★

Then came an opportunity to express his misanthropic view of humanity once more in all its bitterness.

When I said in a review that *HARM* was "the best book [Aldiss] has written in a long time"[20] it wasn't exactly saying much. But *HARM* was informed by an anger that hadn't directly fed into his writing for years, perhaps for decades. The result isn't a great book; it is not one to set alongside *Hothouse* or *Greybeard*, *Report on Probability A* or *Helliconia Winter*, all of which were informed by something intense and personal. By contrast, HARM is jerky, awkwardly constructed, often unconvincing, and generally seems either much too long or much too short for what it is trying to do, yet it has a vigor, a passion that makes it stand out from Aldiss's other late work. This wasn't an old man's rumination on art but, rather, a young man's expression of contempt.

It was the time of the war on terror, when the so-called liberal democracies were behaving with increasing illiberality, the time of Guantanamo and black sites and the use of torture by societies that had supposedly long since gone beyond such barbarities. And in Britain the government had passed an ill-conceived law making it a criminal offense to glorify terrorism, though the law was so poorly framed that it was impossible to tell what precisely was meant by glorification or by terrorism. The novel *HARM* was written out of despair at the muddled, repressive, vicious thinking thus exemplified.

The central character is Paul Fadhil Abbas Ali, a young writer of Muslim descent (though he has an Irish wife and declares that he is "not a believer" [*HA*, 39]) who has written a comic fantasy called *The Pied Piper of Hamnet*. The novel is supposedly Wodehousean, but with the best will in the world, while Aldiss might make a decent fist of most types of writing he could never emulate the effortless, effervescent lightness of P. G. Wodehouse. At least, it is hard to think of a Wodehouse novel that might contain the following labored passage, quoted from Paul's book: "They were laughing together as they walked through the park, where no one could overhear their jokes. Harry said, 'What we need to do is blow up the prime minister'" (*HA*, 40). Paul's friends might laugh uproariously at this scene but the British government does not; the authorities take this seriously as a Muslim openly proposing assassination. As a result, Paul finds himself whisked away to a black site, possibly in Uzbekistan, though it is never clear how much reliance we might place on anything that Paul's interrogators say.

In the hands of the Hostile Activities Research Ministry, Paul is subjected to the expected pains and deprivations, though these pale in comparison to what we know of Baghram and Abu Ghraib. But then, Aldiss isn't really interested in the mechanics of torture but in the Kafkaesque world in which it is situated, a world in which there is no truth, no certainty, and in which there can be no such thing as innocence, and hence the truly innocent person has no defense. To this extent, *HARM* is a direct contrast to *White Mars*. In that earlier novel, Aldiss suggested that rational people might rationally bring about a rational society. In *HARM* he suggests that there is no such thing as rationality, that the more a state is guided by logic, the more it is led into nightmare. It is a view far closer to what we have come to expect in a Brian Aldiss novel, so there is no surprise that he carries it off with such conviction.

But as Aldiss so frequently escaped the uncongenial world (from marital spats to the state of the world) via his imagination, so Paul has a means of escape: "he knew a world called Stygia, where there was more hope and less harm than in this world" (*HA*, 10). Colonists arrived on Stygia aboard the *New Worlds*; they came as downloads—"no one had remained physically whole for the long journey" (*HA*, 97)—and on arrival the Life Process Reservoirs had been implanted in artificially grown bodies to which a computer assigned names at random. At one point Fremant, Paul's avatar, who is familiarly and with heavy symbolism known as "Free," works for "a big, blank-looking man" (*HA*, 96), which in effect is all of them; they are blank people, without history, without identity.

The idea, presumably, is that from this literal blank slate a new, better, utopian society might emerge. It is not to be. The disassociation of the Stygians from the people they once were means that they are not whole; bits of the past filter through but lack coherence or context or understanding. Those who remember something of politics become dictators, those who remember religion establish harsh puritanical communities, and those who remember science create an immoral, unfeeling scientism. Politics, religion, science, all are equally corrupting without humanity, and thus any utopia that draws on such ideas is cruelly distorted before it has started.

As Stygia grows to take over the bulk of the novel, the focus becomes a journey that Fremant undertakes across the blighted landscape. The ostensive quest is to find the last survivor of the intelligent native species that had been wiped out by the colonizers. But really it is an expression of guilt, which Aldiss here considers the natural state of humankind, and the quest is thus a symbolic search for humanity. With the Stygian tale darkening steadily from prospective utopia to distinct dystopia, so the parallels between Paul's two worlds, within his cell and within the confines of his imagination, become ever more distinct. In a sense, therefore, this becomes a novel about writing a novel, or more particularly about Aldiss's career as a novelist, the way his perceptions of the outer world are inevitably reflected within the imagined worlds. And it shows how isolated and isolating it is to be within the Aldiss imagination.

★ ★ ★

If *HARM* had been his last novel, Aldiss's career would have ended, if not on a high, then at least with a bang, with a novel that had something of the impact of his best work.

But there was something compulsive in his writing now. In September 2012 he wrote a short story every day for a month; these were the stories that would comprise *The Invention of Happiness* (2013). It was as though he felt he had to push himself until he dropped. *Walcot* (2009) was another mainstream novel that plundered his own life, following a family from a Norfolk childhood, through the war, and on across the sweep of the twentieth century. Then, after a brief hiatus, came both his last mainstream novel, *Comfort Zone* (2013), and *Finches of Mars* (2013), a novel which he announced in advance would be his last work of science fiction. *Comfort Zone* echoes some of the concerns of *HARM*—prejudices are awakened by plans to build a new mosque in contemporary Oxford—but without the energizing anger of that earlier novel.

Finches of Mars, meanwhile, has a faint echo of *White Mars*. War on Earth, that perennial signifier of failure, has cut off the Martian colony from home. But the colony is in trouble not because of this isolation but because every child born on Mars for the previous ten years has been deformed and stillborn (an echo, perhaps, of the role thalidomide plays in *Moreau's Other Island*). The hope of humanity rests on Mars not because of the creation of a viable utopia, but simply as a place of survival. But that survival is under threat, and the threat is human. As one character perceives in a vision: "mankind had discovered another hell it could occupy . . . [and] . . . was taking great pains to exile there people who would live only in discomfort, creating, spreading, new wickedness" (*FM*, 73). Mars can no more be a utopia than Earth, because humans bring their hell with them.

It is a very typical Brian Aldiss story, but it is not well done. In an interview timed to coincide with the publication of *Finches of Mars* and *Comfort Zone* he claimed: "These days I don't read any science fiction—or do I? Now I only read Tolstoy."[21] That sense of detachment is there in the novel: the writing is weak, the characterization perfunctory. In one of the very few reviews that the book received, Adam Roberts called it an odd swan song: "Some of it is stimulating. Some of it is actively bad."[22] And for Maria Velazquez, "It ultimately offered a premise more interesting than its content, and snippets of plot worthy of better follow-through."[23] The fire that flared briefly in *HARM* had damped down. Aldiss was fast approaching ninety, and he knew his powers were fading. But it was a sad, dispirited end to a career that had seen him become perhaps the most widely recognized and applauded science fiction writer of his generation.

★　★　★

On August 18, 2017, a small group of family and friends gathered at the Oxford home of Brian Aldiss to celebrate his ninety-second birthday. In the early hours of the following morning, Aldiss died.

He had outlived most of his contemporaries, and if the work he'd produced in the last two decades of his career displayed a marked falling-off of quality it was largely because, in his eighties, he was now out of sympathy with the shape of science fiction and with the wider world. But at its best his work had made an indelible impression on the shape of science fiction.

In an appreciation of his old friend, Michael Moorcock said Aldiss could be "brilliant, funny, furiously angry and, above all, enthusiastic." He could also be "generous, petty, tolerant, rude, gracious, charming and cruel—all with the utmost vitality."[24] It is a wonderful tribute to the man, but it is also a perceptive comment on the work. For all of these qualities are found in his best writing. He was a restless writer, uninterested in repeating himself. He wrote only two tightly interwoven sequences of novels, the Horatio Stubbs saga, which drew heavily on the most important influences on his own life, and the Helliconia Trilogy, which covers a period of more than a thousand Earth years, and in which each of the three volumes is set in a very different part of the planet, so that other than setting in the broadest terms and the overarching environmental themes the volumes could as well be three separate novels. (The other apparent sequence, the Squire Quartet, is really four—or perhaps five—very different novels linked only by occasional and generally incidental characters.) Other than these rare exceptions, his whole career can be seen as an effort to find different things to say and different ways to say them. These vary from the bare, unadorned and unemotional prose of *Report on Probability A* to the wild linguistic efflorescence of *Barefoot in the Head*, from the emotional wrench of *Greybeard* to the failure of emotional connection in *The Malacia Tapestry*.

All in all, then, where do we position Brian Aldiss in the history of science fiction? From the 1950s into the 1960s, he used, in the words of Christopher Priest, "familiar generic material [that] gave free rein to his exuberant imagination"[25] and in the process reinvigorated a British science fiction that was becoming staid and unadventurous. With often subtly subversive novels such as *Non-Stop*, *Hothouse*, and *Greybeard* he laid the groundwork for the renewal of that genre in the mid-1960s, when he would become, reluctantly, I suspect, one of what Michael Moorcock has ironically called the "Three Musketeers" of the British New Wave. Older than most of those caught up in the movement, and with a different worldview than many of them, I think it was less that he wrote New Wave stories than that the New Wave aesthetic tended to coincide with the literary experiments he was interested in pursuing at the time. Nevertheless, such stories as "The Girl and the Robot with Flowers" and such novels as *Report on Probability A* and *Barefoot in the Head* came to define what the British New Wave was all about.

By the 1970s he was firmly established in the science fiction community, enjoying a renown that saw the publication of retrospective collections like *Best Science Fiction Stories of Brian W. Aldiss* in Britain and *The Book of Brian Aldiss* in the United States. He started to turn his attention backwards, mining his own life for the three Horatio Stubbs novels, which gained for him a wider literary readership, and establishing a pattern that would recur throughout the remainder of his career. This retrospective mood led him to essay the first major narrative history of science fiction, *Billion Year Spree*, which has had an incalculable influence on science fiction scholarship. True, most scholars now disagree with many of his key points (such as the identification of Mary Shelley's *Frankenstein* as the first science fiction novel), and the historiography of science fiction has changed almost beyond recognition over the course of the intervening nearly half-century, but this book was where it started.

The 1980s saw him undertake a work on a scale he had never attempted before, the Helliconia Trilogy. It was a work that combined romantic storytelling with a doom-laden vision of the human future and startlingly vivid metaphors about the environment. Yet it seems to have been intellectually exhausting, and he would never again (with the possible and partial exception of *HARM*) match the vitality or the necessity of his earlier works. But now, as the twentieth century was drawing to a close, a writer who had been shaped by the war and its aftermath was increasingly out of step. Despite his varied and experimental writing, Aldiss's view of science fiction was forged by the so-called Golden Age, as illustrated not only by the attention it received in *Billion Year Spree* but by the writers he returned to again and again in the numerous anthologies he edited.

Throughout these decades there were consistent themes, often themes that reflected in sometimes oblique ways Aldiss's life experiences. He was perpetually disappointed by humanity, despised political and religious leaders of whatever stripe, saw war as the inevitable expression of failure, considered prudery and sexual repression as indicators of madness, loved the East more than the West, and believed that nature would rightly and necessarily overwhelm human civilization. There are very few of his works in which some combination of these themes cannot be detected. One excellent example might be his story "The Gods in Flight" (1984), which is set on the sort of tropical Eastern island we have met so often in his fiction. Here the locals are getting used to the sudden absence of the Western tourists and military base that did so much for the local economy, while perverting local morals. The West is absent because it has launched a self-destructive war, though from the perspective of the islanders this isn't a total tragedy. But though we might predict where these themes were taking us, he never approached them from the same direction twice. Even when his prose was not overtly experimental, he was always doing something new. In his appreciation of Aldiss, Andy Sawyer says, "My own admiration for him as a writer stemmed from the fact that I was never sure that I would *like* the next book."[26]

That is not an unusual response to Aldiss. When writing about Aldiss within the New Wave, I said that it is hard to see two books that differ so dramatically in tone, approach, and language as *Report on Probability A* and *Barefoot in the Head* as coming from the same writer. That observation could apply to practically everything he wrote, and the unpredictability is both a strength and a weakness. It is a strength in that it makes his work so varied, so unexpected, so challenging: from one book to the next it was impossible to say where his next step might take him. But that is a weakness also, for it means there is no distinctive, readily identifiable trait that immediately marks a book as being by Brian Aldiss. His works were shaped by imponderables such as anger, excitement, restlessness and self-belief, rather than any discernible stylistic quirks, approaches, or subject matter.

Such a weakness may help explain why there is noticeably less scholarship devoted to Aldiss than we might expect for such an important writer. I am not the first person to venture a book-length study of Aldiss's career, but I am the first to do so for thirty-five years, and the most recent of those earlier studies was barely in a position to mention Helliconia. If I have any ambition for this book, therefore, it is not to praise Aldiss but to remind other scholars that he is worthy of serious attention, and in fact he demands such attention.

Simply put, Brian Aldiss was one of the most important science fiction writers of the second half of the twentieth century. He wrote a lot, too much perhaps, and not all of it was good, but when he was at his best his work changed the nature of science fiction and at the same time changed the way we perceive science fiction. There are not many for whom a similar claim could be made. It is impossible to imagine the New Wave without the contribution of Brian Aldiss. It is impossible to imagine postwar British sf without the contribution of Brian Aldiss. It is impossible to imagine the historiography of sf without the contribution of Brian Aldiss. And while there are no writers working in the style of Brian Aldiss, because there is no style of Brian Aldiss, it is nevertheless notable that writers as varied as Christopher Priest, Colin Greenland, and Iain M. Banks have expressed their debt to him. He shaped them, and they shaped the science fiction that was to follow.

Of the eighty books or more that Brian Aldiss wrote, perhaps ten or a dozen will, or at least should, survive. The variety of his work guarantees that opinions will vary as to what they might be, but for my money they would include *Hothouse, Greybeard, Report on Probability A, Billion Year Spree, The Malacia Tapestry,* and the Helliconia Trilogy. That may not seem like much from a career of sixty years, but what books they are!

FICTION

The Brightfount Diaries. 1955. London: Faber [House of Stratus, 2001].

Space, Time and Nathaniel. 1957. London: Faber [Panther, 1979]. Collection.

Non-Stop (Starship). 1958. London: Faber [Grafton, 1987].

The Canopy of Time (Galaxies Like Grains of Sand). 1959. London: Faber [VGSF, 1989]. Collection.

Vanguard from Alpha (Equator and Segregation). 1959. New York: Ace [NEL, 1973].

Bow Down to Nul (The Interpreter). 1960. New York: Ace.

The Male Response. 1961. New York: Beacon.

The Primal Urge 1961. New York: Ballantine [Sphere, 1967].

Hothouse (The Long Afternoon of Earth). 1962. London: Faber [Penguin, 2008].

The Airs of Earth (Starswarm). 1963. London: Faber [Gollancz, 1990]. Collection.

The Dark Light Years. 1964. London: Faber [New English Library, 1971].

Greybeard. 1964. London: Faber [Panther, 1968].

Best Science Fiction Stories of Brian W. Aldiss. 1965. London: Faber. Collection.

Earthworks. 1965. London: Faber [Four Square, 1967].

The Saliva Tree and Other Strange Growths. 1966. London: Faber [Sphere, 1968]. Collection.

An Age (Cryptozoic). 1967. London: Faber [VGSF, 1989].

Report on Probability A. 1968. London: Faber [Sphere;,1969].

Barefoot in the Head. 1969. London: Faber [Corgi, 1971].

Intangibles, Inc. and Other Stories. 1969. London: Faber. Collection.

The Hand-Reared Boy. 1970. London: Weidenfeld and Nicolson [Souvenir Press, 1999].

The Moment of Eclipse. 1970. London: Faber. Collection.

Best Science Fiction Stories of Brian W. Aldiss, rev. ed. . 1971. London: Faber. Collection.

A Soldier Erect, or Further Adventures of the Hand-Reared Boy. 1971. London: Weidenfeld and Nicolson [Corgi Books, 1979].

The Book of Brian Aldiss. 1972. New York: DAW. Collection.

Frankenstein Unbound. 1973. London: Cape [Pan, 1975].

The Eighty Minute Hour. 1974. Garden City, NY: Doubleday [The Friday Project, 2013].

The Malacia Tapestry. 1976. London: Cape [Triad/Panther, 1978].

Brothers of the Head (illus. Ian Pollock). 1977. London: Pierrot [The Friday Project, 2012].

Last Orders and Other Stories. 1977. London: Cape. Collection.

Enemies of the System. 1978. London: Cape [The Friday Project, 2013].

A Rude Awakening. 1978. London: Weidenfeld and Nicolson.

New Arrivals, Old Encounters. 1979. London: Cape. Collection.

Pile: Petals from St. Klaed's Computer (illus. Mike Wilks). 1979. London: Cape.

Life in the West. 1980. London: Weidenfeld and Nicolson.

Moreau's Other Island. 1980. London: Cape [The Friday Project, 2013].

Foreign Bodies: Stories. 1981. Singapore: Chopmen. Collection.

Helliconia Spring. 1982. London: Cape [Triad/Granada, 1983].

Helliconia Summer. 1983. London: Cape [Triad/Panther, 1985].

Seasons in Flight. 1984. London: Cape. Collection.

Helliconia Winter. 1985. London: Cape.

Cracken at Critical (The Year Before Yesterday). 1987. New York: Franklin Watts [Kerosina, 1987].

The Magic of the Past. 1987. Worcester Park, Surrey: Kerosina. Collection.

Ruins (illus. Salim Patell). 1987. London: Century Hutchinson.

Best SF Stories of Brian W. Aldiss, 3rd ed. 1988. London: Gollancz. Collection.

Forgotten Life. 1988. London: Gollancz.

A Romance of the Equator: Best Fantasy Stories. 1989. London: Gollancz [VGSF, 1990]. Collection.

Bodily Functions. 1991. London: Avernus. Collection.

Dracula Unbound. 1991. London: Grafton.

Remembrance Day. 1993. London: HarperCollins.

A Tupolev Too Far and Other Stories. 1993. London: HarperCollins. Collection.

Somewhere East of Life. 1994. London: Flamingo.

The Secret of This Book (Common Clay). 1995. London: HarperCollins. Collection.

White Mars, or The Mind Set Free, a 21st-Century Utopia (with Roger Penrose). 1999. London: Little, Brown [Warner Books, 2000].

Supertoys Last All Summer Long and Other Stories of Future Time. 2001. London: Orbit. Collection.

Super-State. 2002. London: Orbit.

The Cretan Teat. 2002. Thirsk, Yorkshire: House of Stratus.

Affairs at Hampden Ferrers. 2004. London: Little Brown.

Jocasta: Wife and Mother. 2005. London: Rose Press.

Cultural Breaks. 2005. San Francisco: Tachyon. Collection.

Sanity and the Lady. 2005. Hornsea, Yorkshire: PS Publishing.

HARM. 2007. New York: Ballantine.

Walcot. 2009. Uppingham, Rutland: Goldmark.

Comfort Zone. 2013. London: The Friday Project.

Finches of Mars. 2013. London: The Friday Project.

The Complete Short Stories: The 1950s. 2013. London: The Friday Project. Collection.

The Invention of Happiness. 2013. London: The Friday Project. Collection.

The Complete Short Stories: The 1960s, Part 1. 2015. London: The Friday Project. Collection.

The Complete Short Stories: The 1960s, Part 2. 2015. London: The Friday Project. Collection.

The Complete Short Stories: The 1960s, Part 3. 2015. London: The Friday Project. Collection.

The Complete Short Stories: The 1960s, Part 4. 2015. London: The Friday Project. Collection.

NONFICTION

Cities and Stones: A Traveller's Jugoslavia. 1966. London: Faber.

The Shape of Further Things. 1970. London: Faber [Corgi, 1974].

Billion Year Spree: The History of Science Fiction. 1973. London: Weidenfeld and Nicolson [Corgi, 1975].

This World and Nearer Ones: Essays Exploring the Familiar. 1979. London: Weidenfeld and Nicolson.

Trillion Year Spree: The History of Science Fiction (with David Wingrove). 1986. London: Gollancz [Paladin, 1988].

Bury My Heart at W. H. Smith's. 1990. London: Hodder and Stoughton.

The Detached Retina: Aspects of SF and Fantasy. 1995. Liverpool: Liverpool University Press.

The Twinkling of an Eye, or My Life as an Englishman. 1998. London: Little, Brown.

When the Feast Is Finished: Reflections on Terminal Illness. 1999. London: Little, Brown.

An Exile on Planet Earth: Articles and Reflections. 2012. Oxford: Bodleian Library.

EDITED WORKS

Penguin Science Fiction. 1961. Harmondsworth: Penguin.

Best Fantasy Stories. 1962. London: Faber.

More Penguin Science Fiction. 1963. Harmondsworth: Penguin.

Introducing SF. 1964. London: Faber.

Yet More Penguin Science Fiction. 1964. Harmondsworth: Penguin.

Nebula Award Stories Two (with Harry Harrison). 1967. Garden City, NY: Doubleday.

Best SF: 1967 (The Year's Best Science Fiction 1) (with Harry Harrison). 1968. New York: Berkley Medallion.

Farewell, Fantastic Venus! (with Harry Harrison). 1968. London: Macdonald.

Best SF: 1968 (The Year's Best Science Fiction 2) (with Harry Harrison). 1969. New York: Putnam.

Best SF: 1969 (The Year's Best Science Fiction 3) (with Harry Harrison. 1970. New York: Putnam.

Best SF: 1970 (The Year's Best Science Fiction 4) (with Harry Harrison). 1971. New York: Putnam.

The Astounding-Analog Reader, Volume 1 (with Harry Harrison). 1972. Garden City, NY: Doubleday.

Best SF: 1971 (The Year's Best Science Fiction 5) (with Harry Harrison). 1972. New York: Putnam.

The Penguin Science Fiction Omnibus. 1973. Harmondsworth: Penguin.

The Astounding-Analog Reader, Volume Two (with Harry Harrison). 1973. Garden City, NY: Doubleday.

Best SF: 1972 (The Year's Best Science Fiction 6) (with Harry Harrison). 1973. New York: Putnam.

Best SF: 1973 (The Year's Best Science Fiction 7) (with Harry Harrison). 1974. New York: Putnam.

Space Opera: An Anthology of Way-Back-When Futures. 1974. London: Weidenfeld and Nicolson.

Best SF: 1974 (The Year's Best Science Fiction 8) (with Harry Harrison). 1975. Indianapolis, IN: Bobbs-Merrill.

Decade: The 1940s (with Harry Harrison). 1975. London: Macmillan.

Evil Earths: An Anthology of Way-Back-When Futures. 1975. London: Weidenfeld and Nicolson.

Hell's Cartographers: Some Personal Histories of Science Fiction Writers (with Harry Harrison). 1975. London: Weidenfeld and Nicolson.

Science Fiction Art: The Fantasies of SF. 1975. London: New English Library.
Science Fiction Horizons (with Harry Harrison). 1975. New York: Arno.
Space Odysseys: An Anthology of Way-Back-When Futures. 1975. London: Weidenfeld and Nicolson.
Best SF: 75 (*The Year's Best Science Fiction 9*) (with Harry Harrison). 1976. Indianapolis, IN: Bobbs-Merrill.
Decade: The 1950s (with Harry Harrison). 1976. London: Macmillan.
Galactic Empires: An Anthology of Way-Back-When Futures. 1976. London: Futura.
Decade: The 1960s (with Harry Harrison). 1977. London: Macmillan.
Perilous Planets: An Anthology of Way-Back-When Futures. 1978. London: Weidenfeld and Nicolson.
The Book of Mini-Sagas. 1985. Gloucester: Alan Sutton.
The Penguin World Omnibus of Science Fiction (with Sam J. Lundwall). 1986. Harmondsworth: Penguin.
The Book of Mini-Sagas II. 1988. Gloucester: Alan Sutton.
A Science Fiction Omnibus. 2007. Harmondsworth: Penguin.
The Folio Science Fiction Anthology. 2015. London: Folio Society.

SHORT FICTION

1954

"A Book in Time." *The Bookseller*, February 3, 1954 [CSS50].
"The Brightfount Diaries 1." *The Bookseller*, June 12, 1954.
"Criminal Record." *Science Fantasy* 9 [STAN/CSS50].
"The Brightfount Diaries 2." *The Bookseller*, July 17, 1954.
"The Brightfount Diaries 3." *The Bookseller*, July 24, 1954.
"The Brightfount Diaries 4." *The Bookseller*, August 7, 1954.
"The Brightfount Diaries 5." *The Bookseller*, August 28, 1954.
"The Brightfount Diaries 6." *The Bookseller*, September 4, 1954.
"The Brightfount Diaries 7." *The Bookseller*, September 11, 1954.
"The Brightfount Diaries 8." *The Bookseller*, September 18, 1954.
"The Brightfount Diaries 9." *The Bookseller*, September 15, 1954.
"The Brightfount Diaries 10." *The Bookseller*, October 2, 1954.
"The Brightfount Diaries 11." *The Bookseller*, October 16, 1954.
"The Brightfount Diaries 12." *The Bookseller*, October 30, 1954.
"The Brightfount Diaries 13." *The Bookseller*, November 6, 1954.
"The Brightfount Diaries 14." *The Bookseller*, November 13, 1954.
"The Brightfount Diaries 15." *The Bookseller*, November 20, 1954.
"The Brightfount Diaries 16." *The Bookseller*, November 27, 1954.
"The Brightfount Diaries 17." *The Bookseller*, December 11, 1954.
"The Brightfount Diaries 18." *The Bookseller*, December 25, 1954.

1955

"Outside." *New Worlds* 31 [STAN / BSF1 / BSF2 / BSF3 / CSS50].
"The Brightfount Diaries 19." *The Bookseller*, January 8, 1955.

"The Brightfount Diaries 20." *The Bookseller*, January 8, 1955.
"Not For an Age." *The Observer*, January 9, 1955 [STAN / BSF1 / BSF2 / CSS50].
"Breathing Space." *Science Fantasy* 12 [CSS50].
"The Brightfount Diaries 21." *The Bookseller*, February 12, 1955.
"The Brightfount Diaries 22." *The Bookseller*, March 4, 1955.
"The Great Time Hiccup." *Nebula* 12 [CSS50].
"Pogsmith." *Authentic Science Fiction* 57 [STAN / CSS50].
"Our Kind of Knowledge." *New Worlds* 36 [STAN / CSS50].
"Panel Game." *New Worlds* 42 [STAN / CSS50].

1956

"Tradesman's Exit." *The Bookseller*, January 14, 1956 [CSS50].
"Non-Stop." *Science Fantasy* 17 [CSS50].
"There Is a Tide." *New Worlds* 44 [STAN / CSS50].
"The Failed Men" ("Ahead"). *Science Fantasy* 18 [STAN / BSF1 / BSF3 / CSS50].
"Psyclops." *New Worlds* 49 [STAN / CSS50].
"Conviction." *New Worlds* 51 [STAN / CSS50].
"T." *Nebula* 18 [STAN / CSS50].
"Dumb Show." *Nebula* 19 [STAN / BSF1 / CSS50].
"With Esmond in Mind." *Science Fantasy* 20 [CSS50].

1957

"No Gimmick." *Science Fantasy* 21 [CSS50].
"Oh, Ishrael!" *New Worlds* 58 [GGS / CSS50].
"All the World's Tears." *Nebula* 21 [GGS / BSF3 / CSS50].
"Let's Be Frank." *Science Fantasy* 23 [CSS50].
"Gesture of Farewell." *New Worlds* 61 [CSS50].
"The Flowers of the Forest." *Science Fantasy* 24 [CSS50].
"What Triumphs?" ("Visiting Amoeba"). *Authentic Science Fiction* 82 [GGS / CSS50].
"Out of Reach." *Authentic Science Fiction* 83 [GGS / CSS50].
"The Ice Mass Cometh." *Oxford Mail*, December 1, 1957 / *New Worlds* 66 [CSS50].
"The Shubshub Race." [STAN / CSS50].
"Supercity." [STAN / CSS50].

1958

"Judas Dancing." *Star Science Fiction* 1 [GGS / CSS50].
"The New Father Christmas." *The Magazine of Fantasy & Science Fiction*, January 1958 [BSF1 / CSS50].
"The Pit My Parish." *New Worlds* 67 [CSS50].
"Ten-Storey Jigsaw." *Nebula* 26 [CSS50].
"The Carp That Once." *Science Fantasy* 28 [CSS50].
"Poor Little Warrior." *The Magazine of Fantasy & Science Fiction*, April 1958 [BSF1 / BSF2 / BSF3 / CSS50].
"Have Your Hatreds Ready" ("Secret of a Mighty City"). *The Magazine of Fantasy & Science Fiction*, May 1958 [GGS / CSS50].

"Journey to the Interior." ("Gene-Hive") *Nebula* 30 [GGS / CSS50].
"Blighted Profile." *Science Fantasy* 29 [GGS / CSS50].
"But Who Can Replace a Man?" *Infinity* 3 [GGS / BSF1 / BSF2 / BSF3 / CSS50].
"Ninian's Experiences." *Nebula* 31 [CSS50].
"Segregation" ("The Game of God"). *New Worlds* 73 [EQ / SS / CSS50].
"They Shall Inherit." *Nebula* 32 [CT / CSS50].
"Equator." *New Worlds* 75 [EQ / CaC / CSS50].
"Fourth Factor." *Nebula* 34 [CSS50].
"Carrion Country." *New Worlds* 77 [CSS50].
"Sight of a Silhouette." *Nebula* 36 [CSS50].
"Incentive." *New Worlds* 78 [GGS / CSS50].

1959

"The Arm." *Nebula* 38 [CSS50].
"The Unbeaten Track" ("Three's a Cloud"). *New Worlds* 79 [CT / CSS50].
"Intangibles, Inc." *Science Fantasy* 33 [II / CSS50].
"The Lieutenant." *Nebula* 39 [CSS50].
"The Towers of San Ampa." *New Worlds* 80 [CSS50].
"Are You an Android?" *Science Fantasy* 34 [CSS50].
"The Bomb-Proof Bomb." *Oxford Times*, April 10, 1959 [CSS50].
"The Other One." *New Worlds* 82 [CSS50].
"Fortune's Fool." *Science Fantasy* 35 [CSS50].
"Legends of Smith's Burst." *Nebula* 41 [SS / ST / CSS50].
"Safety Valve." *Future Science Fiction* 44 [CSS50].

1960

"Under an English Heaven." *New Worlds* 90 [CSS60.1].
"X for Exploitation." (*Bow Down to Nul*) *New Worlds* 92, 93, 94.
"Faceless Card." *Science Fantasy* 40 [CSS60.1].
"Soldiers Running" ("How to Be a Soldier" / "Hearts and Engines"). *New Worlds* 95 [SS / CSS60.1].
"Stage Struck." *Science Fantasy* 41 [CSS60.1].
"Original Sinner." *Science Fiction Adventures* 15 [CSS60.1].
"A Touch of Neanderthal." ("Neanderthal Planet") *Science Fiction Adventures* 16 [II / CSS60.1].
"Old Hundredth." *New Worlds* 100 [SS / BSF1 / BSF2 / RoE / CSS60.1].

1961

"Hothouse." *The Magazine of Fantasy & Science Fiction*, February 1961 [HH].
"Moon of Delight" ("O Moon of My Delight"). *New Worlds* 104 [SS / CSS60.1].
"Nomansland." *The Magazine of Fantasy & Science Fiction*, April 1961 [HH].
"Undergrowth." *The Magazine of Fantasy & Science Fiction*, July 1961 [HH].
"Hen's Eyes." *Amazing Stories* 35 [CSS60.1].
"Timberline." *The Magazine of Fantasy & Science Fiction*, September 1961 [HH].
"Evergreen." *The Magazine of Fantasy & Science Fiction*, December 1961.

1962

"Basis for Negotiation." *New Worlds* 114 [AoE / BSF1 / CSS60.1].

"Conversation Piece." *New Worlds* 115 [CSS60.1].

"Tyrant's Territory." *Amazing Stories* 36 [CSS60.1].

"Shards." *The Magazine of Fantasy & Science Fiction*, April 1962 [SS / BSF2 / CSS60.1].

"A Kind of Artistry." *The Magazine of Fantasy & Science Fiction*, October 1962 [SS / BSF1 / CSS60.1].

"Matrix" ("Danger: Religion!"). *Science Fantasy* 55 [ST / CSS60.1].

"A Pleasure Shared." *Rogue* 7 / *Science Fantasy* 73 [ST / CSS60.1].

"The Green Leaves of Space." *Daily Express Science Annual* 1 [CSS60.1].

1963

"Comic Inferno." *Galaxy*, February 1963 [BBA / CSS60.2].

"The Under-Privileged." *New Worlds* 130 [SS / BBA / CSS60.2].

"In the Arena." *Worlds of If*, July 1963 [BBA / CSS60.1].

"The Impossible Star." *Worlds of Tomorrow* 1 [BSF1 / BSF2 / CSS60.2].

"The Thing Under the Glacier." *Daily Express Science Annual* 2I *[CSS60.2]*.

"Skeleton Crew." *Science Fantasy* 62 [EW / CSS60.2].

"The International Smile." [AoE / CSS60.2\.

1964

"Counter-Feat." *New Worlds* 139 [CSS60.2].

"One-Way Strait." *New Worlds* 139 [CSS60.2].

"Never Let Go of My Hand." *New Worlds* 142 [CSS60.2].

"Lazarus" (as Jael Cracken). *Science Fantasy* 65 [CSS60.2].

"Pink Plastic Gods." *Science Fantasy* 65 [CSS60.2].

"Unauthorised Persons" (as John Runciman). *Science Fantasy* 65 [CSS60.2].

"Jungle Substitute." *Galaxy*, August 1964 [CSS60.2].

"No Moon Tonight!" (as John Runciman). *Science Fantasy* 66 [CSS60.2].

"Man on Bridge." *New Writings in SF* 1, ed. John Carnell [BSF1 / BSF2 / BSF3 / CSS60.2].

1965

"Scarfe's World." *Worlds of Tomorrow* 2 [CSS60.3].

"Man in His Time." *Science Fantasy* 71 [BSF1 / BSF2 / BSF3 / CSS60.3].

"The Impossible Smile." (as Jael Cracken) *Science Fantasy* 72, 73 [CaC / CSS60.3].

"The Small Betraying Detail." *New Worlds* 150 [CSS60.3].

"The Source." *New Worlds* 153 [ST / RoE / CSS60.3].

"Girl and Robot with Flowers" ("The Girl and the Robot with Flowers"). *New Worlds* 154 [ST / BSF2 /BSF3 / CSS60.3].

"Old Time's Sake." *New Worlds* 154 [CSS60.3].

"The Saliva Tree." *The Magazine of Fantasy & Science Fiction*, September 1965 [ST / BSF3 / CSS60.3].

"The Day of the Doomed King." *Science Fantasy* 78 [ST / RoE / CSS60.3].

"How Are They All on Deneb IV?" (as C. C. Shackleton) *SF Horizons* 2 [CSS60.3].

1966

"The Circulation of the Blood." *Impulse* 1 [MoE / CSS60.3].

"The Oh in José." *Cad* 1 / *Impulse* 5 [SiF / CSS60.3].

"The Lonely Habit." *Ellery Queen's Mystery Magazine*, June 1966 [ST / CSS60.3].

"Amen and Out." *New Worlds* 165 [BBA / NAOE / CSS60.3].

"Heresies of the Huge God." *Galaxy*, August 1966 [MoE / BSF3 / CSS60.3]

"Another Little Boy." *New Worlds* 166 [BSF2 / CSS60.3].

"Lambeth Blossom." *Knight* 5 [CSS60.3]

"Burning Questions." *The Magazine of Fantasy & Science Fiction*, October 1966 [CSS60.3].

"The Eyes of the Blind King." *SF Impulse* 9 [CSS60.3].

"The Plot Sickens." *SF Impulse* 10 [CSS60.3].

"One Role with Relish." [ST / CSS60.3].

"Paternal Care." [ST / CSS60.3].

1967

"Down the Up Escalation." *London Magazine*, February 1967 [MoE / CSS60.4].

"Just Passing Through." *SF Impulse* 12 [BfH / CSS60.4].

"Report on Probability A." *New Worlds* 171 [RPA].

"Randy's Syndrome." *The Magazine of Fantasy & Science Fiction*, April 1967 [II / CSS60.4].

"The Dead Immortal." *Titbits*, May 20, 1967 [CSS60.4].

"Confluence." *Punch*, August 30, 1967 [MoE / BSF3 / TTF / CSS60.4].

"Multi-Value Motorway." *New Worlds* 174 [BfH / CSS60.4].

"Still Trajectories." *New Worlds* 175 [BfH / BSF2 / CSS60.4].

"An Age." *New Worlds* 176, 177, 178 [CZ].

"A Difficult Age." *Nova*, November 1967 [CSS60.4].

"Wonder Weapon." *Nova*, November 1967 [CSS60.4].

"Two Modern Myths: Reflection on Mars, and Ultimate Construction" (as C. C. Shackleton). *Titbits* [CSS60.4].

"Full Sun." *Orbit* 2, ed. Damon Knight [CSS60.4].

"The Night That All Time Broke Out." *Dangerous Visions*, ed. Harlan Ellison [CSS60.4].

"A Taste for Dostoevsky." *New Writings in SF* 10, ed. John Carnell [CSS60.4].

"Auto-Ancestral Fracture" (with C. C.Shackleton). *New Worlds* 178 [BfH / CSS60.4].

1968

"The Serpent of Kundalini" (with C. C. Shackleton). *New Worlds* 179 [BfH / CSS60.4].

"Total Environment." *Galaxy*, February 1968 [CB / CSS60.4].

"Send Her Victorious." *Amazing Stories*, April 1968 [II / BBA / CSS60.4].

"Drake-Man Route." *New Worlds* 182 [BfH / CSS60.4].

"Dreamer, Schemer." *Galaxy*, July 1968 [CSS60.4].

"When I was Very Jung." *Galaxy*, September 1968 [CSS60.4].

"The Village Swindler." *International* 1 [MoE / RoE / CSS60.4].

"The Tell-Tale Heart Machine." *Galaxy*, November 1968 [CSS60.4].

" . . . And the Stagnation of the Heart." *New Worlds* 185 [MoE / CSS60.4].

"Dream of Distance." *Farewell, Fantastic Venus!*, ed. Brian Aldiss and Harry Harrison. [CSS60.4].

"The Worm That Flies." *The Farthest Reaches*, ed. Joseph Elder [MoE / RoE / CSS60.4].

1969

"Ouspenski's Astrobahn." *New Worlds* 186 [BfH / CSS60.4].
"Greeks Bringing Knee-High Gifts." *Galaxy*, March 1969 [CSS60.4].
"Working in the Spaceship Yards." *Punch*, April 9, 1969 [MoE / BSF3 / CSS60.4].
"The Moment of Eclipse." *New Worlds* 190 [MoE / BSF2 / RoE / CSS60.4].
"The Firmament Theorem." *New Worlds* 191 [CSS60.4].
"The Humming Heads." *Solstice* 8 [CSS60.4].
"That Uncomfortable Pause Between Life and Art." *Queen*, July 23, 1969 [MoE / CSS60.4].
"The Soft Predicament." *The Magazine of Fantasy & Science Fiction*, October 1969 [BBA / NAOE / CSS60.4].
"Super-Toys Last All Summer Long." *Harpers Bazaar*, December 1969 [MoE / BSF3 / CSS60.4].
"Since the Assassination." [II / CSS60.4].
"So Far from Prague." *The New SF*, ed. Langdon Jones. [RoE / CSS60.4].

1970

"The Secret of Holman Hunt and the Crude Death Rate." *New Worlds* 197.
"Cardiac Arrest." *Fantastic Stories*, December 1970 [BBA].
"The Weather on Demansky Island." *Quicksilver*, December 1970.
"The Hunter at His Ease." *Science Against Man*, ed. Anthony Cheetham.
"The Day We Embarked for Cythera." [MoE / RoE].
"Orgy of the Living and the Dying." [MoE].
"Swastika!" [MoE / BSF2].

1971

"Sober Noises of Morning in a Marginal Land." [BSF2 / BSF3].

1972

"As for Our Fatal Continuity." *New Worlds Quarterly* 3 [BBA].
"The Ergot Show." *Nova* 2, ed. Harry Harrison.
"Manuscript Found in a Police State." *Winter's Tales* 18, ed. A. D. Maclean.

1973

"A Spot of Konfrontation." *Penthouse*, April 1973 [NAOE].
"Serpent Burning on an Altar." *Orbit* 12, ed. Damon Knight [MT].
"Woman in Sunlight with Mandoline." *Orbit* 12, ed. Damon Knight [MT].
"The Young Soldier's Horoscope." *Orbit* 12, ed. Damon Knight [MT].
"Castle Scene with Penitents." *Orbit* 12, ed. Damon Knight [MT / RoE].
"The Expensive Delicate Ship." *Nova* 3, ed. Harry Harrison [LO].
"The Planet at the Bottom of the Garden." *Edge* 5/6.
"Three Enigmas: The Enigma of Her Voyage; I Ching, Who You?; The Great Chain of Being What?" *New Writings in SF* 22, ed. Kenneth Bulmer.
"Three Enigmas II: All Those Enduring Old Charms; The Eternal Theme of Exile; Nobody Spoke or Waved Goodbye." *New Writings in SF* 23, ed. Kenneth Bulmer [LO].
"Strange in a Familiar Way." *Beyond This Horizon*, ed. Christopher Carrell.

1974

"Melancholia Has a Plastic Core" *Science Fiction Monthly* 1.

"Listen with Big Brother" ("Wired for Sound") *Punch*, January 1974 [LO].

"Three Songs for Enigmatic Lovers: A One-Man Expedition Through Life; The Taste of Shrapnel; 40 Million Miles from the Nearest Blonde" *The Magazine of Fantasy & Science Fiction*, November 1974.

"Diagrams for Three Enigmatic Stories: The Girl in the Tau Dream; The Immobility Crew; The Cultural Side Effects" *Final Stage*, ed. Edward L. Ferman and Barry Malzberg. [LO].

"Live? Our Computers Will Do That for Us" *Orbit* 15, ed. Damon Knight. [LO].

"The Monsters of Ingratitude IV" *Nova* 4, ed. Harry Harrison.

"Three Enigmas III: All in God's Mind. The Unbearableness of Other Lives; The Old Fleeing and Fleeting Image; Looking on the Sunny Side of an Eclipse." *New Writings in SF* 24, ed. Kenneth Bulmer.

1975

"The Aperture Moment: Waiting for the Universe to Begin; But Without Orifices; Aimez-Vous Holman Hunt?" *Epoch*, ed. Robert Silverberg an Roger Elwood [LO].

"Three Coins in Enigmatic Fountains, Three Enigmas IV: Carefully Observed Women; The Daffodil Returns the Smile; The Year of the Quiet Computer" ("Three Coins in Clockwork Fountains"). *New Writings in SF* 26, ed. Kenneth Bulmer [LO].

"What You Get for Your Dollar." *The New Improved Sun*, ed. Thomas M. Disch.

"Year by Year the Evil Gains, Three Deadly Enigmas V: Within the Black Circle; Killing off the Big Animals; What Are You Doing, Why Are You Doing It?" *New Writings in SF* 27, ed. Kenneth Bulmer [LO].

1976

"Excommunication." *New Foundation* 1.

"Nipples as an Index of Character." *Commentary, Journal of the University of Singapore Society*, May 1976.

"Always Somebody There." *Tomorrow*, ed. Roger Elwood.

"An Appearance of Life." *Andromeda* 1, ed. Peter Weston [LO / BSF3].

"The Dark Soul of the Night." *The Ides of Tomorrow*, ed. Terry Carr [BSF3].

"How Did the Dinosaurs Do It?" *Citadel*, 1976.

"Journey to the Heartland." *Universe* 6, ed. Terry Carr [LO].

"Last Orders." *SF Digest* 1 [LO / BSF3].

"A Space for Reflection." *New Writings in SF* 29, ed. Kenneth Bulmer [NAOE].

1977

"Where the Lines Converge." *Galileo*, April 1977.

"Backwater." *Ambit* 69 [LO].

"The Bang-Bang." *A Book of Contemporary Nightmares*, ed. Giles Gordon [BoH].

"Creatures of Apogee." *New Writings in SF* 30, ed. Kenneth Bulmer [LO / RoE].

"The Game with the Big Heavy Ball." *New Writings in SF* 30, ed. Kenneth Bulmer [RoE].

"Horsemen" ("New Arrivals, Old Encounters"). *Cosmos*, September 1977 [NAOE].

"In the Mist of Life." *Winter's Tales 23*, ed. Peter Collenette.
"My Lady of the Psychiatric Sorrows." *Universe 7*, ed. Terry Carr.

1978

"Non-Isotropic." *Galileo 7*, March 1978 [NAOE].
"The Small Stones of Tu Fu." *Isaac Asimov's Science Fiction Magazine*, March / April 1978 [NAOE / RoE].
"Three Ways." *The Magazine of Fantasy & Science Fiction*, April 1978 [NAOE].
"Yin Yang and Jung, Three Galactic Enigmas: Some Transitory Characteristics of Matter; What's Happening to Your Lawn This Month; No Happiness for the Happiness-Bringer." *Vector 87*, May / June 1978.
"Enemies of the System." *The Magazine of Fantasy & Science Fiction*, June 1978 [EoS].
"A Chinese Perspective." *Anticipations*, ed. Christopher Priest [CB].
"Indifference." *Rooms of Paradise*, ed. Lee Harding [NAOE].

1979

"Oh for a Closer Brush with God" ("Bill Carter Takes Over"). *Twenty Houses of the Zodiac*, ed. Maxim Jakubowski [RoE].
"One Blink of the Moon." [NAOE].
"Song of the Silencer." [NAOE].

1980

"Three Evolutionary Enigmas: The Fall of Species B; In the Halls of the Hereafter; The Ancestral Home of Thought." *Something Else 1*, Spring 1980 [SoB].
"The Man Who Saw Cliff Richard." ("Back from Java") *Something Else 2*, Winter 1980 [FB / RoE].
"Modernisation." *Winter's Tales 26*, ed. A. D. Maclean.

1981

"End Game." *Isaac Asimov's Science Fiction Magazine*, December 1981.
"Foreign Bodies." [FB].
"Boat Animals." [FB].
"Frontiers." [FB].
"The Skeleton." [FB].

1982

"Helliconia Spring." *The Times Saturday Review*, February 27, 1982 [HSp].
"Parasites of Passion." *Isaac Asimov's Science Fiction Magazine*, April 1982.
"The Captain's Analysis." *Quarto*, July / August 1982 [RoE].
"Door Slams in Fourth World." *The Magazine of Fantasy & Science Fiction*, October 1982 [BSF3].
"A Private Whale." *Perpetual Light*, ed. Alan Ryan.
"How the Boy Icarus Grew Up." *Fifty Extremely SF★ Stories*, ed. Michael Bastraw.
"Call Yourself a Christian." *Fifty Extremely SF★ Stories*, ed. Michael Bastraw.

1983

"The Blue Background." *Isaac Asimov's Science Fiction Magazine*, April 1983 [SiF / RoE].

"The Girl Who Sang." *Lands of Never*, ed. Maxim Jakubowski [SiF / RoE].

"The Immortal Storm Strikes Again." *Novacon 13 Programme Book*, November 1983.

"An Admirer of Einstein." *The Fiction Magazine*, Autumn 1983.

1984

"Igur and the Mountain." *A Christmas Feast*, ed. James Hale [SiF].

"The Plain, the Endless Plain." *Missouri Review* 7 [SiF / RoE].

"The Other Side of the Lake." *The Fiction Magazine*, Summer 1984 [SiF].

"The Gods in Flight." *Interzone* 9, Autumn 1984 [SiF / BSF3].

"Consolations of Age." [SiF / RoE].

"Incident in a Far Country." [SiF].

"Juniper." [SiF].

1985

"Der Geist von Loch Awe." *Goldmann Fantasy Foliant* III, ed. Peter Wilfert.

"Happiness and Suffering." *The Book of Mini-Sagas*, ed. Brian Aldiss.

"Domestic Catastrophe." *The Book of Mini-Sagas*, ed. Brian Aldiss.

"Another Story on the Theme of the Last Man on Earth." *The Book of Mini-Sagas*, ed. Brian Aldiss.

"The Greatest Saga of All Time" (as C. C. Shackleton). *The Book of Mini-Sagas*, ed. Brian Aldiss.

"Possessed by Love." *The Book of Mini-Sagas*, ed. Brian Aldiss.

"You Never Asked My Name." *The Magazine of Fantasy & Science Fiction*, November 1985 [RoE].

1986

"Operation Other Cheek." *The Words Book, 1985–1986*.

"The Difficulties Involved in Photographing Nix Olympica." *Isaac Asimov's Science Fiction Magazine*, May 1986 [BSF3].

"Vietnam Encore" ("My Country, 'Tis Not Only of Thee"). *The Best of Fiction Magazine* [BSF3].

"The Older Evil" ("North Scarning"). *The Illustrated London News*, December 1986 [MoP / RoE].

"Lies." *All the Devils Are Here*, ed. David D. Deyo Jr. [RoE].

"The Big Question." *Punch*, December 17–24, 1986 [RoE].

1987

"Infestation." *Tales from the Planet Earth*, ed. Frederik Pohl and Betty Anne Hull [BSF3].

"The Price of Cabbages." *Other Edens*, ed. Christopher Evans and Robert Holdstock.

"Tourney." *Tales from the Forbidden Planet*, ed Roz Kaveney.

"Traveller, Traveller, Seek Your Wife in the Forests of This Life." *Science Fiction Blues Programme Book* [SoB].

"The Ascent of Humboldtein." *Science Fiction Blues Programme Book* [RoE].
"Those Shouting Nights." *Science Fiction Blues Programme Book.*
"Thursday." *Words International: The Book, 1987–1988.*
"The Magic of the Past." [MoP].

1988

"How an Inner Door Opened to My Heart." *The Magazine of Fantasy and Science Fiction,*
  April 1988 [RoE].
"Forgotten Life" (excerpt). *Gaslight and Ghosts,* ed. Jo Fletcher and Stephen Jones.
"Confluence Revisited." *Other Edens* II, ed. Christopher Evans and Robert Holdstock
  [TTF].
"Hess." *The Book of Mini-Sagas* II, ed. Brian Aldiss.
"Wordsworth Hallucinates." *The Book of Mini-Sagas* II, ed. Brian Aldiss.
"Conversation in Progress." *Science Fiction Blues.*

1989

"Den Inre Dörren." ("How an Inner Door Opened to My Heart") *Jules Verne Magasinet,*
  February 1989 [RoE].
"The Day the Earth Caught Fire." *The Mail on Sunday,* April 23, 1989.
"Days in the Life of a Galactic Empire." *Zenith,* ed. David S. Garnett [TTF].
"A Tupolev Too Far." *Other Edens* III, ed. Christopher Evans and Robert Holdstock [BF /
  TTF].
"Three Degrees Over." *Dark Fantasies,* ed. Chris Morgan [BF / TTF].
"North of the Abyss." *The Magazine of Fantasy & Science Fiction,* October 1989 [TTF].

1990

"Adventures in the Fur Trade." *New Pathways,* July 1990.
"Better Morphosis." *Nasacon 11 Programbok* [BF / TTF].
"A Life of Matter and Death." *Interzone* 38, August 1990 [TTF].
"Dracula Unbound" (two short extracts). *Interzone* 38, August 1990.
"Sex and the Black Machine." Avernus (chapbook).

1991

"Going for a Pee." [BF].
"People Alone Injury Artwork." *New Pathways,* January 1991.
"Summertime Was Nearly Over." *The Ultimate Frankenstein,* ed. Byron Preiss [TTF].
"FOAM." *New Worlds* 1, ed. David Garnett [TTF].

1992

"Softly as an Evening Sunrise." *Interzone* 62, August 1992.
"Horse Meat." *Interzone* 65, November 1992 [SoB].
"Common Clay." *The Magazine of Fantasy and Science Fiction,* December 1992 [SoB].
"Ratbird." *New Worlds* 2, ed. David Garnett [TTF].

"Enigmas, Her Toes were Beautiful on the Hilltops/Mountains: Another Way Than Death; That Particular Green of Obsequies." *Universe* 2, ed. Karen Haber and Robert Silverberg [SoB].

"Kindred Blood in Kensington Gore." Avernus (chapbook).

1993

"Else the Isle with Calibans." *Weird Tales from Shakespeare*, ed. Martin H. Greenberg and Katherine Kerr [SoB].

"Friendship Bridge." *New Worlds* 3, ed. David Garnett.

1994

"The Monster of Everyday Life." *Interzone* 80, February 1994.

"The Servant Problem." *Crank!* 3, Spring 1994.

"The God Who Slept with Women." *Asimov's Science Fiction*, May 1994 [SoB].

"The Madonna of Futurity." *Universe* 3, ed. Karen Haber and Robert Silverberg.

"Headless." [SoB / SLAS].

"The Dream of Antigone." *Blue Motel*, ed. Peter Crowther [SoB].

1995

"Becoming the Full Butterfly." *Interzone* 93, March 1995 [SoB / SLAS].

"Into the Tunnel." *Asimov's Science Fiction*, April 1995.

"The Eye Opener." *Interzone* 101, November 1995 [CB].

"A Swedish Birthday Present." [SoB].

"An Unwritten Love Note." [SoB].

"Evans in His Moment of Glory." [SoB].

"Three Moon Enigmas: His Seventieth Heaven; Rose in the Evening; On the Inland Sea." [SoB].

"How the Gates Opened and Closed." [SoB / CB].

"If Hamlet's Uncle Had Been a Nicer Guy." [SoB].

"Making My Father Read Revered Writings." [SoB].

"Sitting with Sick Wasps." [SoB].

"The Mistakes, Miseries and Misfortunes of Mankind." [SoB].

"Travelling Towards Humbris." [SoB].

"Compulsory Holidays for All." *Overload* (Novacon 25 chapbook).

1996

"Dark Society." *Dante's Disciples*, ed. Peter Crowther and Edward E. Kramer [SLAS].

1997

"The Enigma of the Three Moons." *Asimov's Science Fiction*, May 1997.

"Death. Shit. Love. Transfiguration." *New Worlds*, ed. David Garnett.

1999

"An Apollo Asteroid." *Moon Shots*, ed. Peter Crowther and Martin H. Greenberg.

2000

"Cognitive Ability and the Lightbulb." *Nature*, January 20, 2000 [SLAS].
"Steppenpferd." *The Magazine of Fantasy and Science Fiction*, February 2000 [SLAS].
"Apogee Again." *Art After Apogee*, ed. Brian Aldiss and Rosemary Phipps [SLAS].

2001

"Supertoys: Play Can Be So Deadly." *Playboy*, July 2001.
"Supertoys: What Fun to Be Reborn." *Playboy*, July 2001.
"A Whiter Mars." [SLAS].
"The Pause Button." [SLAS].
"Nothing in Life Is Ever Enough." [SLAS].
"Supertoys in Other Seasons." [SLAS].
"Supertoys When Winter Comes." [SLAS].
"Three Types of Solitude." [SLAS].
"A Matter of Mathematics." [SLAS].
"Beef." [SLAS].
"Galaxy Zee." [SLAS].
"III." [SLAS].
"Marvels of Utopia." [SLAS].
"The Old Mythyology." [SLAS].

2002

"Aboard the *Beatitude*." *Daw 30th Anniversary Science Fiction*, ed. Elizabeth R. Wollhein and Sheila E. Gilbert [CB].
"The Man and a Man with His Mule." *Pataphysics* 2002 [CB].
"Near Earth Object." *Mars Probes*, ed Peter Crowther.

2003

"Commander Calex Killed, Fire and Fury at Edge of World, Scones Perfect." *Third Alternative* 33 [CB].
"The Hibernators." *Asimov's Science Fiction*, October/November 2003 [CB].

2004

"Tarzan of the Alps." *Postscripts* 1, Spring 2004 [CB].

2005

"Pipeline." *Asimov's Science Fiction*, September 2005.
"Tralee of Man Young." [CB].
"Dusk Flight." [CB].
"The National Heritage." [CB].
"Ten Billion of Them." *Constellations*, ed. Peter Crowther.

2006

"Building Sixteen." *British Fantasy Society: A Celebration*, ed. Paul Kane and Marie O'Regan.
"Tiger in the Night." *Elemental: The Tsunami Relief Anthology*, ed. Alethea Kontis and Steven Savile.
"Safe." *Asimov's Science Fiction*, December 2006.

2007

"Life, Learning, Leipzig and a Librarian" *Postscripts*, Autumn 2007.
"Four Ladies of the Apocalypse." *The Solaris Book of New Science Fiction*, ed. George Mann.

2008

"Peculiar Bone, Unimaginable Key." *Celebration*, ed. Ian Whates.
"Mortistan." *A Prehistory of the Mind* (chapbook).
"Fandom at the Palace." *Postscripts*, Summer 2008.

2010

"The First Born." *Gateways*, ed. Elizabeth Ann Hull.
"Hapless Humanity." *Catastrophia*, ed. Allen Ashley.

2011

"Benkoelen." *Welcome to the Greenhouse*, ed. Gordon van Gelder.
"Less Than Kin, More Than Kind." *Lemistry*, ed. Ra Page and Magda Raczynska.

2013

"The Hungers of an Old Language." *xo Orpheus: Fifty New Myths*, ed. Kate Bernheimer [IH].
"The Invention of Happiness." *Flotsam Fantastique*, ed. Stephen Jones [IH].
"The Mighty Mi Tok of Beijing." *Twelve Tomorrows*, ed. Stephen Cass.
"After the Party." [IH].
"The Apology." [IH].
"Belief." [IH].
"Beyond Plato's Cave." [IH].
"The Bone Show." [IH].
"Camões." [IH].
"Days Gone By." [IH].
"Flying and Bombing." [IH].
"Flying Singapore Airlines." [IH].
"The Great Plains." [IH].
"How High Is a Cathedral?" [IH].
"Illusions of Reality." [IH].
"Lady with Apple Trees." [IH].
"The Last of the Hound Folk." [IH].
"The Light Really." [IH].

"A Middle Class Dinner." [IH].
"The Mistake They Made." [IH].
"Moderns on Ancient Ancestors." [IH].
"Molly Smiles Forever." [IH].
"Munch." [IH].
"The Music of Sound." [IH].
"Old Mother." [IH].
"Our Moment of Appearance." [IH].
"Peace and War." [IH].
"The Question of Atmosphere." [IH].
"The Sand Castle." [IH].
"The Silent Cosmos." [IH].
"The Village of Stillthorpe." [IH].
"The Vintage Cottage." [IH].
"What Befell the Tadpole." [IH].
"Writing on the Rock." [IH].

2015

"Finches of Mars" (excerpt). *Lightspeed*, August 2015.

2016

"Abundances Above." *Postscripts* 36/37.

CHAPTER 1. WARRIOR

1. Hatherley, Aldiss, and Edwards, 1990: 14.
2. See Hatherley, Aldiss, and Edwards, 1990: 101–102.
3. Aldiss, M., 1992: quoted at 16.
4. Pringle, 1985: 69. (Emphasis in the original.)
5. Griffin and Wingrove, 1984: 7.
6. Jameson, 2005: 261. (Emphasis in the original.)
7. Knight, 1967: 243.
8. Pringle, 1985: 70.
9. Jameson, 2005: 261.
10. See Aldiss, M., 1992: 10.
11. Kincaid and Speller, 2015: 6.
12. See http://fancyclopedia.org/Dena_Brown (accessed January 20, 2020).
13. Aldiss, M., 1992: 23.
14. Knight, 1967: 244.
15. Griffin and Wingrove, 1984: 58.
16. Griffin and Wingrove, 1984: 65.
17. Mathews, 1977: 14.

CHAPTER 2. NATURALIST

1. See Atheling, 1964: 128.
2. Collings, 1986: quoted at 6.
3. Carey, 2009: quoted at 188.
4. Gillespie, 2001: 189.
5. Manlove, 1986: 61–62.
6. Aldiss, M., 1992: quoted at 31.
7. Darlington, 1977: 13.
8. Pringle, 1985: 88.
9. Roberts, 2016: 358.
10. Atheling, 1970: 99.
11. Atheling, 1970: quoted at 11.
12. Mathews, 1977: 27.
13. Harrison, 1964: 31.

14. Aldiss, M., 1992: quoted at 36.
15. Greenland, 1983: 70.
16. Griffin and Wingrove, 1984: 72.
17. Malcolm, 1964: 24.
18. Aldiss, M., 1992: 34
19. Platt, 1965: 25.
20. Griffin and Wingrove, 1984: 121.
21. Aldiss, M., 1992: quoted at 299.

CHAPTER 3. EXPERIMENTALIST

1. The discussion that follows originally appeared, in somewhat different form, in Kincaid, 2020.
2. Ferman and Malzberg, 1974: 89.
3. Gillespie, 1978: 20.
4. Gillespie, 1978: 20.
5. Greenland, 1983: 79.
6. Greenland, 1983: 70.
7. Atheling, 1970: 129.
8. Strick, 1973: 32.
9. Aldiss, M., 1992: quoted at 299.
10. Collings, 1986: quoted at 2.
11. See Greenland, 1983: 69–72.
12. See Taylor, 2016: 339–42.
13. Griffin and Wingrove, 1984: 111.
14. Mathews, 1977: 44–45.
15. March-Russell, 2015: 143.
16. Atheling, 1970: 139.
17. Gillespie, 1978: 16.
18. Greenland, 1979: 34.
19. Greenland, 1979: 34.
20. Atheling, 1970: 140.
21. Gillespie, 1978: 16.
22. Griffin and Wingrove, 1984: 187–88.
23. Disch, 2005: 106.
24. March-Russell, 2015: 127.
25. Collings, 1986: quoted at 48.
26. Mathews, 1977: 55.
27. Clute, 1988: 100.
28. Masson, 1975: 201.
29. Ferman and Malzberg, 1974: 90.
30. Bulmer, 1973: 67.
31. Bulmer, 1973: 67.
32. Hosty, 1979: 96.
33. Griffin and Wingrove, 1984: 194.
34. Wingrove, 1978b: 30–31.

CHAPTER 4. HISTORIAN

1. Griffin and Wingrove, 1984: 151.
2. Aldiss, M., 1992: 55.
3. Aldiss, M., 1992: quoted at 26.
4. Lewis, 1966: 86.
5. Lewis, 1966: 90.
6. Lewis, 1966: 91.
7. Ballard, 1996: 197.
8. Merrick, 2009: quoted at 103.
9. See Wolfe, 1986: 109–111.
10. Adlard, 1974: 65.
11. Adlard, 1974: 68.
12. Butler, 2012: 28.
13. Griffin and Wingrove, 1984: 169.
14. McLeod, 1980: 162.
15. Ruddick, 1997: 80–81.
16. Watson, 1974: 76–77.
17. Adlard, 1975: 30.
18. Collings, 1986: 60.
19. Shakespeare, *The Tempest*, I, 2, 283–284.
20. Collings, 1986: 62.
21. James, 2012: 67.
22. Aldiss, M., 1992: quoted at 308.
23. Higgins, 1980: 18.
24. McAuley, 1991: 64.
25. Clute, 1995: 281.
26. Pringle, 1977: 95.

CHAPTER 5. SCIENTIST

1. Wingrove, 1978c: 41.
2. Stableford, 1979: 96.
3. Wingrove, 1978a: 44.
4. Burgess, 1984: 122.
5. Clute, 1995: 260.
6. Clute, 1995: 263.
7. Clareson, 1983: 89.
8. Gentle, 1982: 43.
9. Meadley, 1983: 74.
10. Clareson, 1984: 184.
11. Clareson, 1984: 185–86.
12. Caracciolo, 1985: 70.
13. Gentle, 1982: 43.
14. Langford, 2002: 97.

1. Clute, 1995: 262.
2. Kincaid, 2014: 10.
3. Kincaid, 1993: 19.
4. Clute, 1995: 263.
5. Jones, 1987: 78.
6. Wallace, 1987: 18.
7. Clute, 1995: 260.
8. Wolfe, 2010: 152.
9. Clute, 2003: 219.
10. Clute, 2003: 219.
11. Greenland, 1999: 99.
12. Greenland, 1999: quoted at 99.
13. "Letter," *Foundation* 94, Summer 2005, 118.
14. Bailey, 2000: 97.
15. Leane, 2005: 18.
16. "Letter," *Foundation* 94, 118.
17. Kincaid, 2014: 11.
18. Hurst, 2005: 14.
19. Clute, 2009: 202.
20. Kincaid, 2014: 12.
21. Kelly, 2013: n.p.
22. Roberts, 2013: n.p.
23. Velazquez, 2013: n.p.
24. Moorcock, 2017: 6.
25. Priest, 2017: n.p.
26. Sawyer, 2017: 8–9.

Adlard, Mark. "A Labour of Love." *Foundation* 6, May 1974, 61–69.

———. "Frankenstein Unbound." *Vector* 69, Summer 1975, 28–30.

Aldiss, Margaret. *The Work of Brian W. Aldiss: An Annotated Bibliography and Guide.* Bibliographies of Modern Authors 9. San Bernardino, CA: Borgo, 1992.

Atheling Jr., William (James Blish). *The Issue at Hand.* 1964. Reprint, Chicago: Advent, 1973.

———. *More Issues at Hand.* Chicago: Advent, 1970.

Bailey, K. V. "White Mars." *Foundation* 79, Summer 200, 93–97.

Ballard, J. G. *A User's Guide to the Millennium: Essays and Reviews.* London: HarperCollins, 1996.

Bulmer, Kenneth, ed. *New Writings in SF.* Vol. 22. 1973. Reprint, London: Corgi, 1974.

Burgess, Anthony. *Ninety-Nine Novels: The Best in English Since 1939.* London: Allison & Busby, 1984.

Butler, Andrew M. *Solar Flares: Science Fiction in the 1970s.* Liverpool: Liverpool University Press, 2012.

Caracciolo, Peter. "Helliconia Summer and Helliconia Winter." *Foundation* 35, Winter 1985/1986, 70–73.

Carey, John. *William Golding: The Man Who Wrote* Lord of the Flies. London: Faber, 2009.

Clareson, Thomas D. "Nebula Time Again." *Extrapolation* 24, Spring 1983, 88–91.

———. "Three Major Novels Show Diversity of Field." *Extrapolation* 25, Summer 1984, 180–186.

Clute, John. *Strokes.* Seattle: Serconia, 1988.

———. *Look at the Evidence: Essays and Reviews.* Liverpool: Liverpool University Press, 1995.

———. *Scores: Reviews, 1993–2003.* Harold Wood, Essex, UK: Beccon, 2003.

———. *Canary Fever: Reviews.* Harold Wood, Essex, UK: Beccon, 2009.

Collings, Michael R. *Brian Aldiss.* 1986. Reprint, Rockville, MD: Borgo, 2006.

Darlington, Andrew. "Hothouse and Cryptozoic." *Vector* 82, August 1977, 13.

Disch, Thomas M. *On SF.* Ann Arbor: University of Michigan Press, 2005.

Ferman, Edward L., and Barry N. Malzberg, eds. *Final Stage: The Ultimate Science Fiction Anthology.* 1974. Reprint, Harmondsworth: Penguin, 1975.

Gentle, Mary. "The Three Ages of Man." *Vector* 109, August 1982, 42–44.

Gillespie, Bruce. "Cheerfulness Keeps Breaking In." *SF Commentary* 54, November 1978, 12–21.

———. "A Valediction Forbidding Melancholy: Aldiss and the Far Future." In *Earth Is But a Star: Excursions Through Science Fiction to the Far Future*, ed. Damien Broderick, 184–196. Crawley, WA: University of Western Australia Press, 2001.

Greenland, Colin. "The Times Themselves Talk Nonsense: Language in *Barefoot in the Head*." *Foundation* 17, September 1979, 32–41.

———. *The Entropy Exhibition: Michael Moorcock and the British "New Wave" In Science Fiction*. London: Routledge & Kegan Paul, 1983.

———. "When the Feast Is Finished." *Foundation* 77, Autumn 1999, 98–99.

Griffin, Brian, and David Wingrove. 1984. *Apertures: A Study of the Writings of Brian W. Aldiss*. Westport, CT: Greenwood, 1984.

Harrison, Harry. "Greybeard." *Vector* 29, November 1964, 31–32.

Hatherley, Frank, with Margaret Aldiss and Malcolm Edwards, eds. *A Is for Brian: A 65th Birthday Present for Brian W. Aldiss from His Family, Friends, Colleagues and Admirers*. London: Avernus, 1990.

Higgins, Steev. "Moreau's Other Island." *Vector* 99, October 1980, 17–18.

Hosty, Tom. "Last Orders." *Foundation* 15, January 1979, 94–96.

Hurst, L. J. "Jocasta: Wife and Mother." *Vector* 241, May/June 2005, 14–15.

James, Simon J. *Maps of Utopia: H. G. Wells, Modernity, and the End of Culture*. Oxford: Oxford University Press, 2012.

Jameson, Fredric. *Archaeologies of the Future: The Desire Called Utopia and Other Science Fictions*. London: Verso, 2005.

Jones, Gwyneth. "Cracken at Critical." *Foundation* 41 Winter 1987, 78–80.

Kelly, Stuart. "Brian Aldiss: 'These days I don't read any science fiction. I only read Tolstoy.'" *Guardian*, December 13, 2013. https://www.theguardian.com/books/2013/dec/13/brian-aldiss-science-fiction-author-review (accessed May 22, 2020).

Kincaid, Paul. "Remembrance Day." *Vector* 173 June/July 1993, 19.

———. *Call and Response*. Harold Wood, Essex, UK: Beccon, 2014.

———. "The Girl and the Robot with Flowers." *Vector* 291, Summer 2020, 44–46.

Kincaid, Paul, and Maureen Kincaid Speller, eds. 2015. *Best of Vector*. Vol. 1, *The State of the Art*. British Science Fiction Association, 2015.

Knight, Damon. *In Search of Wonder*. 2nd ed. Chicago: Advent, 1967.

Langford, David. *The Complete Critical Assembly*. Holicong, PA: Cosmos, 2002.

Leane, Elizabeth. "Reading Aldiss and Penrose's *White Mars* as 'Science Faction.'" *Foundation* 93, Spring 2005, 18–25.

Lewis, C. S. *Of Other Worlds: Essays and Stories*. London: Geoffrey Bles, 1966.

Malcolm, Donald. "The Dark Light Years." *Vector* 25, March 1964, 24.

Manlove, C. N. *Science Fiction: Ten Explorations*. London: Macmillan, 1986.

March-Russell, Paul. *Modernism and Science Fiction*. Basingstoke: Palgrave Macmillan, 2015.

Masson, David I. "The Eighty-Minute Hour: A Space Opera." *Foundation* 7–8, March 1975, 201–203.

Mathews, Richard. *Aldiss Unbound: The Science Fiction of Brian W. Aldiss*. San Bernardino, CA: Borgo, 1977.

McAuley, Paul J. "The Triumph of Hugo." *Interzone* 49, July 1991, 63–64.

McLeod, Patrick G. "Frankenstein: Unbound and Otherwise." *Extrapolation* 21, Summer 1980, 158–166.

Meadley, R. G. "Half and Eye and Tono-Bungay." *Foundation* 27, February 1983, 71–78.

Merrick, Helen. "Fiction, 1964–1979." In *The Routledge Companion to Science Fiction*, ed. Mark Bould, Andrew M. Butler, Adam Roberts, and Sherryl Vint, 102–111. London: Routledge, 2009.

Moorcock, Michael. "Brian W. Aldiss." *Foundation* 128, 2017, 6–8.

Nicholls, Stan. *Wordsmiths of Wonder*. London: Orbit, 1993.

Platt, Charles. "Earthworks." *Vector* 31, March 1965, 24–25.

Priest, Christopher. "Brian Aldiss Obituary." *Guardian*, August 21, 2017. https://www.theguardian.com/books/2017/aug/21/brian-aldiss-obituary (accessed 22 May 2020).

Pringle, David. "Time Must Have a Stop." *Foundation* 11–12, March 1977, 93–96.

———. *Science Fiction: The 100 Best Novels*. London: Xanadu, 1985.

Roberts, Adam. "Finches of Mars." *Guardian*, June 5, 2013. https://www.theguardian.com/books/2013/jun/05/finches-of-mars-aldiss-review (accessed 21 May 2020).

———. *The History of Science Fiction: Second Edition*. London: Palgrave Macmillan, 2016.

Ruddick, Nicholas. "The Brood of Mary: Brian Aldiss, *Frankenstein*, and Science Fiction." In *The Dark Fantastic: Selected Essays from the Ninth International Conference on the Fantastic in the Arts*, ed. C. W. Sullivan III, 77–84. Westport, CT: Greenwood, 1997.

Sawyer, Andy. "Brian W. Aldiss." *Foundation* 128, 2017, 8–10.

Stableford, Brian. "Enemies of the System." *Foundation* 15, January 1979, 96–97.

Strick, Philip. "Reporting on Possibilities." *Vector* 63, January/February 1963, 32–34.

Taylor, D. J. *The Prose Factory: Literary Life in England Since 1918*. London: Vintage, 2016.

Velazquez, Maria. "Finches of Mars." *Strange Horizons*, September 2, 2013. http://strangehorizons.com/non-fiction/reviews/finches-of-mars by brian-aldiss/ (accessed 21 May 2020).

Wallace, Jon. "Cracken at Critical." *Vector* 141, December 1987/January 1988, 17–18.

Watson, Ian. "The Aldiss Lamp and the Bright Radiance of Eternity." *Foundation* 6, May 1974, 76–83.

Wingrove, David. "Brothers of the Head." *Vector* 86, March/April 1978, 43–45.

———. "Last Orders and Other Stories." *Vector* 87, May/June 1978, 30–31.

———. "Enemies of the System." *Vector* 89, September/October 1978, 39–41.

Wolfe, Gary K. *Critical Terms for Science Fiction and Fantasy: A Glossary and Guide to Scholarship*. Westport, CT: Greenwood, 1986.

———. 2010. *Bearings: Reviews, 1997–2001*. Harold Wood, Essex, UK: Beccon, 2010.

Lewis, C. S., 86–87, 88

Life and Adventures of Peter Wilkins, The (Paltock), 90

Life in the West (Aldiss), 120, 141

Little, Brown, 156

Lloyd, John, 59

London, 37

Long Afternoon of Earth, The (Aldiss). See *Hothouse*

Look Back in Anger (Osborne), 27

Lovelock, James, 135, 145

Lucian of Samosata, 89

Lyell, Charles, 91

Lysenko, Trofim, 113

Madkind (Berg), 42, 75, 116, 143

Magazine of Fantasy and Science Fiction, 24, 30, 54

"Magic and Bare Boards" (Aldiss), 147

Make Room! Make Room! (Harrison), 44

Malacia Tapestry, The (Aldiss), 3, 4, 6, 32, 81, 106–9, 111, 113, 121, 151, 163, 166

Male Response, The (Aldiss), 26

Malzberg, Barry N., 83

"Man in His Time" (Aldiss), 112

Man in the Moone, The (Godwin), 44, 90

Manlove, C. N., 34

March-Russell, Paul, 69, 76

Masson, David I., 81

Mason, Margaret. *See* Aldiss, Margaret

Mathews, Richard, 7, 26, 37, 69, 77

McEwan, Ian, 110

McLeod, Patrick, 96

"Meaning of Death, The" (J. Huxley), 29

Meaning of Liff, The (Adams & Lloyd), 59

Memoirs of Elizabeth Frankenstein, The (Roszak), 93

Midnight's Children (Rushdie), 139

Mind at the End of Its Tether (Wells), 150

Modern Utopia, A (Wells), 152

Moment of Eclipse, The (Aldiss), 85

Monet, Claude, 52

Montieth, Charles, 10

Moorcock, Michael, 6, 49, 55–57, 59, 60–61, 68, 69, 87, 89, 163

More, Thomas, 152

Moreau's Other Island (Aldiss), 6, 98–102, 114, 127, 162

More Penguin Science Fiction (ed. Aldiss), 86

Morris, Desmond, 121

National Book League, 27

Nebula, 9, 11, 24

Nebula Award, 49

"Never Let Go of My Hand" (Aldiss), 59

"New Accelerator, The" (Wells), 22

"New Father Christmas, The" (Aldiss), 24

New Wave, 3, 5, 6, 49–50, 53, 54, 56–58, 68, 69, 76, 85, 87–89, 92, 93, 157, 163, 165

New Worlds (ed. Garnett), 157

New Worlds (magazine), 6, 10, 11, 23–25, 49, 54, 59, 61, 68, 69, 71, 87, 89, 144

New Writings in SF, 59, 83, 105, 118

Nicolson, Ian, 121

Nicolson, Marjorie Hope, 90

Nineteen Eighty-Four (Orwell), 113

"Nomansland" (Aldiss), 30

Non-Stop (Aldiss), 3, 4, 6, 13–18, 29–32, 45, 70, 73, 79, 88, 101, 111, 121, 123, 127, 129, 134, 137, 139, 140, 147, 148, 157, 163

"North Scarning" (Aldiss), 48, 117–18

"Not For an Age" (Aldiss), 10, 11

Nouveau roman, 60

Nouvelle vague, 60

Nova Publications, 59

Observer, The, 10, 34

"O Ishrail!" (Aldiss), 20

"Old Hundredth" (Aldiss), 23–24, 39

"Old Time's Sake" (Aldiss), 54

"O Moon of My Delight" (Aldiss), 23

Orbit (publisher), 156

Orbit 12 (ed. Knight), 105

Orphans of the Sky (Heinlein), 13

Orwell, George, 113, 116

Osborne, John, 27

Otranto, 1, 2

"Our Kind of Knowledge" (Aldiss), 12, 13

Ouspensky, P. D., 75, 97

"Out of Reach" (Aldiss), 18, 19–20

"Outside" (Aldiss), 10–11, 148

Oxford, 9, 37–38, 55, 98, 104

PAUL KINCAID is a Clareson Award-winning critic. His previous volume for Modern Masters of Science Fiction, *Iain M. Banks*, won a BSFA Award. His other books include *What It Is We Do When We Read Science Fiction* and *The Unstable Realities of Christopher Priest*.

MODERN MASTERS OF SCIENCE FICTION

John Brunner   *Jad Smith*

William Gibson   *Gary Westfahl*

Gregory Benford   *George Slusser*

Greg Egan   *Karen Burnham*

Ray Bradbury   *David Seed*

Lois McMaster Bujold   *Edward James*

Frederik Pohl   *Michael R. Page*

Alfred Bester   *Jad Smith*

Octavia E. Butler   *Gerry Canavan*

Iain M. Banks   *Paul Kincaid*

J. G. Ballard   *D. Harlan Wilson*

Arthur C. Clarke   *Gary Westfahl*

Joanna Russ   *Gwyneth Jones*

Kim Stanley Robinson   *Robert Markley*

Roger Zelazny   *F. Brett Cox*

Brian W. Aldiss   *Paul Kincaid*

THE UNIVERSITY OF ILLINOIS PRESS

is a founding member of the

Association of University Presses.

———————————————————

University of Illinois Press

1325 South Oak Street

Champaign, IL 61820-6903

www.press.uillinois.edu